My Road Home

A 13 month journey from Wall Street to behind the walls of a NY State Prison.

Jerry Byrne

authorHOUSE®

AuthorHouse™
1663 Liberty Drive
Bloomington, IN 47403
www.authorhouse.com
Phone: 1-800-839-8640

First published by AuthorHouse   5/25/2011

ISBN: 978-1-4634-0028-6 (e)
ISBN: 978-1-4634-0029-3 (hc)
ISBN: 978-1-4634-0030-9 (sc)

Library of Congress Control Number: 2011908267

Printed in the United States of America

It's never too late to be what you might have been.
-George Elliot

When it is dark enough,
you can see the stars.
-Persian Proverb

This book is dedicated in memory of my Mother and Father.

It is also dedicated to my sons, Brooks and Philip.

I cannot fully express my thanks for the multitude of family and friends who helped me survive this journey. While I may have been the one alone in that cell, I simply had to glance over my shoulder and I knew you were there with me. Thank you especially to my brothers and sisters, Joe, Liz, Jack, Virginia and Susie. No doubt I have tested the bounds, but you have never left my side. You'll never know what your numerous visits and letters meant; they carried me through my darkest days. Joe thank you for looking after my sons while I was gone, I know you were always there when they needed to lean on someone. Jack, your sage advice and unhindered wisdom comforted me during the darkest of days. You've been there for me.....always.   Liz, Virginia & Susie, I felt your prayers, tears, and love, even behind those thick prison walls. Thank you for your unending faith.

Thank you to my 'lifeline,' Eileen. Your extraordinary 33 visits, combining 3 different prisons is truly amazing. Not to mention your countless food packages, books and magazines. How can I ever thank you! My journey would have so much worse without you, you carried me from start to finish. Truly not a day goes by when I don't think of you.

Thank you to my cousin George Maguire. You were my rock, always there to help, from the day of my indictment, to the day I was released, you never left my side. I look back at the numerous times, prior to my sentencing I would stop by your office. I didn't know what awaited me, your encouraging words lifted my spirits, giving me the strength to get through. You gave, and gave, and gave. Please know how incredibly grateful I am. To Mr. & Mrs. J. Robert Maguire, (Uncle Bob & Aunt Polly) your wisdom, support, faith and friendship have never wavered. You've done so much, I don't have the words to express my gratitude, so I'll mearly say, I love you.

Thank you to James J. Maguire, not only were you there by my side the day I was led away, but you have always been there for me. I love you Uncle Jim. Thank you Diane Maguire. Thank you to all the Maguire cousins, for your letters, books, and support. Thank you to my brother-in-laws, Bob Gett, Doug Marzonie, and Bob Sargent. Some families are lucky to have one decent brother-in-law, well we have three of the best, and I'm grateful for you're always being there.

Thank you Abby, I've placed a lot on your shoulders, I'm so sorry for my absence and what I've put you through. Thank you John Boozan. Thank you to my ex in-laws, your supporting letters and the books you sent touched my heart. Thank you to all my ex sisters in law, Kate, Josie, and Molly.

Thank you Stephanie DeSesa, for your never ending faith, friendship, & love. Thank you Sara McDonald, one of the nicest & caring women I have ever known. What a breath of fresh air you are.

Thank you to my nieces and nephews, when I received your letters, it was an automatic tear. I'm so proud of you all......Bobby, Laura, Peter, Kristy, Samantha, Abby, Holly, Julie, Bridgett, Vanessa, Joey, Caroline, Kyle, and Michael.

During my thirteen months away there were literally only 2 days when I did not receive at least one letter. That is amazing! To all of the following, thank you. It's true what they say, 'there is nothing like a letter,' and nowhere is this more so than prison. Your letters were read countless times, never failing to bring a tear. Thanks to Katie Nolle, who upon hearing the news of my incarceration wrote me a letter nearly every single day day, without fail. Thank you Aunt Claire. Thank you Cynthia Shook, my cousin, who had a Hallmark card waiting for me every Friday. Thank you Laurie and Jim Clarke for the countless times you treated my boys to dinner in my absence, I'll never forget it.

Thank you to the Christian Brothers of Manhattan College for all their generosity, friendship and support as I reentered society. Thanks to all my colleuges at Manhattan College O'Malley Library, you never judged me during my most vulnerable days; Melinda, Rose, James, Andre, John, Dennis, Peggy W, Maura, Barbara, Amy, Kate, Fred, Olga, Noreen, Ellen, Gina, Doris, Peggy M., Thank you to Brother Frank Byrne, you took the ball and ran with it, making my post release environment simply the best possible. Thank you Aunt Virginia Maguire for your daily prayers.

Thank you Henry & Holly for always being my friend. Thank you Ted Lawrence, you refused to let me hide, I treasure our good times on the courts. Thanks to Darlene & Brian, my paddle friends, but you're so much more than that. Tom Mangan, thank you, you'll never know the feeling when I saw your smiling face in the Visitor's Room. Thank you Sherian Edgreen, the guidance you gave Brooks helped him so.

Thank you Debbi, Bill, Devon, John, Sue, and Curt; we've lost touch, but the memories of our fun times I'll never forget. Thank you Caren Rossi, your energy is inspirational. I wish I had shared this story with you sooner.

Thank you Ed Dratch. Elizabeth Ruhland, Jim Harrison, Howard & Allsion Bunn, Lisa & Joe Corcoran, Philip O'Cone, Hon. James Zazzali, Nancy & Tony Maguire, Jane Maguire Gross, Helen Graham, Margaret Sullivan, Aunt Bobby & Uncle John Schulte, Mary Lou & Betty Ann Clarken. Thank you to my loyal friends, on and off the course, Rick Jenkins, Dave Lindstrom, Chris Scott, and Jack Gilbert. Thank you to Bonnie Gannon, Ann and Neil McLean, Suzanne Burkner, Father Tom Walsh, Karen Walters, Margaret Sullivan, Gina Ingrassia, Elise & Rob Redmond, Regina Fernicola, Julie and Patrick Caulfield, JoAnn Korba, Rita Jordan, Margaret Jordan, Jody Wagner, Katie & Randy Roessle, Laurie and Fred Gertner. Thank you Carolyn Lemone, Virginia McBride, Cynthia Boatwright, Sally Cole. So many parents helped my sons while I was incarcerated, I can't tell you what a comfort that was & I can't thank you enough, but I'll try. Thank you Cara and John Moxley, Melissa and Mark Nugent, Jean and Paul Funk, Maureen and Ed Bednarski, Cynthia and Mike McChesney, Randy and Jeanie Riley. Thank you Trina and Tory Rennie, Ralph, Heidi, and Sam Davies. Thank you to the women of Roberts Circle; Gail, Jane and Jody.

Thank you Patricia Carniglia, you let me know my past is acceptable, I'm sorry to have hidden it from you. Thank you Dr. and Mrs. Kapsimalis. Thank you Dale Feeney. Thank you Mauri Clarke, I told you this story right off the bat and you never flinched. Your faith is inspirational. Thank you Dave Broderick, you arraigned for me to be looked after up at Mohawk, I never knew that until then end. Thank you Nicole Finnigan, you jump started this project. Thanks to Allison Parker and Jenna Lyons, I told you my story and your artistic talent took over, your sketches are spot on. Thank you Lyn Turner, what a friend you are! Thank you Robert Pell, I miss you. Thank you Jim Powers for preparing me. I'm sorry to all those I have let down or hurt, it was never my intention. I hope you can forgive me someday.

Friday June 22nd, 2007

I wake up at 5:00 a.m. knowing this will be my last day of freedom for quite some time. Perhaps as long as nine years. Once again I hardly slept, in spite of numbing myself with more cocktails than I had a right to. But why not, for I know there won't be any alcohol in prison. Not being able to face them this morning, I bid tearful goodbyes to my parents last night, as well as my two teenage sons. The pattern of continuing worst moments of my life seems to have no end, today's sentencing will sadly keep that streak alive.

You don't exactly pack a bag for prison, so knowing I will be in the same clothes for at the least the next 2-3 days I try to pick out the most comfortable and inconspicuous clothes I own: khaki pants, blue Brooks Brothers shirt, and Nike sneakers.

I get into my car and head to the local Starbucks. Real coffee is a pleasure I won't be experiencing again for, well, longer than I want to imagine. I treat myself to a latte and look around at all the familiar faces I have come to know these many months, as far as their concerned it's just another day for me as they extend their greetings. Little do they know I won't be seeing them for quite some time. The first hint of a tear begins to fall, before the day is over many more will come.

I get on the train heading to Manhattan, specifically 100 Centre Street where I await sentencing at 10:00 for Securities Fraud. I look around at my fellow commuters, engrossed in their NY Times, and Wall Street Journals, a scene that I participated in for 20 years as I made the trek from the suburbs to the streets of Lower Manhattan. "How the hell did it come to this?," I think to myself. I look out the window at perhaps the bluest sky I have ever seen, not a cloud to be had on this first official day of Summer. I make my way to the court house, walking slowly, and hoping the sidewalk might just open up, swallow me whole so I can disappear and avoid the humiliation that awaits. I'm in sort of semi-shock I think. Wait, what if I just turn around and run? I'll head out West, start over, and avoid all this shit. But of course I can't. I'd be

1

a fugitive, constantly looking over my shoulder. And worst of all, I could never see my family again. I enter the building and take the elevator to the 13th floor. In a matter of minutes I'll be handcuffed and no longer a free man.

Waiting for me in the courtroom are my lawyers, my oldest brother Joe (I have two, along with three sisters) , cousin George Maguire, who has been by my rock since the day I was indicted 16 months ago. Also my Uncle and mentor, the man who got me my first job on Wall Street way back in 1980, James J. Maguire. Shortly before I am called to appear in front of Judge Michael Opus, I reach into my pockets and hand Joe my cell phone, wallet, and car keys. I will no longer have a use for any of these things. We've already said our goodbyes, out in the hallway. When I go to hug them I know it'll be for quite awhile. I don't want to let go, but my time has come.

The sentencing is a blur, the prosecution makes a few closing remarks, stuff like what a pleasure it's been to work with the defense, the shared cooperation, blah, blah, (oh how lovely for all of you I think to myself, one big happy family) . Then my lawyer stands before the Judge asking for leniency, the fact that I have never been in trouble with the law before, that this is a non-violent 1st time offense The whole time I just sit there, in shock really, staring at the floor, trying to hold back the tears I promised I would not let fall. Minutes pass, and now it's my turn to speak. I know the Judge has already decided my fate, nothing I say will change that, but for some reason I feel the desire to say a few words. This is probably my 10th visit to the courtroom, and I have never once had the opportunity to speak. I want the Judge and everyone else to know how sorry I am, how I can't believe where my life has taken me; literally minutes from being led away in handcuffs. I rise out of my chair, I've given a lot of thought to what I want to say, but immediately I go blank, I stand there frozen, my rehearsed speech all but forgotten. I faintly recall saying how much I will miss my sons, the pain I have caused them along with the rest of my family. I admit my guilt, ask the Judge to be lenient, thank my lawyers, and my family for their love. I begin to sob. I can't feel anything; my body is numb. Finally I run out of things to say and sit down. Now it's Judge Opus's turn. I wait to hear the number; is it 1 year, 3, or worst case scenario, 9 years that I am being sentenced to. He's speaking, but very little registers. Why can't I just faint, or better yet wake up, because really, this is all just a bad dream isn't it. Next thing I know, I hear him say "2 1/3rd to 7. Good

2

luck to you sir." There it is, right smack in the middle of the best/worst case scenario. Four hundred thousand it cost my family in legal fees to get a result I probably would have received if I had pled guilty at my arraignment….16 months ago.

At the same time the Judge was meting out my sentence, 2 court officers stepped up directly behind me. I could see one of them reaching for his handcuffs, the other one pulling out my chair as he began to utter the words I had come to dread, "Place your hands behind your back sir." The tears are still running down my cheeks, I'm almost gasping for breath; my legs wobble like a rubber pencil. Will I even be able to stand up? I hear the clicking of the cuffs, then I feel them. Thankfully not to tight. I look back at my Uncle, my cousin, and my brother, I'm helpless now, and there is nothing they can do for me. But their hearts reach out, I can see it in their eyes. The holding cell I am being led to is off to the side of the court, step through a door, and I will be gone. The guards are holding on to me, I want this walk to take forever, but considering it's only about ten yards long, that won't happen. The door opens, I look back one last time.

Handcuffed to a steel bench in a windowless room, I sit. My initial thoughts are how am I going to survive this; at least 2 years of incarceration, possibly up to a maximum of seven. The cuffs begin to pinch my skin. After about an hour I am led to the first of many holding cells that I will occupy before the day is over. This one already has about 20 prisoners in it when they open the door for me; everyone stares, I stare, quickly realizing I am the only white guy. Not to mention my khaki pants and button down shirt, I don't think I dressed properly. They look at me like I'm an alien, funny; I was thinking the same about them. I quickly become aware of two things; it's hot, and there is an awful smell in this room, it reeks of body odor. And it's only 11:00 a.m. Two long benches run side by side in the middle of the room, they are fully occupied. Actually there might be a bit of room if a few guys would move closer together, but I think better of asking anyone to squeeze in. So I stand.

Two hours later the cell door is open again and cheese sandwiches, wrapped in cellophane are brought in. I pick one up, I can barely look at it, much less eat them. The bread is soft, mushy & wet. The cheese is a color I have never seen before, it has kind of a greenish look. Ugh. I glance around, doesn't seem to be bothering anybody else; they're all eating away happy as could be. I quickly learn an important rule; you're in prison now, forget everything you were used to out in the real world. Unless I want to starve I will have to eat this type of food sooner or later. I manage to take a few bites. Then I sit, and sit some more. All of a sudden some career criminal comes over and asks if I'm going to finish my cheese sandwich. He looks like he's going to take it regardless, so I hand it over. A few hours later my name is yelled out, "Let's go Byrne, we got to hurry up and get you on the 3:00 p.m. bus to Rikers." Apparently the 3:00 one is the last bus each day heading out there, so it's either that or stay in this holding cell all night, I don't know which one will be worse. About 30 prisoners are lined up waiting to board, the sun is shinning, it's a hot and beautiful summer day. It means nothing to me though. As boarding begins I'm to be shackled at the ankles & wrists with the guy standing next to me. As luck would have it, standing next to me would be Carlos, a methadone addict coming off a 5 day binge, who hasn't bathed in God knows how long!! He was anxious to inform me that he "hasn't taken a shit" in 4 days." Carlos and I grab the very last seat in the back. The bus temperature must be in the 100's, I don't see a single window open, just hot air being blown around by a fan that barely runs. The huge metal gates of the Manhattan Detention Center open up and the bus begins it's journey to "the island" as Rikers is commonly referred to. As we inch our way through Chinatown, young boys, on their way home from school, spot the "prison bus" and begin to mock and taunt us. Through the windows I can hear and see them yelling out stuff like, "Losers, you guys suck, hope you die in prison, etc......" I just can't believe this is happening.

An hour into the ride Carlos begins to scream, "C.O., I need to take a shit, stop the bus." This goes on for a solid 20 minutes. The guards pay him not the slightest bit of attention. Unless you've been stabbed, or are having a heart attack, they don't want to hear it. We arrive around 5:00 p.m. and the thirty of us are unshackled and led to various holding cells. Thankfully Carlos and I go our separate ways. The bouncing back & forth from holding cell to holding cell continues throughout the night. Each one more crowded and dirtier than the next. At times I am called out to give my name, sign some papers, get my picture taken, yelled at for no apparent reason other than they (the guards) can. I spend the bulk of my time lying on the cold, smelly, dirty floor. I try to catch some sleep, or at least rest my eyes, when all of a sudden I feel a water-bug crawling up my arm.

Eventually we all get a turn to see the Doctor who makes sure no one is entering the Island with some horrendous disease. Twenty of us are led into a class room like anti-room before seeing the Dr. It's 3:00, Saturday morning. We sit upright at desks while a movie is playing on a lone TV screen bolted into the wall. "Starsky & Hutch" is being shown. There is no talking allowed. We sit, stare, try to stay awake, and wait for our names to be called. I'm hungry, incredibly tired, sad, and afraid.

It isn't until 4:00 p.m. on Saturday, thirty hours after my sentencing, when I am finally taken into a dorm like setting, kind of like a tiny gym. For the time being it's my new home. There are 50 cots spread out, side by side. Other than a bite of that disgusting cheese sandwich, I haven't eaten or slept. All I want to do is call my parents to let them know I'm alive, and for them to relay that news to my sons. And then eat whatever horrendous food is available, crawl on top of my cot, and drift off to sleep.

When you enter your dorm room initially each prisoner is given a pin # from which you can make three phone calls, courtesy of the State. I didn't know this at the time, but using your pin requires you go through a series of steps before you get an outside line. I was in no condition to sort my way through this maze. I guess the look of desperation must have been written all over my face, because quickly a fellow inmate was at my side, offering to help. "Hey man, let me take care of this for you, you're new here right, I got this for you." At last I think, an act of human kindness, on Rikers of all places. Hey maybe I can survive this after all. Little did I know however, I was committing a cardinal sin of prison life, NEVER give out your pin #!! As it turned out, my "guardian angel" was actually stealing my pin number for his own use.

I begin to think that maybe when I wake up this will only be a bad dream, my mind plays tricks with me, yeah that's it Jerry, this is simply a dream. Sadly it's not a dream, but a nightmare that is just beginning.

Sunday, June 24th

I wake up at Rikers from my first real sleep in 48 hours. I'm still in a shock and expect I will be for some time. Today is Visitors day and my girl friend Eileen is coming to see me. How loyal and supportive she has been, from the minute I learned I had to "go away." She has promised to bring the NY Times and three paperbacks, what a treat. Already I have discovered that those little things, ya know the ones we all take for granted, like a newspaper, will become precious as my time rolls on.

To gain access to the Visitor's room I have to change out of the clothes I'm wearing and into a gray, 100% polyester jump suit that probably hasn't been washed in years. It is beyond filthy. I also have to put on old rubber sandals, again ones that seem to have never been cleaned or fumigated. Some kind of foot disease can't be far away. I dread Eileen seeing me like this (I will not allow anyone else to see me during my Rikers stay) but I am desperate for company and to get out of my cell for an hour.

Eileen looks great and we hold off the tears for as long as possible, but inevitably they flow. The one hour of allotted visitor time flies by. It seemed like just five minutes when the guard informs us it's time to leave. We hug and Eileen is whisked away, I must remain seated, the strip search awaits. Again I wonder how can I survive this. I'm craving a cup of coffee.

Monday June 25th

I have been befriended by one of the top prisoners in "3 Main," the dorm room I am currently housed in. His name is Tyson and he's been in prison for eight years. Built rock solid, and amazingly positive for a guy who has 5 years remaining on his sentence. I think Tyson sees how vulnerable and lost I am in this environment. But I ask myself, does he have an ulterior motive? Hmmm, he just might after seeing me enter the dorm fresh off my visit with Eileen, laden down with goodies such as a newspaper, t-shirts & magazines. Being a veteran, he knows eventually it'll be my turn to head upstate, to one of the processing prisons. When that day comes (hopefully soon, so I can get the hell out of here) I won't be allowed to bring anything but the clothes on my back, so Tyson will be the beneficiary of Eileen's largess. But for now I'm glad to have someone actually reach out to me. He pulls me aside, "Jerry, if anyone fucks with you, just let me know." I come to learn that everyone in this system has their own little scams and will do whatever it takes to survive. But he does appear genuine. I'm as fresh as a Daisy, Tyson senses this loud and clear.

I need to eat more! It's taking some time getting comfortable with this food, but of course I have no choice, I had better learn to like it. I miss my sons terribly; they are all I think about. Falling asleep has been difficult, there are 49 other men in this dorm and it seems everyone of them snores loudly.

This morning was the first time since my sentencing that I was able to see daylight. I was allowed a grand total of 1 hour recreation. As it turns out, only ten other fellow inmates line up at the door at the assigned time, 9:00 a.m. I think to myself, how could these other dudes not want to get out for some fresh air, to escape this filthy, smelly dorm for just an hour?

Guards escort us outside to a high school type of field, with a track, weight lifting area, and basket ball court, all surrounded by barbed wire of course. I soon notice particular areas being claimed by the inmates. Like the weightlifting area, a bunch of bad looking dudes hanging out there. All I want to do is run on the track, and breath in the fresh air. I have no interest in anything else. Rikers, or "The Island" as the prison veterans refer to it as, is right next door to LaGuardia airport, where it seems a plane flies overhead every 60 seconds. They appear so close, I can almost make out the tread of the tires as they take off and land. All I can think about is the freedom I no longer have, the freedom to be on one of those planes, and fly somewhere. As I walk the track I daydream about being in the sky again. The sun is shinning and the hour goes by way too quickly. The guards blast the siren, it's time to line up and return to the cell.

Tuesday June 26th

Constantly I find myself going back to where I was a week ago. Not sure why I punish myself with this train of thought, but I can't help it. The contrast from where I am now is two different worlds. I was playing golf with my sons Brooks & Phil, enjoying our last days together as I thought about all the special moments (Birthdays, holidays, Brooks High School graduation, Sr. college tour, etc...that I will miss out on. I am so sad and depressed. We had gone out to dinner, and I sat there stealing glimpses of the looks on their faces, the smiles. I am almost certain I will not want them to visit me while I am away.

The lights here at Rikers go out at Midnight, but that means nothing; the noise and hollering continue until the wee hours. I am so tired, hopefully I can fall asleep quickly tonight. My cot is at the end of the dorm, as far away from the night CO on duty as possible. I'm a little nervous with this but it was the only bed available when I arrived. Out of the 50 in this room, about 2 or 3 are white. Wake up is at 4:00 am, I have no idea why so early. Breakfast is wheeled in on a cart, we grab a tray, the slop is spooned out and then we head back to our beds to sit and eat. Oh God please help me survive.

Wednesday June 27th

It's 4:00 a.m., I'm sound asleep when I receive a tap on the shoulder waking me up. For some reason they are moving me into a new dorm. I dress quickly and look for Tyson to give him some of the clothes Eileen as given me. These are items I just won't feel comfortable wearing around here; like a bathrobe! Some of these guys could get away with it, but not me. As I prepare to leave, Tyson goes from being one of the most important people (my protector) in my current world, to someone, once I leave this room, odds are I will never see again.

The new dorm is only about a quarter mile away but after all the processing & waiting, it ends up taking me 10 hours to get there. I spend the bulk of that time in a holding cell the size of a closet. There are eleven of us, the heat is sweltering, the toilet doesn't work, and I feel like I am going to pass out. The guards don't give a shit if we all drop of heat exhaustion. I have to stay strong.

Thursday June 28th

As much as you can like anything in this horrid place, I do like my new dorm, much improved over the old place. For starters, it's somewhat air-conditioned, and that's a huge relief. Same layout as the other one, a large, flat open room, with 50 cots lined up side by side. The majority of the men are black & hispanic, the caucasian count totals four! Next to me is Mike, 63 years old, former CEO of an engineering consulting firm. Since we're half the white population, we got to chatting. He was arrested for cocaine possession and is awaiting trial. I observe Mike spending his days combing through the obituaries. Curious as to what he was up to, I asked him why he pours over them so. Apparently he looks for someone about his age and appearance, with no immediate family, so he can one day assume their identity when he gets out. I wait for him to smile, thinking he might be just kidding me. Well I'd be waiting a long time, he's serious!

This place is crawling with characters, petty thieves who would steal you blind or sell out their very own Mother for a few dollars. One of them I've encountered is Giovanni, who claims to be from an aristocratic family in Italy. He's here for credit card fraud & seems more than willing to share his tale of woe. Just last week he was arrested at a trendy NYC hot spot called Bungalow 8. "Jerry what are we doing here, only a few nights ago I was sipping champagne with three gorgeous models." I'm skeptical however, he looks like he doesn't have a dime to his name, I'll have to watch out for Giovanni, a real con-artist. But he is entertaining, and is facing a 2-4 year sentence.

Friday June 29th

In a very short time I have come to discover prison is something akin to a hate factory, with pain & suffering coming at you from all directions. The hate and sadness seems to permeate through the walls like maple syrup flowing through a tree in Vermont. Yes I am here doing the time, but the ripple effect of my crime is far-reaching. I have hurt (and let down) my loving parents along with my 5 siblings. Not to mention the two most important accomplishments of my life, my sons Brooks and Philip, ages 17 & 14. I couldn't have been more blessed, nor ask for more.

I will certainly have a lot of time for reflection here. I grew up upper middle class & never in a million years did I ever foresee so much as a minute of prison in my future. I began my career on Wall Street in the Fall of 1980, & while I did indeed have many productive years working there, they were off-set by the destruction that inevitably would befall me; the inability to look myself in the eye and say "I can't handle this, I'm not strong enough." Surrounded by 'action' on a daily basis would prove to be too much for me. I could go years and years without the desire to make trades for my personal account, but then something (I never have understood 'what' it was) would toggle a switch in my brain, and off on a binge I would go; throwing hundreds of thousands dollars around recklessly. More often than not, on the losing side of a trade. This sort of behavior went on for years, eventually leading me down the road to divorce, and eventually prison, as I cut one too many corners.

Sunday July 1st

Because I have been sentenced to more than one year in prison, Rikers Island will be only a temporary stop. The next shit hole will be a processing jail where I will be evaluated, tested both mentally & physically, have my hair shaven, and receive all my state prison garb which I'll have to wear for only God knows how long. After a brief (usually 3 weeks from what I understand) stay there I will eventually be bussed up north to one of the 70 prisons throughout NY State.

Along with my family, my hope and prayer is to be assigned to a Minimum Security facility. Considering that I am a 1st time felon and my crime is of a non-violent nature, I would think I fall into that category. As I overhear the other veteran inmates talk about "going upstate" they promise me there is no comparison to Rikers. 'Like a Four Seasons Hotel compared to this dump' they stress. I pray they're right.

A brief scuffle in the TV room earlier, punches about to be thrown until cooler heads prevailed. One idiot wanted to watch pro wrestling, the other a baseball game......wrestling got the nod. I had to go to bed, I'm sad, lonely and becoming more and more depressed. I miss my sons so much.

Monday July 2nd

I come to find the only highlight of my day here is the one hour I am allowed to go outside. It is sunny and warm, and when I step outside the building, I look straight up and see the nothing but blue sky, it's never looked so perfect. I know I only have 60 minutes, so I want to soak up every second.

I did not sleep well and this isolation is weighing heavy, and it's only my 2nd week. How will I survive this I keep asking myself. I continue to read about a book a day. I refuse to sleep the day away or take naps as most other inmates seem to do. I tell myself that would be a form of surrender to the system, to roll over (literally) feels like giving up. If I am to survive this I must never give up hope, I have to believe in myself, I must stay strong.

Tuesday July 3rd

Mike who sleeps in the cot next to mine, and whom I have become friendly with, drinks about 15 cups of coffee per day. Each one containing 4 packs of sugar. I watch him methodically prepare; pouring in the freeze-dried coffee, adding a drop of hot water, sugar, then he will whip it up into a kind of paste. Once the paste hardens Mike pours in the hot water. He was kind enough to make me a cup as well, I must admit, for instant coffee, it tasted pretty darn good.

Mike's trial is coming up in a few weeks; he faces anywhere between a year and six. Besides his drug charge he ran a small escort service along the side. His girls would not only offer their bodies to the clients, but deal Mike's drugs to them as well. Call it one stop shopping. Like me he reads books all day & night. The lights go out here @ Midnight, but it's meaningless, the noise level even at that hour sounds like Times Sq. on New Years Eve. I can already see that to the majority of men in this dorm, the whole prison thing is no big deal. You see it in the way they carry themselves, looking totally relaxed and at ease, playing cards with their buddies, like they were back home or something.

Tomorrow is the 4th of July & Eileen is coming to visit. Not only will it be a relief to get out of this dorm for an hour, it will be great to see her. She's promised me a few books, a newspaper, and earplugs.

Wednesday July 4th

I hate to keep harping on it, but one of the toughest adjustments is simply trying to fall asleep each night. Forty-nine other men (actually most are young kids, in their late teens, early twenties, gangster wannabes) living in this hell-hole they call a dorm, and you should hear the screaming, hollering and attempts at singing that take place every night. It's wearing me down, I'm exhausted. These are the dudes who sleep all day, the night is their time; probably similar to the way it was back when they were on the streets dealing. To make matters worse, those earplugs Eileen tried to give me, well the guards wouldn't let me have them, for what reason I can't even fathom. Probably because it would make too much sense.

I wake up at 2:00 a.m. or so, and observe over in the corner the usual poker game taking place. Yes, even at this hour. Instead of chips, tiny bars of soap are being used, kind of like the ones the hotels give out. As I rubbed my eyes to get a closer look, who do I see but the night guard, who's supposed to be in charge of watching the room, right in the thick of the game, playing along with the inmates! Oh great, I feel really safe now.

No fireworks for me this year, for the 1st time since I was a little boy I haven't heard the sound of crackers going off in the distance. I try not to think about it, all I can do is hope and pray I'm home to enjoy the 4th a year from now.

Thursday July 5th

I hope to be leaving here soon! One of these mornings I will be awoken early (3:30) and ordered to get dressed, but not packed. Apparently we are not allowed to bring a single stitch of clothing or anything else upstate. Off to the processing jail I'll go, either a place called Downstate or Ulster. Both a few hours north of here.

I've heard of the feeding frenzy that takes place when you're told to leave; all the slimy vultures come out of the woodwork to queue up for whatever clothes or food you leave behind. It doesn't matter that the entire time I've been here they haven't said one word to me, now I'm their best friend. These dudes have no shame. I can't wait to get the heck out of here.

Friday July 6th

I met an inmate named Gilly today. Normally, other than Mike, I don't associate with anybody, but Gilly seemed friendly enough, approachable, and with his cot directly across from mine, it's hard not to have at least some eye contact. In speaking with him briefly I found him to be mild mannered, intelligent, and aware of his surroundings, not a nuckel-head. Hmmm, might not sound like too much to ask, but in here it's like a needle in a haystack. Gilly carries himself like he's done this prison thing before, again like most of the guys here. He could see that I was out of my element, scared, and came across the way to offer some words of encouragement. As it turns out, he's served a total of eleven years so far, various crimes here and there adding up to that number. So I was thinking what did he do this time to end up back on Rikers Island.

Well why not just ask him I thought. Gently I broached that subject as a somber look appeared on his face. "Jerry, it's the biggest mistake I ever made, and I've made a lot of them. I killed my brother." Just like that, it was out in the open. All of a sudden I was silent, I mean what the heck could I say? "Shit happens Gilly, don't sweat it." No, I don't think that would be the answer. So lamely all I could muster was, "Oh wow, geez, I'm sorry to hear that, hang in there." Hang in there? Quietly I slinked back to my cot, with an understanding not to ask anybody again what they are here for.

Saturday July 7th

Remember the clothes vultures I mentioned a few days ago? Well Mike & I turned into "bed vultures" early this morning. Let me explain. Both of our cots had been in the middle of this long , windowless, dull room. The noise level seemed to be ground zero right where we were. So at 3:30 a.m. when we saw two guys getting the nod signaling they were departing Rikers (Steve was one of them, serving 2-4 for hitting his next door neighbor over the head with a brick, and John sentenced 6-9 years for massive credit card fraud) and whose beds were along the coveted wall area, (no one behind you & quieter) we sprang into action. Quickly we switched our mattresses & sheets with theirs, and just like that, we had moved into a more desirable (quieter?) neighborhood. And to think, a mere week ago I would never have had the nerve to make such a move. Hopefully tonight I can finally get some sleep.

Sunday July 8th

The dorm was raided this morning! There I was getting ready for my precious one hour of outdoor recreation, the hour that keeps me sane, keeps me going throughout the day, when all of a sudden 30-40 officers come storming in, most dressed in riot gear, with their helmets, long shields, night sticks, looking just like a group of Ninja Turtles, but a whole lot meaner. What the hell was going on?

Well apparently it all stemmed form 1 idiotic inmate the night before who had put on such a scene; screaming, cursing at the night guard, refusing to shut up for a solid hour. As they do I guess, the night CO recorded all of this in his daily log, so when the Sergeant came around to inspect the book, well that's all he needed to see. Game over for this dude, and the rest of us as well. Time to show these inmates who is really in charge. What struck me as weird was that none of these other bad asses in the room bothered to challenge this lunatic. No one yelled over, telling him to sit the fuck down or something to that effect. And believe me, there are some hard core dudes living here who take no shit from anyone. Because even a rookie like me knew there would be consequences for his actions.

Once the Ninja Turtles took charge of the room, we were all ordered to strip naked, our clothes then tossed in every direction. Then each man's bed was striped, lockers overturned, food spilled every which way. There was shit thrown about the entire room. If contraband was found on anyone, that would be a bonus for the guards, but the main goal was simple shock & awe. To create the largest mess and headache for us. The raid was a particular blow for me, not only did I never get my hour of rec, my sneakers were confiscated. They were the Nike Air Max 360's. The problem is they had the tiny plastic bubble soles along the base of the shoe. Big deal, right? Well the guard claimed they could be used to insert and hide various drugs. What? In addition, they had a trace of red on them, which is a gang color, so red is abolished throughout Rikers. I'm so pissed as they were my running shoes. Now I don't have a pair. Of any shoe! So I was given a pair of orange slip-ons (Pataki's they call them, after the former NY State Governor who cracked down on prison reform) which are absolutely repulsive & make me look like a convict more than ever.

Monday July 9th

I've just completed my third weekend of prison! So much of this existence is brutal; but I have come to find the weekends particularly hard. They are filled with too much time on my hands, which leads to memories of happier days. Days spent with my sons, families and friends. For the past ten years as Brooks & Philip were growing up, they played in countless town baseball, soccer, and basketball games. In all those years I missed maybe one or two of those games. What a joy I would get, sitting in the stands, watching the two of them compete, the innocence of the surroundings protecting us all at that moment. What a proud father I was. While I sit in prison I recall taking them out for a treat or lunch afterwords, I wanted to soak up every single minute of being in their space. And as I look around at my current surroundings, I miss the connotation of Saturday mornings; the errands, trips to the local coffee shop where I would hang out reading the papers, planning a busy day ahead.

I have begun to realize that I almost have to force myself not to look back on those days. As harsh as that sounds, it's true. While yes they define my past and my days as a father, it's just too damm painful. It is almost like I have to block the boys & my family from my mind, they can't exist inside my head while I stay here, perhaps just quick little pit stops her & there. Because to dwell on the past will just make me sad and weak, and to get through this, I need to be the total opposite. I have to tell myself that kids are resilient, they are healthy, they are getting tons of support from family and friends, and someday we'll all come out of this in one piece. Maintaining a strong psyche, I realize more and more, is the key to survival here. Prison is a hate factory, and if I'm not careful it will strip me of my remaining dignity and self-esteem.

Tuesday July 10th

It is commissary day. I have the opportunity to purchase a few snacks, instant coffee, soap, shampoo, stamps and shower shoes. I don't want to load up on too much as I have a feeling I'll be leaving here any day now. At least I hope that's the case.

Last night I witnessed an inmate trying to sell his collection of hardcore porno (don't know how he managed to get it in here) magazines for a combination of coffee and phone call minutes. A deal was struck (who says there is no honor amongst thieves) and both sides seemed content.

My first week here I could barely stomach the food, but it's amazing how the body and mind soon take over. After all, no matter how disgusting it is, I have to eat something, plain and simple. The temperature outside is a sunny 95 degrees. I can catch a glimpse of the blue sky through the windows in the hall, as we line up single for dinner...at 4:00 p.m! Why so early? My thoughts will then drift to happier more normal days, when I would be at work right now, finishing up at the office or whatever the days chores would be, getting ready to head home for a run, see the boys, and have a cocktail. I miss going to the movies, watching TV, making a sandwich, or grabbing a fresh cup of coffee whenever I want. I miss fresh air, not this circulated stale, smelly air that permeates throughout Rikers. I miss putting on clean clothes, throwing them into the washer instead of having to wash them in the showers and sinks with a bar of soap like I do now. But more than all this, I miss my family, brothers, sisters, and my Mom & Dad.

The word "nigger" is bandied about amongst the inmates all day long. It's a bit of a shock to me, but it seems not a sentence is spoken amongst the black inmates without that word being used constantly. I don't get it, I thought they found that word offensive.

I received a pair of sneakers today; my Mother sent them. Yes, like Christmas morning. Now at least I can shed those hideous orange slip-ons.

Wednesday July 11th

This is the fourth straight day of 90 degree plus temperatures! Needless to say it's hot in here, which might explain the uptick of tension swirling around lately.

Around 8:30 this morning I witnessed my first fight in prison. What triggered it was so minor, but within these confines apparently thats all it takes. It was a simple matter of one inmate cutting in front of another when it was time for soap bars to be passed out. As soon as this guy cut in front, hat happened a cry rang out, "Hey man, what the fuck do you think you're doing." I knew trouble was not far behind. And wouldn't you know it, my lucky day, I found myself right smack in the middle of these two gigantic black inmates, with no escape. Call it a super-sized Oreo with just a tab of creme filling on the inside. Somehow I did manage to quickly sidestep the mayhem, because it doesn't matter if you're involved or not, if the guards see you around this, you're guilty until proven innocent. Two quick punches were thrown, both of these dudes connecting, my guess is they've done this before. But before you knew what was happening, 3 Corrections Officers (CO's) were on the scene, breaking it up before anything further could spread. I bet this is just how riots start. Both guys were led away in cuffs, a trip to "the box" (a prison within a prison) was in their future.

One guy I've spoken to a few times since being here got the tap on the shoulder early this morning. Dean (serving 2-4 on a drug charge) is now on his way to one of the two processing centers run by NY State. He's off to Downstate CF, in Fishkill, NY. From what I understand this part of the journey lasts about 3 weeks. After that, you're bussed to your permanent "home." I keep waiting for someone to tap me on the shoulder so I can get the hell out of here. Before Dean left he gave me his comb and nail-clipper. So for the first time in 19 days, since I was sentenced, I was able to run a comb through my hair. The mirrors in the bathrooms here are not real mirrors, but rather plastic ones, plastic reflecting glass. It's kind of like looking at yourself in one of those mirrors you find at the circus. Combing my hair and cutting my fingernails and toenails is the highlight of my day.

Thursday July 12th

It's nothing concrete, just a bunch of little things, but I feel really down today. From the minute I woke up (at 4:30 for breakfast) I've had this cloud of sadness overhanging. I am so fucking depressed. I knew a day like this was looming. For days now I have been trying to convince myself that this ordeal is doable, I'm strong enough to get through it. Today the dark forces took over. I can't stop thinking about my sons.

In attempt to cheer myself up, I called my younger son Philip. he brought me up to date on his summer, typical teenage boy activities; hanging out with his friends, sleeping late, playing sports, etc. No matter how shitty I feel, no matter how helpless and removed I am, I will never let them know the depths of my sadness. It is critical that I always stay strong when speaking or writing to them. I will always try and maintain the same composure when dealing with my Mother & Father. I know they are suffering right along side of me, and my Mom, if given the chance, would want to do this time for me. I have put them through a lot, no doubt. Dad is 85, my Mom 81. And no matter how sharp and strong they are, these ages don't lie; it takes a toll, witnessing your child sent off to prison. They have such faith however, never have I seen such love and devotion, their hearts ache for me. As mine does for them. I will never forget walking into their bedroom the night before sentencing, knowing there was a strong possibility this would be the last time I saw them, God forbid something happens to them while I'm gone.

Four inmates left this morning, sure enough only hours later their beds were already being occupied with new prisoners. The beat goes on.

18

Friday July 13th

I heard noises, my head immediately sprang up from the pillow. Quickly checking my watch I saw that it was 3:30 a.m, Friday the 13th. Right then and there I should have known the day was not going to bode well. I saw a flashlight coming towards me, the night officer standing over my cot. "Time to go Byrne, get dressed." This is it; I was leaving leaving Rikers, for good! I jumped into the shower, thinking I will not miss this mildew-infested excuse for a shower room. From there, given I am not allowed to bring anything Upstate except the clothes on my back, I put on my khakis and blue button down shirt, which have served me so well, the ones I was wearing when sentenced. Everything else I had accumulated (thanks to Eileen) would have to be left behind, not for the vultures, but for Mike, who I have become very close with. We hugged goodbye, this guy I had eaten all my meals with, read books side by side with, and slept next to for 3 solid weeks. I knew deep down I would never see again.

It's about 4:00 when I walk into the holding cell, awaiting the trip up North. There is only one other inmate in there at the time and I remember thinking to myself, "Hmmm, this isn't so bad, just the two of us, I can handle this." Little did I know that number would eventually grow to 16, in a cell that fits maybe 8. Here I would sit (stand is more like it) for the next 6 1/2 hours! During this time I come to learn I am in this cell with guys whose sentences range from 2 years to life. There was 'Ray Ray,' already 14 years under his belt with 15 remaining. I looked at him in amazement, thinking, how could anyone do that much time? And then there was 'Speedy,' serving 15 to life. There was only one other white guy besides me, I did my best to remain in his space. What a sight; the two of us, looking like two lost sheep. His name was Sean, serving 1 1/2 to 3 for stealing a car high on drugs.

Right out of the movie "The Fugitive" with Harrison Ford, when a prisoner is moved from one facility to another, you must be shackled at the wrists and ankles. Your ankle is then cuffed to another inmate. Joined at the hip you could call it. I was chained up with Sean, the only other white guy. Can't be a coincidence I thought, the guard did that for a reason. So we hip-hoped our way down the hall, and eventually, quite gingerly, climbed onto the bus. Sean got the window seat.

I was on my to Downstate Correctional Facility in Fishkill, NY. Exit 11 off of Route 84 West. I couldn't help but think of the last time I travelled on this road; my sons were in the backseat, my ex-wife upfront, and we were on our way to maine for a summer vacation. I was a successful Wall Street broker, proud father, loving husband, and the future was boundless. Look at me now.

There is no talking allowed on the bus, two guards in the front seats, one in the back. I stare straight ahead, my wrists are killing me. Don't even think about going to the bathroom or asking for something, it's not going to happen. Eventually lunch is 'served.' Brown bags are passed out, each one containing a cheese sandwich, plastic container of grape juice, and 2 stale cookies. Have you ever tried to eat while handcuffed? No? Well let me tell you, it's not easy, I slobbered all over myself. The ride takes 3 hours.

Our bus sits for 30 minutes outside the barbed wire gates of Downstate. Just another delay in a day already filled with them. Eventually we head in and are ordered off the bus. Sean and I gingerly manage to get out, my muscles ache from sitting so long, my ankles & wrists are killing me. All of us (there are about 35 prisoners on the bus) make our way into another holding cell where we are verbally abused by a collection of CO's. One of the C.O.'s tries to pick a fight with the entire lot of us, "I'll bring full-force down on all of you, c'mon! Full-force!" He screams. We sit and wait some more. Eventually it's time to be strip searched, then thrown in cold showers to clean up. Guards watching and grinning the entire time. From there it's into the barber's chair, where your hair will be 99% shaved off. Any ounce of dignity I had been able to cling to is now gone. I was feeling so very low, and scared. My spirit was being broken, I could feel it. Don't let up I kept saying to myself, you must stay strong for the boys and your family. There is no other option. I have to go through this, to get through this, was all I could think of.

Saturday July 14th

Downstate is a reception facility, it's main purpose is to get me and all the other inmates "state ready" and be classified as to which facility we'll end up at. From what I'm told there are 3 different classifications,

Minimum, Medium, and gulp......Maximum. Of course my family and I are praying for minimum. As a 1st time offender, with a non-violent crime, I have a decent chance, I think. Another term for the Minimum facilities are "camps."

Yesterday I also received my lovely state greens. These hideous, polyester infested clothes will be the clothes on my back for the length of my term. I have been given heavy duty black work boots, 3 pairs of green pants, 3 short-sleeved shirts, all with my name and Identification number (07A3830) on them, and a winter jacket for the freezing cold weather I'll be looking at in a few months time.

Sunday July 15th

I am confined to my cell 23 hours a day! Other than being marched, under ground through a maze of tunnels, over to the mess hall 3x per day, I sit in this tiny cell and stare at the walls & out the tiny window. No books (only my Bible is allowed) no paper, no nothing. The only paper I have is the pages inside my Bible. At night, during the one of Rec time, I am given a tiny pencil, with just a trace of a lead point. This is when I do my writing....quickly. Through the window I look out at tree tops in the distance, along side a mountain here in Duchess County. A slew of Canadian Geese constantly are strolling by, I look down at them, jealous of their freedom. What I wouldn't give for my feet to be touching that grass right now. I sit and daydream about happier days, the world was my oyster, and I fucking blew it. I try to convince myself that life is not over for me; yes this is a major hurdle, when I will eventually climb over.

I think of my ex wife and son Brooks who are up in Vermont right now, doing a college tour, and here I am, sitting in this depressing cell. Some father, aren't I. This special moment in his young life is one I will never get back, gone to me forever. How many more moments will I miss out on before I return, whenever the hell that might be.

It's a beautiful sunny day, one of those summer days you never want to end, if you have your freedom that is. Since I don't, I can't wait until the darkness comes and I can shut it down. I'm quickly learning a prison mantra the other veteran inmates have stressed......just look at the end of each day "as another day down." That's all it is. "You do the time, don't let the time do you," I hear so many of them say. Most seem to live by that creed.

I'm looking forward to next Sunday when my parents will be coming to visit, as well as my brother Jack. Looking at Mom & Dad you would never guess their ages to be 85 & 81; they appear and act so much younger. I can't stand the thought of them seeing their son in a place like this, but they insist on coming. Jack has been my rock throughout this ordeal, I've leaned on him hard. Currently he lives in Honduras, back in the States now for summer break.

Earlier today, those of us who wanted to, were able to attend Catholic Services, which began at 8:30. I must say I found it to be not only peaceful and spiritual, but reinforced a sense of hope, a temporary sense of normalcy. For the 1st time since coming to prison, I felt calm. Well, all those wonderful feelings came to a crashing halt as the other inmates and I were led back to our cells. Thanks to one brutal corrections officer who went on profanity laced tirade towards me and the other guys. "You mother fuckers don't deserve forgiveness, you're all a bunch of hypocrites. I bet you like to touch 11 year old girls, don't you." Oh man did I want to lash back at this angry and miserable person. It was just so ugly and hurtful, made especially so given where we had just come from. And the fact that I had, for the 1st time since being sentenced, achieved a feeling of hope and calm. But you know what, there was absolutely nothing any of us could do about it, we had to stand there and take it. Sure, you want to be a hero and say something to this piece of shit, go ahead, next thing you know you'll be in the box! And lose what ever small privileges you do have. I got back to my cell and felt horrible all over again.

Monday July 16th

I broke down tonight. God I hated to, but I couldn't help it. While I was on the phone speaking with my Mom, it just happened. Of course she did her best to console me. I quickly checked myself, for as I mentioned, I especially need to remain strong for my folks. The last thing they should have to hear is their son crying over the phone.

With all this free time, my mind drifts amongst a slew of various thoughts. Earlier today I found myself wishing that instead of reporting to the courts for sentencing a month ago, I had said "fuck it" and become a fugitive. Yes I'd be on the run right now, but hell, it would have to be better than this miserable existence, at least I'd be on the outside. That's crazy thinking though, I snapped back to reality. The thought that perhaps I would never see my boys again, not freely anyway. No, can't do it. To always be looking over my shoulder, not knowing when I'd be caught, well that's not living either. That has to be the worst option!

Tuesday July 17th

When I arrived here last week I wound up siting next to a 55 year old white guy who seemed approachable. I was scared of course, my new surroundings and all, and just wanted to have someone I could talk to, cling to I guess you could call it. His name is Don, an ageless hippie sort, long grayish hair with a laid back attitude. He didn't seem to mind my coming into his space a little and engaging him in conversation. Don gave me brief rundown on his story. He had been living a successful, comfortable life in Arizona for the past 8 years or so. He told me he was a chef at a high-end restaurant out there, a part-owner, had quite a reputation as a mildly famous chef, and was married to a beautiful woman 20 years younger. Also, a few of his recipes have been featured in Bon Appetite magazine. Life was good he mused. So I was thinking to myself, what the hell had happened to Don to end up here, back in a New York state prison.

With all this spare time we had sitting and waiting in the holding cell, Don was willing to share. Apparently about 10 years ago Don had sold a "dime bag" of heroin (now I have no idea how much drugs that is, but I assume a decent amount) to an undercover cop. Well he got busted and was sentenced to 2 years in prison. After 15 months served he gets out on a work release program, and is sent to a facility in the Bronx where he must report each night to sleep. After numerous times of being shaken down and extorted in & out of the facility, (apparently a real crappy area of the Bronx) Don said the hell with this and took off. An immediate violation! He heads out West and begins this new life I just mentioned. His wife never knew of his past, Don never thought he would get caught, never thought the past would come back to haunt him. And it didn't, until just a few short months ago.

Don and his wife were driving back home after a lovely night out for dinner. He had had a drink or two, and didn't realize he was now speeding. Sure enough a cop pulls him over. The cop runs a routine check, and bingo, eight years later, there was still a warrant back in NY for Don's arrest. His wife is going hysterical, all this a shock to her, she knows nothing of it. Don is taken out of the car in cuffs and eventually extradited back to New York. And here he is, sitting next to me. Oh man life, ya never know.

The beat goes on here, same old loneliness and depression. I have found out that tomorrow I will finally get some free/rec time (1 hour) and be able to head to the library. You're only allowed 1 book at a time, but to me it'll feel like I'm browsing through the world's largest Barnes & Noble store. I'm so excited. The past 6 days I have had no paper to write on; I keep having to tear pages out of my Bible so I can continue this story.

Wednesday July 18th

I didn't just wake up one day and end up in prison. Sadly to say, it was years and years of cutting corners, making bad choices, and losing my moral compass. The majority of the above fueled by my inability to face my weaknesses, most notably, an addiction to financial gambling and recklessness. I had it all, was given every tool to succeed, and look what happened. Ashamed doesn't begin to describe my feelings.

Shortly after graduating from Villanova University in 1980, I began my career on Wall Street, at the prestigious brokerage firm; Paine Webber. Earning the princely sum (to me it felt like I had hit the jackpot) of $12k per year. I worked hard, was one of the first ones on the desk every morning, and felt exhilarated by the excitement of the financial arena I stepped into each day. Shortly afterwords I became intoxicated by it all and had to have the accouterments that went with it all; stuff like the Rolex watch, along with the leased BMW 3 series.

About eighteen months later I had saved enough to make my 1st stock trade, plus I was ready to jump on board this financial casino. It was about time to conquer the markets. Remembering the day like it was yesterday, I deposited $8000 in my brokerage account and purchased call options (betting the stock would move higher in price) on a California

24

S&L by the name of First Charter Financial. I had done my homework, the stock had taken a beating the past few weeks and I felt it was ready for a bounce back. Sure enough, only hours after I bought in, the stock went up, on paper I was richer by $2k.....a lot of money back in 1981. My exuberance took hold and I screamed to everyone on the trading desk, "shoe shines are on me today." I was a big-shot, my time had come, look out Wall St!

Well no sooner had I paid the shoeshine man, to the tune of $60, did the market begin to collapse, my options along with it. "What the hell is going on," I shouted to no one in particular. Nobody answered, but something indeed was going on. In hindsight it should've been a sure omen that the stock market was no place for me. As it turns out, the day I decided to make my 1st trade, was the same day the President of the United States was shot. Yes, Ronald Reagan was shot. The stock exchange quickly closed down for the day, and my investment was just about gone. Not to mention my shine money.

However I failed to heed this omen and proceeded to continue on with my life on Wall Street. In spite of myself I was able to forge a pretty lucrative career as a bond broker, earning on average, depending on the year end bonus, anywhere between $200-300k per year. My sons were born, and along with my wife, we lived in the exclusive suburb of Short Hills, NJ.....the same town I grew up in. We belonged to private country clubs, took trips, drove nice cars, etc, etc. But for every step forward, there was that eventual step or two backwards. I was surrounded by action, 12 hours of day of money changing hands, millions and millions of it. The lure wore me down, I could hold out only so long before I would binge and turn into 'Jerry the reckless trader' who looses all sense of of reality. During that time nothing else (and I mean nothing) matters except my trading, my bets on the market.

This pattern continued on & off over the years, my marriage taking a toll from the ups and downs, the highs and lows. I remained on the street but morphed a bit of my career over to the media side of finance. I was hired by various news organizations to report and comment about the markets, going on live TV for Bloomberg, CNBC, as well as the leading financial network in India, NDTV. I worked hard at these appearances, took pride in my reporting, always trying to present the best trading advice possible. And I was good at it, invited back time and again. I was the 'good Jerry' when I did this.

Then I got arrested/indicted. This world came to a screeching halt, no one wanted to know me or take my calls. I was finished. Every shred of credibility I had worked so hard at establishing had vanished in a heartbeat.

Thursday July 19th

No writing today, simply not up to it.....too depressed.

Friday July 20th

A month ago today, I was sentenced! While I never want to relive that day, and yes, there have been some horrible moments in between, the time has gone quickly. Already a month down. I sit here in my cell anxiously awaiting my next and final destination, a bus ride somewhere up North, where exactly I have no idea. The question is; how much longer will I remain in this hellhole. From what I hear the veteran prisoners say, once you get to your permanent housing facility (sounds so much nicer than prison, doesn't it) life becomes a whole lot smoother, easier to handle. They say the guards are more laid back, there is all sorts of Rec available, free time to go running, walking weight lifting, basketball, the library, etc, etc. I doubt it's as rosy as all that, but anything would be an improvement over this place.

The CO's here take absolutely no shit, none at all. I thought the guards at Rikers were brutal, well compared to these guys, they are like choirboys. You could be on deaths door here and it would not mean shit to these dudes. In fact if you did die, the only thing they'd be upset about would be the paperwork that needed to be filled out.

Inmates get shuffled around constantly. In the brief time I've been, two new faces have come & gone in the cell next to mine. As I peer through the tiny slot of my cells heavy steel door, I witness my new neighbor checking in. Sounds kind of like a hotel, doesn't it. Immediately I can tell this guy is no stranger to prisons; not a shred of panic on his face, a swagger that exudes "gangsta." Also referred to as the pimp role.

26

You would have thought cat was walking into a restaurant or nightclub they way he carried himself. What really is the dead give away is that all the other inmates surrounding his cell seemed to know him, from the "hood" or some place like that. It was like a homecoming. I heard shouts of, "Yo, Big Dog, what up my man." Or "Big Dog be in the house!" Looking at him I'd say he was about 6'8, 300 pounds easily. Someone yells out, "Big Dog, what they get you for?" He screams back, "I didn't do shit, these crackers accuse me of murder and kidnapping." Lovely I thought, here's my new neighbor for the foreseeable future. When you are called out for meals you have to line up single file, one cell mate next to another. So this means Big Dog will be in back of me as we proceed to the mess hall, and will be seated right next to me during all our meals. He's looking at life imprisonment, do you think he'll insist on taking my food? Do you think it will matter if I tell him no? Do you think he'll simply ring my neck one day?

Compared to Rikers, the food here is a major step up. I can actually eat it, and there have been a few times, not that I would be allowed to, that I have actually wanted seconds. The portions are tiny and you have ten minutes to eat. Upon leaving the mess hall you deposit your plastic "spork" (combo fork & spoon) into the trash, place your tray on the conveyor belt, and get back in line. The guards are of course watching your every move. No food is allowed out of the mess hall with the exception of the 4 slices of white bread you receive. I always take my bread, mostly so I can feed the geese that gather outside my window. I can entertain myself for a few hours doing this. I have to be careful however, if caught a trip to the box would most likely be the result.

I made my first visit to the library today. Calling it a library is certainly a bit of a stretch, but it did have books, and that was good enough for me. It had about 200 old and tattered paperbacks, the newest one probably at least 5 years old. The most up to date newspaper was from over two weeks ago. In searching I managed to find a book by one of my favorite authors, William Goldman, called "The Color of Light." Normally I would tear through this in a day, but not this time, I needed to treasure it, for who knows when I'll be able to get back in the library. I'd scoop up ten books if I could, but you're only allowed one at a time.

I find manners here to be nonexistent. Something as simple and common as a "thank you" or "please" would be seen as a sign of weakness. Since I'm in the habit of saying these words I have to learn to refrain from using them. Already, the first sign of my being forced to alter my demeanor so as I can 'fit in.'

There is a father & son here. Yes, can you imagine the heartache of being in prison with your son? Apparently the entire family was busted on some extortion charges. The son, who is a few cells away from me doesn't appear to be all that bothered with his circumstances, he's actually been quite boastful. I have to keep reminding myself that I am in another world at the moment; one that is so incredibly foreign. But one I must adapt to.

Saturday July 21st

At Rikers breakfast was served at the early hour of 4:00 (so the inmates going to court could eat and be ready for the bus ride into Manhattan) but here at Downstate it is much more civilized. (Again, a bit of a stretch, civilized?) Here we gather at 7:00. Oh, and it's never referred to as either breakfast, lunch, or dinner, it's all called just one thing.....chow! I know I will come too detest that word. Before we line up to go to meals you get ready to hear the guards scream out, " On the chow." That means it's time to get the state greens all buttoned and tucked in, then lineup for food.

I have to say I'm grateful there are no mirrors to be found, anywhere. I dread to see what my shaved head must look like. Laundry is done once per week You put all your clothes, underwear, and t-shirts, into a net-bag, tie it up, and then your bag is thrown into the wash along with everyone else's. Disgusting! I get three showers a week, Mon-Wed-Fri. Considering it's the dead of summer, 90 degree temps everyday, you can imagine the horrid smell of some of these dudes. On shower day I stand by the cell door, soap and towel in hand, ready to go when the guard bushes a button from the control room to unlock it. You're sent in one at a time, you have 3 minutes.

Sunday July 22nd

My writing is sporadic, I know that. It all hinges on the ability to score a few pieces of paper, not to mention a pen or pencil. These items are precious here.

The past few days have been mostly quiet, the only highlight being a visit from my parents, and brother Jack. I had not seen Mom & Dad since the night before I was sentenced and went into their room to say goodbye, not knowing if I would ever see them again when I wasn't behind bars. As much as a strain as I have endured, they have been with me on this journey in equal fashion, suffering on the inside at the thought of their son locked away. But I am happy to report they both looked amazing. Their strength is my strength. It's how I will survive this nightmare.

What a sight it was, the three of them entering the visitors room. My father wearing his ever present blue blazer (he opted to forgo the tie), Mom sporting a needlepoint belt and shoes, and Jack, who is just always dressed as if he was stepping onto 5th Ave. I think it's safe to say the Downstate CF visitors room doesn't see this sort of attire all too often. In fact one of the guards who spotted them going through the processing line even had to ask, "Uhm, excuse me folks, are you sure you're in the right place?"

Monday July 23rd

Before being sentenced I read quite a bit about the effect that doing prison time has on a person, both before & after. While yes, I know it's only been very brief so far, I'm sure the post-traumatic stress never fully leaves you. Already I carry such an amount of sadness, remorse, guilt and shame. Negativity is rampant. I fight hard against wallowing in it however, I will be looking for the positive spirit that I know can be gained here, somehow. Only a month in and I can tell you, that when I do regain my freedom someday, there will never be a time when I am not so utterly grateful for all the Lord has given me. I can't help but think of all the complaining and negative energy I have given off for so many years now. Rarely living in the now, soaking up all the beauty that was in front of me.

In the town where I grew up (Short Hills, NJ) and resided most my life, the majority of folks know what as happened to me. I try not to think of the gossip or the nasty, mean-spirited words that are being used to describe me. A good 'ol fashioned kick him while he's down. Fine, say what you want, but please, please, don't let my sons come under this type of fire, don't you dare say anything to them. I am so sorry I am here!

I have friends who never left my side during all this, I will forever be grateful. There are others, even though I haven't hurt them in anyway, have already written me off. I understand though, I do.

Tuesday July 24th

The temperatures remain in the low 90's, the heat in this cell is unbearable at times. I am sweating constantly. Outside these walls, one would describe it as a perfect Summer day. In here however it is something different entirely. No showers yesterday, so it's been 4 days since water or soap has touched my skin. I have been using the sink water to clean my body as best I can. So as not to sit the entire time I pace back & forth, back & forth. Three whole steps before I have to turn around. I stare out the tiny window, summer has always been my most favorite season. I think it would be easy to go absolutely mad here, just fucking lose it, become broken. The days seem to last forever. At 7:00pm we get one hour of TV time, or if you prefer, card playing. Plastic chairs arraigned in front of the TV, six rows of five each, positively no talking allowed. Majority rules in terms of what we watch, this of course means watching some mindless sitcom or reality show, something along the likes of either Jerry Springer Show, or Bernie Mac. I sit there in a trance, alternating between staring out the window at the setting sun, to the ridiculous show. The sad thing is, just about all the guys watching the TV are loving it, laughing their stupid heads off. Like their in the comfort of their own homes, the only thing missing is a Lazy-Boy chair. I think to myself; 'Why can't I be happy like that?' Where is the stress on these dudes, why don't they seem to feel the shame that I do?

Wednesday July 25th

Sadly I'm still here. Each day when I wake up I think well maybe this is the day I'll receive word that I'm on tomorrow's bus headed up North. The final leg on this journey. The veteran inmates continue to drone on about how much "nicer" it is there, the freedom you get. The way they speak it's almost like we're all going to Club Med. Recreation galore, a gym, basketball, bocce, handball, running track, library, free dental and medical, commissary, food packages, etc.....the only thing missing is the fruity drinks with the umbrellas. As they speak of these upstate prisons I can notice a look in their eye, a look of contentment, as if the life up there is so much better than anything they experienced back in the projects. It begins to dawn on me that perhaps the reason the recidivism is so high (83%) is because a lot of these guys prefer it to back home.

Downstate CF is so over the top, a guy in my dorm received a disciplinary ticket for taking an extra slice of bread out of the mess hall. Yeah, that's right. You're permitted to carry out 4 slices, he took 5. The procedure is to wrap it up in your napkin and quickly show it to the guard standing at the door. The CO on duty must have noticed the additional girth within the napkin, pulled this guy over and before you knew it a whole slew of cops had him up against the wall, legs spread. You'd think he just robbed a bank.

Thursday July 26th

Big Dog left Downstate this morning! I have no idea where they took him, but I have to assume he'll be on the bus headed to a maximum facility. Maybe even a super-max, from what I understand there are three of them in NY State. While it's horrendous the crimes he's committed (murder/kidnapping), it presents such a stark contrast to the scene in the Visitor's room yesterday. There he was, playing with his 5 year old son, his wife sitting next to him as well. (I assume it's his wife, perhaps his Baby Mamma). This a scene that will be repeated throughout this young boys life; visiting his Dad behind bars. So sad.

Friday July 27th

I've had a wicked headache all day; it continues and doesn't seem to want to go away. Thankfully I don't get too many of these, but I think it's just the general day-to-day anxiety of being here. Tomorrow will mark two weeks that I've been at this hell hole. I continue to pray that any day now the guards will tell me to pack up, that I'm "On the draft." What this entails is; you gather up your belongings (mostly just the depressing state clothes you've received) the afternoon before you leave, you bring it all to the reception building, where they are then dumped out and searched. After the search, we have to pack it all up again, in these large draft bags, kind of like gigantic lawn & leaf bags. They take these bags from you, hold them overnight, then when it's time to be bussed the next morning, they are ready to go. Of course this all means that I will once again, have to be chained and shackled for another bus ride. Let me tell you, I already have knots in my stomach thinking about it. On average, with stops and starts, you're talking a 6 hour bus ride.

So after dropping the bags off, I go back to my cell, where I will be locked down (not that I have much freedom now) with no phone calls, no outside contact at all. I suppose for security reasons. I guess some of these lifers heading up North, with nothing to lose, might just try to make contact with their peeps back home, maybe roll the bus, hijack it or something. Ok, farfetched? Yes, maybe a little, but you never know, the Department of Corrections take no chances. I guess that's why the guards aboard the bus all carry loaded weapons.

It was a beautiful sunny day, but not for a minute did I set outside. We were allowed Rec twice, an hour each, but it consisted of watching mindless TV. The majority rules when it comes to that. You should've seen the looks I got when I suggested we tune in the CBS evening news. I swear some of these dudes looked like they wanted to stab me.

After dinner tonight I went back to my cell, gave 2 pieces of my bread to the geese.......I think they'll miss me when I leave.

Saturday July 28th

As of earlier this morning I am now living in a new cell. Unfortunately however, it's just as depressing. All of us (29) from the old dorm were moved out of G block and dispersed throughout the other prison dorms. Now instead of the view of the mountain tops I look out onto a parking lot.

Each weekday approximately 25-30 inmates are moved out of Downstate and herded upstate. So as a block/dorm gets depleted here, the administration then moves everyone out in order to make way for the daily busloads of incoming prisoners, just like I was 2 weeks ago. Kind of like a revolving door.

The weather continues to be gorgeous but I get the chance to enjoy very little of it. Today I got outdoors for whopping thirty minutes. I've been told that tomorrow we'll have a full hour of outdoor yard time, but as luck would have it, the forecast is for rain.

Sunday July 29th

I met an inmate named Ron yesterday, interesting guy to say the least. He's in my new dorm and I saw him talking with another guy I know, so I sort of worked my way into the conversation. Ron is white, the big and burly type, huge gut, tattoos everywhere. After some small talk I asked him gingerly how long he was in for. Ron informed that he already has a 20 year sentence under his belt, and had most recently been convicted of a new crime, and sentenced to 7 years. Incredibly enough Ron knew the exact date of his release, seven years from n ow, and also knew exactly what he would be doing. "Man I'm getting out on a Friday, September 27th, 2013. And since I won't have to see my Parole Officer until that Monday, I'm going to get fucked up all weekend long." I was speechless. I looked for a crack in his smile, please some sort of sign that he might be kidding. No, afraid not, no smile. Ron was completely serious about his plan. Six years from now and already knows exactly what he'll be doing....violating his parole. There is no doubt in my mind Ron will return to prison for a 3rd time, he's a lifer, this is his world now, all he's ever going to know.

Monday July 30th

There is no such thing as "yesterdays news" here. Earlier today I was able to get my hands on a NY Daily news, and even better, it was only 10 days old!! Hey, that's practically current. I savored it like a piece of swiss milk chocolate, with butter creme filling. I read it for two whole days, going over and over the columns, the feel of newspaper print on my fingers. Oh my, how I miss the old morning routine of coffee and the paper.

On Wednesday my Mom, sister Virginia, and brother Joe are coming to visit. I can't wait to see them all. Joe was with me on the day of my sentencing, I haven't seen him since. I know it's a day he'll never forget either. Their impending visit will carry me through the next few days.

Tuesday July 31st

When it became clear a few months ago that I was going to have to serve time, my family & friends all promised to visit. I was adamant for just the opposite; it would be too emotional and painful for me to see anyone in this environment. Well, that wasn't the first time I was wrong. Yes of course the visits are emotional (I've broken down each time so far I've been visited by someone in my family) not to mention humiliating as I am marched out from lockup, guards accompanying me as I wear these hideous state green uniforms, along with my newly shaved head.

But for those 2-3 hours (and they do fly by) it is a happy link back to my old world, being with the people I care about the most. We laugh and reminisce about happier days, past and what's to come. They bring me up to date what is happening back home and never fail to instill courage so that I can get through this nightmare.

It's only when I realize there are just a few minutes left in our visit that the pit in my stomach returns. I so desperately don't want them to go. Why can't I just walk out with them? I promise I've learned my lesson. This is all a horrible mistake, isn't it? These thoughts race through my head as I try to stay composed; I can't let them see me breakdown, I must stay strong. My strength is their strength. But leave they surely do, the visit is now over. I must remain at the table until a guard tells me it's okay to get up. I watch their backs as they head towards the exit, they turn one last time to wave goodbye. I love you & I am so sorry is all I can think of. Eventually I am escorted out to a small holding area, finding a spot on the cold steel bench, waiting for the guard to come along and order me to strip. And then to bend over. The post visit nightmare is about to begin.

Wednesday August 1st

Still here at Downstate...ugh. Hopefully my days are numbered as it will be three weeks tomorrow since I arrived. Earlier today some of us were allowed out for 1 hour of Rec time. Oh just being able to walk around, my shoes touching grass for a change, gazing up at the bluest of skies, and breathing in nothing but fresh air. It felt incredible. While I was busy getting lost in my own little world another inmate approached, looking to strike up a bit of a chat. His name was Joe and he seemed normal enough. Like me, he was white, mild-mannered, and we both seemed happy to have someone to talk to.

We got to speaking about our crimes and why we were both here. Joe G. is serving 2 1/3-7 for vehicle manslaughter, and leaving the scene of an accident. He's 42 and prior to this, was living in Kingston, NY, and had never been in trouble with the law before this one fateful night. He started out by saying, "Jerry I left the scene of an accident." Hmmm, I thought to myself, that seems like a rather stiff sentence, there must be more to it than that." I didn't press, I waited for him to tell me more. "I was driving home one night after a couple of beers," Joe said, "when all of a sudden there was this guy in front of the car, on a bicycle. he came out of nowhere." Joe hears a loud thud, but is convinced he missed the guy and continues to drive on. He slows down about a mile up ahead, thinking that maybe, just maybe I did clip this guy. No he convinces himself, I couldn't have, and drives home, goes to bed.

The next afternoon there is a knock on Joe's door, it's the police asking to take a look at his car. Tragically he had indeed struck and killed this man on the bike. Apparently a witness had seen Joe's SUV speed away. In that split second Joe's life had changed....as did the victim of course. A minute earlier and this story would not be told. Fate. "Jerry

35

I think of that night every day now, and I will for the rest of my life," he said. Joe will spend at least 4 years behind bars, in addition he faces a huge civil suit from the family of the deceased.

Everyone here has a story to tell, I will hear many more before this is all over.

Thursday August 2nd

In a Correctional Facility (sounds so much more civilized than a prison doesn't it) it's the little things that count. I have touched on this before, but it bears repeating. For instance, when I can get my hands on a pencil with lead in it, or a pen that actually works, and heaven forbid writing paper, well you'd think I just won the lottery. It's that special. Or perhaps a book, without half the pages torn out, or a newspaper less than a week old. Less than two months ago I never gave these items a 2nd thought, there was no need to. And don't even get me started about a cup of coffee.

It's been a banner day for me; I got outside for Rec once again, was able to get to the library for ten minutes, and tonight I even received three pieces of writing paper!! Wait, there's more....the guy in the cell next to me, gave me my very own pen. He bought an extra one at commissary for me.

A familiar face arrived here today; Greg, a guy I had met while at Rikers. Kind of like me, he stands out. he's approximately 55 years old, wears these fancy tortoise shell eye glasses, and he's white. He's serving 3 to 9 for credit card fraud. Well as we were leaving the mess hall earlier, in single file, and Greg was just ahead of me. Well all of a sudden he's surrounded by three guards, right in his face. Thrown up against the wall, he begins to be frisked and berated. I'm thinking, what the hell is going on, what did he do? As it turns out, Greg tried to leave the room with a tiny packet of mayonnaise. Yes, true story, I kid you not! With the way these lunatic guards were carrying on you'd have thought Greg had a machete in his pocket. He'll now be written up and lose whatever miniscule privileges he has, for two weeks. He'll also be confined to his cell (including meals) the entire time.

Late this afternoon I received wonderful news: I'm on the draft!! Tomorrow I will be on the bus headed upstate towards my final

36

destination. The only thing I know for sure is I have been assigned to a medium security facility. In one sense I am relieved and happy to be leaving here, but I can't help the pit in my stomach that as already reared its ugly head. There is the anxiety of not knowing what awaits me, the long bus ride, my ankles and wrists shackled. Who will I be shackled to? Some murderer like BigDog, or someone more normal, like Joe? How will I get along at the new facility, what will the guards be like, who will be in the cell next to me? So many questions, with no answers at the moment.

Since I will be traveling and cut off from paper & pen for the next day or so, this will be my last posting until I reach and get settled in at the new prison.

Friday August 3rd

I am now residing at the final leg of my journey, Mohawk CF in Rome NY. The following is an account of what took place on this day, my trip up North. It's now Saturday, and the events of yesterday are still fresh in my mind.

I was awoken at 4:30 a.m. and ordered to get dressed quickly. With just my state greens to choose from, it's an easy chore. My stomach remains in knots, for I know a long day is ahead, but a day that had to finally come. The sooner it ends, the better.

About 100 of us will be headed up North today, a big moving day. We are herded down to the mess hall, cold cereal and toast await. Nightmarish thoughts begin to race through my head; what if there was a clerical mistake (bet it happens from time to time) and I am listed for a maximum prison, perhaps some state employee hit the wrong button or something, it could take months to fix while I rot in a max. Some place like Attica. Why am I always thinking the worst?

After breakfast (and I'm sure not to drink too much, cause if I have to take a piss on the bus, forget about it) we are taken into a large room where we sit and wait for our names to be called. Once my name is called, I am ordered to strip naked. After that humiliating ordeal I put my clothes back on and go sit in another room, one which has been designed to hold maybe 50 people, certainly not the 100 who are here now. Its literally standing room only. The few chairs that are lying around have been grabbed by the hard core guys, tats all over their bodies, most likely on the way to a max. Not for a second to I think about asking them to squeeze in so I can sit. I simply lean against the brick wall when I spot my sort of new friend Joe, the one I met in the yard the other day. Cool, he's leaving today as well, I wonder if we'll end up in the same facility. With 70 of them spread throughout the State it's doubtful, but hey you never know. We begin to discuss our similar fears and prepare for the long day ahead. Mentally I tell my body that we are facing some pain, my wrists and ankles will be tightly shackled, it's going to hurt. Sitting in a tiny bus seat, for 5-6 hours, no movement, cold steel digging into your skin, not a pleasant thought.

After much sitting around, finally there seems to be movement, names are being called, buses are being loaded. From the look of things, the hardcore dudes are the first ones shipped out of here. Makes sense I guess, as the Maximum prisons are furthest North, hence a longer bus ride.....ugh, those poor guys, I can't even imagine how brutal a max must be. Their bus ride could be as long as 10-12 hours, what with stops (so the guards can stuff their faces at McDonald's) and all. Thank God my name isn't called for this first group. No clerical mistake after all. Soon more names are called, finally I hear mine; I am going to a Medium security facility, called Mohawk, located in Central New York, in a town by the name of Rome. This will be my "home" for at least the next year, and who knows how much longer after that. And I guess God was looking out for me, because the very next name that was called is my new friend Joe. We will be shackled to each other.....a huge relief! He's about my size, so no one will be hogging the seat, and he doesn't smell. A lot of these dudes are 300 lbs plus, and don't believe in showers, I could have been stuck with one of them.

I was awake this morning at 4:30, but by the time the bus pulls out of Downstate , it's 11:30 a.m. It's going to be a long one I keep telling myself, heck, it already is. But I also repeat to myself a new mantra, "in order to get through this, I have to go through this." And this horrendous day is just another step closer to going home someday. On the bus I have the window seat, Joe on the aisle. As we make our way North on the NY Thruway, I do a lot of staring out the window, cars passing us by. Cars packed with families, most likely headed off for a week of summer vacation. The kids in the back seats, Mom & Dad in the front, eagerly awaiting the fun times that await them all, wherever they're going. It wasn't that many years ago I was one of those dads, taking my own boys off on a vacation. "How did I go so wrong" I keep thinking to myself, as I sit on this stifling hot bus with 40 other prisoners, all of us off to begin our sentences, of varying lengths. What kind of fate awaits me at Mohawk; will I get the shit beaten out of me, by some dude who doesn't like white guys, or white collar criminals? Will someone find me cute and attempt to rape me someday. Can I find the strength and courage to get through this? Will my parents stay alive while I'm incarcerated? God forbid the worst, I won't be allowed to attend their funerals, as they would be in NJ, and being a NY State prisoner, my request would be denied. These are just a few of the horrible thoughts that I ponder as I stare out the window, the open road passing my by. How long before I one day take this trip going back the other way.....when will I see this road again? God only knows.

Saturday August 4th

Think of your 1st day of school, or that 1st day on the new job, that moment when you have to walk through the front door for the very first time. Remember how nervous you were, that anxious feeling in your stomach? Well now, try if you can, that feeling of walking into a prison for the very first time. All eyes staring you down, hundreds of inmates trying to spot any sign of weakness. Fresh meat has arrived.

I am now writing from Mohawk CF in Rome, NY. About 20 of us arrived yesterday, late afternoon. After going through processing where we receive our blankets, mattresses, shaving razor and a pillow, we were then sent for our first night, to a Reception Dorm, #75A. At some point this afternoon I will be assigned to permanent housing. No matter what dorm I end up in, I will be relegated to a bunk bed, forced to take the upper bunk. All rookies get this treatment. The more time I stay in that particular dorm, I will eventually be moved down to the lower bunk, and then (hopefully) after a few months, really begin to live large, I'll get my very own 7x7 single cube. Think of an office cubicle, but instead of a desk, you have a cot and a foot locker.

I've already called my parents, to let them know I have arrived safely, in one piece. I rang my sons as well, trying to sound as upbeat as possible. I ache for them. Here it is, only August, and already I am so homesick. How will I possibly last another year (at minimum) of this?

It is now late on Saturday as I write. Earlier tonight, at 6:00, I was moved to my new dorm.....# 74D. My new home. I didn't know it at the time, but this particular dorm is considered the cleanest within the facility. It houses 39 inmates, there are 20 single cubes, the rest are bunks beds with 2 guys squeezed into a space the same as a single cube. So not a whole lot of elbow room. Each cube also holds a metal chair. The chair can be carried out to the TV room, but then always needs to be brought back to your cube when you're finished watching. I will be sitting quite a bit on my chair, I plan to read as many books as I possibly can.

Saturday nights I quickly learn, is when Catholic Services are held, so I drop off my draft bags atop my bunk, and head to the chapel. Movement within the facility is restricted after a certain amount of time (about 8 minutes is alloted for us to scurry to wherever we need to go, after that, if you're caught walking around outside the dorm, you'll receive a ticket) so I have to hustle. I notice my bunkie (cell mate) is sound asleep on the bottom bunk as I head off. Later that evening we introduce ourselves; he is Jamaican and goes by the name of 'Rome,' short for Jerome. He's here on a drug charge.

Sunday August 5th

There seems to be a rule for everything at Mohawk. I come to learn quickly that I best get up to speed right away, for there are no excuses, like "oh I'm new and didn't know that." Bullshit. The guards could care less. Each inmate is allowed 2 care packages per month, not to exceed a total of 35 pounds. There are all sorts of food rules for your care packages you must strictly adhere to. For example, nothing may be contained in a glass, all must be alcohol-free, no packages are to arrive unsealed, (for example a pack of store bought cookies, they must be completely sealed) clothing can only be a handful of colors (my favorite, navy blue is not allowed) and nothing can be multi-colored. No logos (Nike swooshes) of any kind, and no lettering or symbols on any clothes. Colors of clothes are restricted because some are considered gang colors.....such as red, black, orange, and blue.

My friend Eileen has already sent two packages of clothes, but little did we know that I will receive not a stitch of it. Yes it got to Mohawk, but because she had her business address attached as the return address, and not her home, they would not let me have it. The next package sent is from my sister, but this one will also be sent back because although she did leave a return address, she used an initial for her fist name, instead of spelling out the entire name. I thought I was going to cry. Welcome to the world of state bureaucracy and prison rules. I stood there in the package room, begging the guard to let me have one of the packages, asking for a little "rookie mistake" leniency. He looked at me like I was crazy. His reply, "Well you shouldn't have come to prison then, now get out of line." I suppose he's right, I shouldn't have come here.

Monday August 6th

Yesterday, for the first time in 7 weeks, I was outside and my feet were touching grass for longer than an hour. From 1-4:00 p.m. Joe and I went to one of the two Rec yards here at Mohawk. It was a beautiful sunny day, very hot. The only negative was that since it was so hot, my shaved head got completely scorched. A major case of sunburn. But hey, that's ok, this was a day I had been waiting for. Since Joe and I know nobody else, we stuck together like glue. We sat down on one of the many cement benches lining the yard and talked about our loved ones back home. Sad. I did some push-ups and we walked along the perimeter of the barbed wire fence. Within the yard there are two hard-top basketball courts, 4 handball courts, a bocce ball pit, volleyball nets (no one was playing) and a big field for soccer games. You can choose to participate in any of the above, or simply walk/run around.....or even, as many seem to do, just lounge around on the grass, soaking up the rays. The two of us standout, what with are bald white heads, and that look which just screams of "new jacks."

I am informed I will be meeting with my counselor soon. He (or she) will bring me up to speed in regard to programs available, as well as which prison job (every inmate as some sort of job) best suits me. I will make a point to ask about work release (yes, I know it's early, I just got here, but I have to cling to something) and when I might be eligible. I'm thinking I might like to work in the horticulture department. There happens to be large greenhouse on the grounds and being inside it might make me feel removed from my situation. It might be nice surrounded by flowers and plants.

Tuesday August 7th

It's been only a matter of days since my arrival and already I can tell which of these many inmates (there are aprox 1000) know their way around a prison. With years of experience at this sort of thing, they glide around here doing their time without what seems, a care in the world. As Joe and I were sitting yesterday there was a conversation going on next to us. Apparently this guy's name was David, and his buddy asked him how long his sentence was. Now David had the required display of tattoos that adorn some of these repeat offenders, along with a pretty viscous scowl. "Yeah, the fucking Judge gave me 12 years, but I'll only have to do 9 of them." Only nine I think to myself??? What is he kidding, only nine? He makes it sound like a walk in the park. Like nine weeks maybe. No, we're talking 9 years! This seems to be the type of guy walking around Mohawk, and probably throughout the prison system. They carry an air of such nonchalance, who view a stay in prison so much differently than me. I'm beginning to get a warped idea that some of these dudes actually like it here. (I will eventually learn how accurate a call that turns out to be).

One piece of advice that continues to be drummed into my head is, "don't trust anyone while you are here." Thats really not my nature, but then I harken back to my 1st day at Rikers, when that lowlife stole my pin number. I hate to be a cynic, but I do have to keep telling myself, that this is state prison, and there are rapists, murderers, kidnappers, child molesters & drug dealers everywhere you turn. I'm not looking to make any friends, I want to do my time, get through each day, stay under that radar, survive, and finally, get the hell out someday. But I'm finding this is easier said than done. Let me explain. If some of these guys perceive you as aloof, or giving off an air that you're better than the rest, well thats going to spell trouble. Finding the right balance between fitting in and mixing it up a little, versus keeping your independence and keeping to yourself as much as possible. I'm going to have to work on this.....I can tell it's going to be very important for me to come across as "not aloof." I will need to have a few 'friends.' I have Joe, but he's been moved to another dorm, on the other side of the facility, odds are won't be seeing him much anymore.

I have been approached a few times by a guy in the dorm whose goes by the name Dino. His bed/cot is a few down from mine, he has a single, has been been here awhile Looking at Dino you would best describe him as resembling the "OddJob" character from the James Bond film, Goldfinger. Without the funny hat. Now Dino has reached out to me kind of, he heard that my package was denied which meant I still don't have any deodorant, and kindly offered me one of his. Well, it was like someone offering my $1000. I would no longer smell, I could not have been more grateful. He also offered me a plastic mug (used, but thats ok) for my coffee, loaned me some creamer, coffee, sugar, and writing paper. It felt like Christmas morning. On the outside it might not seem like much, but in here, it was the mother lode. . "Whatever you need" has been Dino's daily reply to me. Hmmm, should I be on the lookout, is this too good to be true, everything comes with a price, right. Especially in here. Or maybe Dino is just looking out for me, I do notice he isn't overly friendly with everyone in here....but then again I am new, a fresh target. Will he eventually come at me? These are all questions I have running through my mind, but I'm desperate for the coffee, not to mention wanting to smell normal again. Will Dino be all over my food packages when they finally start to arrive? (He's very overweight). Dino has been in prison for 13 years so far, kidnapping and forgery charges, having spent the first 8 or 9 years doing his time in a maximum, and was moved to a medium a few years ago.

Wednesday August 8th

I've been trying to settle into a routine both within the confines of the dorm and the surroundings of Mohawk. As the new kid on the block I adhere to "be seen but not heard." Three new guys came into 74D last week and one of them as already alienated himself by trying "to be the man." The old timers here, guys like Dino & Willie, don't take kindly to young punks coming into their house, and disrupting things.

I haven't mentioned Willie P. yet, but I have come to learn that he pretty much runs this dorm. He arrived at Mohawk about 8 years ago, after serving 20 years at a maximum. He is serving a life sentence for rape and double murder, committed back in 1978. His cube is directly next to mine, keeps to himself, but at the same time, if he likes you, he'll reach out and extend some help in any way he can. For example, when I first arrived here I hadn't received my clothes yet, so I had no hat. Well my first day in the sun I got badly sunburned. The next day before heading out again, I spotted an extra baseball cap in his cube. At the time not knowing anything about him, I simply asked if I could borrow one (looking back, it was kind of nervy of me). Now Willie has a bit of a stuttering problem, but he managed to get the words out, that yes, I could use his extra cap.

He seems to know everything that goes on in this dorm, like what CO's are decent/fair, which ones to avoid, which ones you can get over on, and those you don't even want to consider trying. He wears wire rim glasses, stands about 5'8, lean, black, and totally unassuming. Never would you look at him and think; murderer. His cube is exceedingly neat and organized. With nearly 30 years under his belt, you could say he's got this prison thing down pat. I get a chuckle when I see him in the TV room, right on the dot of 12:30 p.m., so he can tune into his favorite soap opera, "The Young & the Restless." He'll be good to have on my side, with all the gravitas he carries around this place. I'll make an extra effort to reach out and be respectful.

Thursday August 9th

I have not seen my sons, Brooks & Philip, since the night before I was sentenced. From the day they were born I don't think there was a day or two that went by without my not seeing them. More than anything else which has been thrown my way these past eight weeks, their absence from my life has been without a doubt the biggest struggle. I'm sure that will be a constant for no matter how long I am incarcerated.

Like all teenagers, they have been enjoying their summer, spending the bulk of it outdoors. Upon hearing how active they are, allows me to cope so much easier, frees my mind up so I can concentrate on survival. Thank God for all the love and support they receive from my family, Abby's family, and all our friends. As desperate as I am for them, I struggle with the notion of them coming up to visit. I just can't bare the thought of the boys seeing their Dad in prison garb, behind barb wired fences and walls. Do I want them, for even one second, to have that kind of memory of me, seeing this shit hole? This hate factory where darkness, despair, and sadness prevail? I don't have the answers yet, but what I do know is, that I will do whatever is best for them. If they have a burning desire to come see their dad, then by all means, thats what we'll do.

Friday August 10th

In about 30 minutes (8:00 a.m.) I will head over to the main building for orientation. During the next 2 weeks twenty or so newly arrived inmates will learn the in's & out's of this place, and what is expected of us. This mornings class will (and I'm serious here) cover such topics as how to use a ladder, and the proper way to use a buffer machine while waxing the floors. Good grief, taxpayers money hard at work.

For the past few days my folks have been attempting to send me clothes along with my first food care package. Seems it might just be easier to win the war in Iraq than it will be to get these items past the package room. The Department of Corrections has very, very specific rules as to what can & can't come in from the outside. As I mentioned, colors of clothes for instance. Black, blue, red & orange, forget about it.....all considered "gang colors." Shirts have to be one solid color, not a trace of stripe anywhere. No logos, brand names, no Nike swooshes. Everything sent it must be brand new, receipts included, nothing costing more than $50. Toiletries have to be hermetically sealed or in a box. No alcohol may be contained in any product, mouthwash for example. Nothing may come with a pump attached, like moisturizer. Now what am I going to do with a pump?

So this afternoon the first couple of packages arrive and I get the call to head up to the package room. Kind of like walking down the stairs on Christmas morning, waiting to see what Santa brought. After waiting in line for 15-20 minutes, the CO on duty informs me that nearly half of what my parents sent, I can't have, due to rules I mentioned above. I have five seconds to decide what to do, he tells me. "Ok Byrne, what is it, donate, destroy, or send back home?" Don't think for a second either

45

that you're going to reason with this guy, or gal, as there are female CO's here as well. You have to show restraint, you cannot argue, you do, it could be a trip to 'the box,' (a prison within this prison) or worse, you get a reputation for being a troublemaker. The anxiety levels will kill you unless you can reign them in, really there is no other choice. "Send it back," I tell the CO. The final indignity awaits, he informs me I must pay the shipping costs.

Saturday August 11th

Weekday mornings from 8-11:00, if you don't yet have a prison job, requires that you head out for mandatory Rec. The yard is huge and you can partake in any of the following (sounds like a day camp brochure) activities; handball, basketball, soccer, volleyball, and bocce. I have found I prefer to just run around the track, do push-ups, or sit at one of the many cement benches that dot the yard. If it's sunny I will bring a book and read on the grass.

There are cliques here, you see them walking together, laughing, joshing, and probably scheming. They could be buddies from the projects or members from the same gang. For the time being I'd rather be by myself. I wish Joe was around, but as I mentioned, he's been moved to another dorm and I will see him less and less. While half of the prison is using this yard, the other half uses yard #2. Joe is part of that group. In fact, I've been told by a few guys here that there is a chance I might not see Joe during my entire time at Mohawk. The other half of the prison (Group 2 it's called) may as well be in a whole different zip code.

On the occasional morning when it's raining out, you have the option of going to the library, but as it only holds 25, you better get there quick, or else you'll be forced to stand in the yard. In the pouring rain, fenced in like a dog.

Sunday August 12th

Every dorm has it's own laundry porter, ours in 74D is a guy named Fritz. It's his job to take care of everyone's sheets and laundry, three times a week if you can believe it. Let me tell you, some of these dudes back home would be lucky to have their laundry done three times a year! Fritz is a dead ringer for a young Paul Newman, think of his character in the movie "Cool Hand Luke." Handsome face, strong muscular build, about 5'9. And he seems to have a perpetual tan. Throw in a few stamps or a bag of coffee and Fritz will even fold your laundry for you.

I look at certain guys and wonder what the heck are they doing here. I'd certainly like to include myself in that category, but I am here, so be it. Fritz is one of those guys too. We've been hitting it off okay so I thought I would ask how he landed here. He's currently towards the end of a ten year sentence for burglary, quite a few burglaries actually, and I think the Judge finally had enough and threw the book at him. He didn't want to talk so much about his crimes, but rather the only woman he ever loved. Prior to his arrest they were engaged to be married, apparently she knew nothing of this other life he led. So Fritz gets himself arrested, and is sentenced to a maximum security prison. For weeks she never knew what happened to him, until finally he writes from his cell, explaining all the bad mistakes he made in his life, culminating in his sentencing. But she promises to stick by him, makes repeated visits (every weekend practically) way up North to show her support and love for her fiance. This goes on for a year, when all of a sudden, one weekend comes, and she's not there to visit. No letter, no call, no nothing. Another weekend comes & goes, the same treatment. Eventually, 3 months later, Fritz gets the letter he's been dreading; she can't take it anymore, and is breaking off the engagement. She never will see him again. Fritz tells me that was the last visit, and last letter he has ever received, from anyone, in over 8 years. He keeps a picture of her in his locker.

Monday August 13th

Weekends continue to be the most painful time. They represent the realization of all that I am missing in my life. A weekend here allows me so much (dreaded) time to sit around and remanence about all the wonderful memories of weekends past. I used to live for them, when Friday would roll around and represent the end of the work week, off I would go to spend as much time with my sons as possible. I have to check myself in the 'looking back dept,' as it really is too painful.

I pass the time by reading as many books as I possibly can. Right now I average about one per day. It's my only escape.

Tuesday August 14th

I'm discovering there is actually such a thing as prison etiquette. Yeah I know, seems crazy right. Well this afternoon I was having lunch with Dino and another guy from our dorm, Dino's buddy, 'Country.' Country is a neo-nazi skinhead, with a swastika tattoo on his stomach, about the size of a mini-pizza. Anyway, I had finished eating and not really wanting to be like "buds" with these guys, I decided to pick up my tray and head for the exit. I did happen to notice a strange look or two from the table as I did so, but thought nothing of it. Well no sooner had I returned to the dorm when Dino pulls me aside to scold me for not sticking around until everyone at the table had finished their meal. "Mo, I know you're new here, but let me tell you something, you never get up from the table until we're all done, especially a table of white guys, we stick together." I looked at him expecting a trace of a smile, like he might have been half joking. But no, no smile, Dino was totally serious. He even had more, " And when you're finished, tap your knuckles on the table to signify that's it's been cool sitting and bonding together." Oh geez, what have I gotten myself into, I just want to be left alone. I don't want to be a part of prison nomenclature, I just want to do my time and get the fuck out of here. I have a feeling it's not that simple though.

Wednesday August 15th

Over the years Hollywood and TV studios have created a side of prison life that, at least here, doesn't have a thing in common with how they portray it. While yes I have seen some horrible things so far in my two months, I have yet to witness the brutality you see on the silver screen. Is it because this a medium security jail? I doubt that, as there are some awfully mean dudes here.

The 74D dorm is spotless! I wake up each morning to Willie polishing and buffing the floors out in the dayroom and hallway. We have a porter for every task you can think of; from garbage, to dusting, to laundry, even a guy who is in charge of watering the plants. We have microwaves, toaster ovens, a giant hot water pot for coffee all day and night, and two TV's, both loaded with just about every cable channel available, including HBO. Not all the dorms here are this clean, but all of them do contain the same amenities I just mentioned.

And this I have discovered, in a very short time, is part of the problem.......a recidivism rate of 83%!! Prison life is so much better than anything nearly all of these guys ever had back home. Believe it or not, a great deal of them actually like it here. I know, it's crazy, but true. These career criminals receive 3 (relatively) good meals per day, 6-8 hours of Recreation (or sleep, if they'd rather) with all the basketball, handball, and weightlifting you could want. At your disposal you have free medical and dental, no bills to worry about, hot showers, a comfortable bed, and clean laundry 3x per week. Yes there is family back home that you miss, but I find so many of these guys have some sort of family right here. Either their selling drugs on the street family, prison family, or real life blood family. When they get together it's a race to see who can tell the most war stories about the good 'ol days, back on the streets. If the taxpayers of NY could see the inside of a prison & see how their hard earned money is being spent/wasted, there would be a revolt. No wonder NY State is going broke.

Thursday August 16th

Being one of the very few here that has a college degree, I've been asked to be a teacher's aide, or TA. The job entails correcting tests, some tutoring, along with helping many of the inmates read and write correctly. I think I'll enjoy this job, it'll keep me busy, and at the same time I'm happy if I can actually help someone. Some of the veterans have told me otherwise though. "You'll hate it, it's only going to lead to trouble," says Dino. I don't know, I kind of feel otherwise. There is so little that is good about this place, if I can help just a few inmates, well it'll really make me feel good.

Friday August 17th

Beginning next week along with the week after, I will be reporting to "Phase 1." It is the orientation period for new inmates. There will be 22 in the class, all of us having arrived within days of each other. The teacher (actually a fellow inmate) will go over all the shit we need to know about surviving here. There are so many little rules (for instance you can get a ticket for walking too fast, or not having your shirt tucked in) to be adhered to. We will learn about "good time, or merit time" which are basically days you can get shaved off your sentence for good behavior. They will go over work release and who is eligible.

So this is my world now, a classroom full of convicts, young and old; here for every crime imaginable. It would be so easy for me to sink into the depths of depression.

Saturday-Sunday August 18-19th

Sad, lonely, and depressed.....no energy to write this weekend. Plus my stomach has been a jangle of nerves with very irregular bowel movements. No doubt a combination of the food and my anxiety level.

Monday August 20th

For the first time since my sentencing, I was too depressed to write. In fact I went the entire weekend not wanting to sit in front of my "writing table." Which is in actuality a tiny card table, in the day room. This weekend just seemed like it would never end, the hours dragged on and on. Perhaps it's because my birthday is only days away, and this is where I'll be celebrating it......behind bars.

Today however brought the first laugh in a long time. A laugh that captures in a nutshell, the world which I now reside in. Our instructor at Phase 1 was discussing merit time and who might be eligible and which type of crimes committed simply don't qualify for merit. Like an inmate who is found guilty of a violent crime would never be granted merit. As he was going over the ground rules one of the guys raised his hand. He was curious if he himself would be considered for good time. "Well, what was the nature of your crime," the instructor asked. "When I did my crime I didn't use a gun or knife, so I think I should qualify" replied the inmate. Then the teacher inquired, "Ok, so why are you here, what did you do?"

"Well, there was this drug dealer and he owed me some money, so I decided to suffocate him, but I only used a plastic bag, " the inmate replied with the straightest of faces. A second or two of stunned silence elapsed before we all just broke into absolute hysterics. It didn't stop this lunatic inmate from screaming out, " It ain't violent my nigger, I got my rights, my rights be violated." Like I said, the first laugh I've had in months.

Tuesday August 21st

A dull cool and dreary morning, not very summer like. I've become close with an inmate named Gordon. He's white, about 40 years of age, and to look at him you'd be reminded of the GI Joe cartoon character.... solidly built, crew cut, tattoos, and all. Gordon was originally sentenced for dealing drugs, receiving a 5-7 year sentence. Well, he wound up doing 13 years! He bought himself all that extra time by messing up in prison, things like fights, possessing contraband, and doing drugs. He's educated, comes from an upper middle class family, and divorced due to a drug addiction he could not contain. Gordon is back in Mohawk on a parole violation, serving 9 months this time around. Needless to say he knows his way around a prison, has clearly concluded that I do not, and has somewhat taken me under his wing.

It's funny how I first met Gordon; we were both in the yard, and as I looked across the way I noticed this guy mimicking a golf swing. Now let me tell you, this is not something you see in the yard very often, if ever! So I kind of felt that, hey, this is a guy I at least have something in common with, as I am a life long golfer, and have been to known to practice my swing from time to time. So I went up to him, we got a chuckle about it, and have been kind of hanging with Gordon ever since. He's a good guy.

Wednesday August 22nd

Phase 1 continues to muddle along, this 2 week orientation program could have easily have been wrapped up in a few days. But, whatever. The teacher opens every session by asking if there are any questions, none are asked of course (half the dudes are asleep in the back row) and with that, we all begin to doodle, read books, or stare out the windows. One guy brushes his hair non-stop for two hours, I kid you not!!

In the afternoon class we had two topics raised; the first was, which gun is the gun of choice to own, either for show or actual use. And the other discussion centered around whom was richer, the comedian/actor Eddie Murphy, or the singer Beyonce. This was a heated discussion. These are the times where I close my eyes and think I have landed on another planet.

My friend Joe (vehicle manslaughter) and I sit back and take it all in. To openly laugh or mock one of these guys would be huge no-no, a sign of disrespect. Like it our not, this is our world now, we have to live in it and follow the rules. I've managed to survive this far (2 whole months) by keeping to myself, being polite when need be, and standoffish when necessary. Within my dorm it certainly has helped that I've been befriended by Dino and Willie, who are serving time for kidnapping and double murder respectively. Willie has been down nearly 30 years so far. His sentence was 25 to life, but each time he's come before the parole board he has been denied, or "hit" as prison slang goes. If you are denied parole you have to wait two years until you become eligible again. To look at him you would never know it however. he is slight of build, polite, quiet, keeps to himself, and very hard working. Twenty years in a Max, the remainder at Mohawk, I can only imagine the shit he's witnessed.

Thursday August 23rd

The weather continues to be cloudy & cool. I think I should tell my family to bring sweaters when they come to visit. No classes today so I ran a few miles at Rec this morning, followed by a routine of push-ups and sit-ups. Like the plaque I avoid getting involved in any of the team sports that take place, like handball or basketball. It seems almost a daily occurrence that a heated argument or fight breaks out over whether a dude was fouled taking a shot, or if someone calls a ball out, that was clearly in. This is prison don't forget, these guys will cheat at sports if they can get away with it. And if you do fight, well consider that a one-way trip to "the box." Remember the box is a prison within a prison, where the lights are always on, 3 showers a week, and one hour of Rec every other day, which consists of standing outside in a tiny dog-like cage.

It's my birthday on Saturday, I'll be turning 49. Don't go there Jerry! Oh God, never in my worst nightmare did I envision celebrating a birthday in prison. I keep thinking about the boys & my family, and how much I miss them. The veterans here will tell you how you almost need to block them from your mind, almost like they don't exist. Point well taken, I get it;; but I can't do that. Not yet anyway. The past few days have been repeated bouts of loneliness, depression and anxiety. For all these reasons this week has been the toughest one since my sentencing. I need to snap out of it, and I will. There is no other option. Stay strong.

Friday August 24th

I try to stem off the wave of depression but it's overwhelming at times. How the fuck could I have allowed my life too spin so out of control that I ended up surrounded by drug dealers, kidnappers, rapists, child molesters, and a murderer or two. Life is so short, there is an incredibly beautiful world passing me by outside these walls. At the moment I am about as far as you could possibly be from that world. It's only been two months and I feel myself slipping. Enjoy your birthday tomorrow Jerry.

Saturday August 25th

Saturday mornings are meant for mandatory cleaning. Everyone has to sweep their 7x7 cube, then mop it. Afterwords the CO takes a walk around the dorm making sure each cube is spotless. There is no Rec on saturday mornings, just the cleaning followed by supplies being passed out. At 10:00 a.m. we all line up for razor exchange. You stand in front of the guard holding up your old razor (so he can see the blades, making sure they haven't been removed) from the previous week. Once he nods approval, you drop it in a bucket, and he hands you a new one until next saturday. Whatever you do, don't lose it!!! When I get mine I immediately place it at the very back of my locker, hidden in a sock. Remember, losing your razor means an automatic 30 day trip to the box, no questions asked. You could even lose out on your 'good time' when you appear before the parole board....this could mean the loss of six months.

This happened just last week, an inmate walked away from his unlocked locker for just a few minutes,, apparently a rival gang member swooped in, stole it, and then when the dude couldn't produce it on saturday, he's looking at being removed from the dorm. And headed to the box. So the Sergeant was called, the inmate is cuffed, and thats that! The rival gang ember wanted him out of the dorm, and since there is no ratting out of anybody, he gets away with it. For now that is. I'm sure eventually there will be a 'get even' moment.

I couldn't wait for the day to be over so I could crawl into bed and put it behind me.....another day down as they say here.

Sunday August 26th

Catholic services took place last night at 6:00, I was there as I have been every Saturday since arriving at Mohawk. I'd say on average about 30 inmates attend. Yes a decent number, but out of 1000 inmates, not a very strong percentage. The Deacon gives a moving and relevant sermon having to do with what we face on a day to day basis.

As I was leaving the chapel (actually a classroom in the school building) I got to chatting with James, a guy I've seen at Mass a few times before. Besides being white, he stands out for other reasons; with his slicked-back hair he's a dead ringer for Harrison Ford. Or throw a 3 piece suit on him, and with his tortoise shelled glasses, he could pass for a Wall St. investment banker. Certainly not a look you see walking around here very often. We exchanged small talk until James volunteered how a guy like him ended up in a place like this. Apparently he was arrested for burglary at the famed Waldorf Astoria Hotel in NYC. The District Attorney originally offered James a plea deal of 2-4 years, but James and his lawyer thought they could win their case at trial. Well long story short they lost in court and he was sentenced to 7 years!! James is divorced and has a young son whom he hasn't seen in a couple of years.

Monday August 27th

Mohawk is 'closed' between now and the day after Labor Day. While not fully closed of course, as it's open for prison business, but rather the schools and any programs are on hiatus. Truth be told, I'd much rather be working, as it keeps me occupied and out of the dorm. These next 10 days or so will bring an abundance of free time to stew, reflect, and wallow in the sadness. I dread these days. I'll try to stay as busy as I can by going to the yard and the library.

Many of the crowd up here seem to be relishing this week however, for it's ' sports championship week.' Yes that's right, we will be having finals in soccer, bacciball, volleyball, and basketball. Just like a day camp for adults/inmates. I sense these games are extremely meaningful to the majority; the trash talking goes on continuously in my dorm and the mess hall. I see guys getting fired up, like they are getting ready to suit up for the Super Bowl. Gone are the scowls or frowns that usually pervade the grounds of Mohawk, in its place are smiles, backslapping, and high fives. So many guys don't get this kind of camaraderie back in the 'hood, so it feels to me like they (at times like this) are much happier being in state prison. They have this kid in a candy store look to them.

Tuesday August 28th

I haven't been to the mess hall in about a week. Let me tell you why. Gordon and Dino love to cook, so ever since Gordon received his 35 pound food package, (including Tupperware bowls of all sizes, enough to feed the entire dorm) the two of them have been whipping up meals for themselves at breakneck speed. Luckily, since I'm friendly with both, I've been a recipient of a meal or two. Ever since Gordon and I met out in the yard (when I saw him practicing his golf swing) we've sort of come together. Before either one of us heads to the mess hall, we will always look for each other so has to head over together.

But to watch them prepare their meals is quite comical, sort of like the prison eating scene straight out of the movie "Goodfellas." They fuss over the amount of ingredients; Dino insisting on more olives and peas for the macaroni salad, while Gordon insists on more mayonnaise. And let me tell you, this salad is delicious, and as tasty as anything you'd find in a gourmet deli back home. Now for me, as I'm not a big foodie/ eater, the salad alone would have been plenty. But for these guys, it's just the beginning. Dino will commandeer one of the two microwaves in the dorm, and slave over a chicken (you can get chicken from the commissary) dish, or he'll prepare an egg & cheese sandwich to tide him over. That is until it's popcorn time an hour or two later while he takes in a HBO movie in the TV room. So I'll skip the mess hall this evening, as Dino & Gordon have prepared a tuna fish sandwich on white toast, with lettuce & tomato. Amazing isn't it.

Wednesday August 29th

As I feared, the week is dragging on. I find the days so long and lonely. With the abundance of free time on my hands, inevitably it triggers a chain reaction of sadness. And it always seems to come back to how much I miss my sons. From there the path leads to either remorse or guilt, or both. A path I try hard to avoid going down, but it's no use really. I'm back on it again. The mental checklist of people I've let down pops out, starting of course with my family. Ever since the indictment back in December of '05 they have been suffered right along side me, witnessing my despair and grief. During that time they have endured a multitude of phone calls, emails, and letters from me, as I needed their encouragement to keep me strong. Throw in the legal fees (eventually they will rise to nearly half million) the family as seen to, and I really began to go over the edge. Then my mind goes to another horrible thought, ' who will be a father figure to the boys' while I'm away? This one probably weighs me down the most. The pain and anguish I have put everyone through. No parent, at any age, should have to witness their child being handcuffed and led away. Some golden years I've given them.

Thursday August 30th

There are men here who have committed every crime imaginable; and even a few you can't quite fathom. Even with my limited time in the prison system I still think I might be reading a Stephen King novel. I go back to Mike whom I met @ Rikers. He'd rummage through the obits looking for an identity he could eventually assume when released. He'd pull me over, "Jerry, do you think I look like this guy?" Or there is Willie, a double-murderer & rapist, who sleeps in the cube right next to mine. We have a bit of everything in this dorm; sex offenders, kidnappers, white collar crimes (like myself), drug pushers, and one or two dudes here for vehicle manslaughter.

This morning I was having breakfast with Gordon when he leaned over and said, "Jerry do you see that guy at the other table, the one with the glasses?" "Yeah, why do you ask" I said. "Well the story is (and I believe Gordon, he knows prison and absolutely no reason to bullshit me) this sicko, while working as an orderly a hospital, raped a woman patient while she was in a coma. And that's not at all. She comes out of the coma, becomes pregnant and now this guy is attempting to sue the woman and her family to gain custody of the child." I sat there in disbelief, c'mon, really, you can't make this shit up.

Friday August 31st

Peter (the diamond thief) along with Joe and I, were sitting together out in the yard this afternoon. Take away the barbed wire and the watch tower and you'd think ' three normal looking white guys sitting out on a park bench.' Yeah right, if only.

I've been spending some time with Peter, getting to know him a bit. He's the father to three girls, and wrestles with the same dilemma I have; should we or shouldn't we have our kids come and visit us? As much as we ache for them, do we really want them to have this memory of seeing their Dad's in prison jump suits, being led into the Visitors room? And then surrounded there by every type of scummy inmate you could ever want to imagine? Do we really want that? Well, right now I most definitely do not. But eventually I wonder, will time wear me down, will I become so desperate to see their faces that I eschew the fears of the memories they will hold from being in the visitors room? I don't know that answer yet......I can only hope and pray I am able to hold out.

There are three "counts" per day here, the main one being at 4:00 p.m. Every single inmate in a NY State prison is counted at that time. Just as it sounds, a count is when all inmates have to be standing at the front of their cubes, no talking allowed. The C.O. then walks the floor, stopping in front of every cube checking us off. He then calls in the number to the admin, building, and they in turn call it into Albany. After the count, it's time for the mail to be handed out. Everyone queues up in front of the C.O.'s desk in the hope of receiving even a single piece of mail. I know some guys who have been here for years & years, and to this day have not had their names called out indicating a letter is waiting. I was blessed to receive 3 letters this day, plus the NY Times.

One of the dudes behind me uttered out, "Hey man, you be having a good day."

The other counts take place at 11:15 a.m and 11:00 p.m. For the evening one you're allowed to asleep in your bed, no standing necessary.

Gordon is all excited; earlier today he and his partner won the handball finals. That's big stuff in prison, kind of like winning the World Series. In prison, handball is America's favorite pastime. For their efforts they will each get a box of chicken, two cans of soda, and three honey buns. Honey buns are a big staple here, they only cost 22 cents, are about the size of a discuss, and will tack on about 600 calories.

Saturday September 1st

The weather continues to be sunny & hot, the entire week has been like this. I have developed a routine of going to the yard for two out of the three breaks, usually the afternoon and evening sessions. Although tonight I will skip it and instead attend catholic services. Thankfully all this free time will come to a halt this Tuesday when school and programs start up again. It'll also be my first day as a teacher's aide, or TA. I'll be working with Mr. Z., a civilian who has taught at Mohawk since its inception, about twenty years ago. I haven't the faintest idea of what to expect, but I'm looking forward to it. However Gordon has warned me that, "I'll hate it." " You think you're going to make a difference, put some meaning into their lives, don't fucking count on it" he says. Then he continues some more, " They are going to look at you and think 'what man, you're a teacher's aide, you got a college degree, you think you're fucking better than me?". Personally I think Gordon is jaded and I would like to prove him wrong.

Sunday Sept 2nd

I saw Peter earlier this morning, there was a bright, late summer sky, the sun beaming, and it was crystal clear. We met at the yard and proceeded to run/walk four miles. Naturally we got to talking about our families and how much we missed them. Peter is still married (to a doctor) and has three daughters. Although I have sons, the ages of our kids are about the same. As we walked around the perimeter of the yard, reminiscing about the joys of fatherhood, I began to do something I hadn't done in about a month; I began to cry. Right there in the yard, right in front of Peter. It started when I began to tell him how I had spoken with my youngest son Philip the night before. Phil is about to begin his freshman year of high school. He's always been a keen and skillful athlete with the rarest of talents; natural instincts. On the court, the baseball diamond, or the soccer field, he simply knew where to be...... you can't coach that. And competitive to boot! Almost to the point where my ex-wife and I would worry about him, he'd take the losses so hard, not surfacing from his room for hours after a stinging defeat.

So it was during this call that Phil informed me that he had quit the Freshman soccer team, not even lasting a tryout or two. I was shocked and saddened. My first instinct was to blame myself, for it had to be he fact that I was in prison, thus weakening any desire he had to compete. Or was it the possible embarrassment he might inevitably face from his peers or worse the teasing, when they learned his Dad was behind bars. I mean what else could it be, why now, he'd never quit anything in his life. It had to be my fault. But what's even worse, is that I realized I am so helpless right now, what could I possibly say? I can't look him in the eye or be stern with him, for what credibility do I have right now, behind bars? It hit me, I can't be a real father for the time being. Thats why I cried. I'm nothing right now.

Monday Sept. 3rd

My family often inquires about the food served, is it edible? Well I must admit, its not delicious by any means, but it's not terrible either. The servings are decent sized, but you only pass through the line once, there is no such thing as seconds. The only shot you have there is if the guy next to you doesn't want to finish what's on his plate, then you can reach over and grab it.. But don't let one of the many C.O.'s patrolling the mess hall spot you doing that. Nor is there any table hopping!

When you walk into this cavernous room you pick up your spoon and fork which is wrapped in a napkin. You can also grab some packets of salt & pepper. Down the way a bit you take a tray and proceed single file through the serving line, where fellow inmates will hash the stuff on your tray. There are no plates, you eat everything off of the tray. You then choose from one of the 70 or so steel tables bolted to the floor. At each table are three metal stools on each side, also bolted to the floor.

For breakfast you're looking at something like cold cereal, such as Rice Krispies. The hot cereal is usually cornmeal or oatmeal. You get one shot-sized glass of juice and two tiny cartons of milk. Along with the constant prison staple; four slices of white bread. There is not a meal served without those 4 slices. Lunch is anything from Mac & Cheese, tuna salad in a plastic container, under-cooked hot dogs, or grilled cheese sandwiches.

There are some nights I can't bring myself to face the dinners and will instead make myself a peanut butter & jelly sandwich, and simply eat in my cube. But mostly, simply to get out of the dorm, I'll head over to face the usual "mystery meat" du jour or some sort of chicken dish. I need to keep eating vegetables, so such as they are, I'll always head to the mess hall when spinach or carrots are on the menu. And there is one dessert thats actually tasty; an apple crumb cake. Other than the slices of bread, no food is allowed out of the mess hall. Of course this being prison, rules are made to be broken. So you'll see these guys stuffing milk cartons in their "hoodies," pants, or in the winter, the big parka like jacket the state gives everyone. There is usually a bid (a price) back at the dorm for anything that might be decent. You can sell a milk for a stamp or two, and good dessert (like ice cream) can bring you at least a stamp. Hot dogs or hamburgers (tough to smuggle out however) are worth 3 stamps.

Tuesday Sept 4th

"When's our next vacation?" This was the very first question asked by a fellow inmate within minutes of the class sitting down this morning. Of course everyone was just coming off a two week break, so this gives you a quick indication as to just how serious these guys are in the learning department. Hmmm, maybe Gordon is right. Well I'm still going to keep an open mind, but I'm beginning to think my teacher's aide services aren't going to be in much demand. I've been assigned to Mr. Z's GED 2 class from 8-11:00 a.m.. I also have been asked to work his GED 3 class as well, in the afternoon from 1-3:00. This would be equivalent to a high school 9th and 10th grade respectively. There are 18 inmates/students to a class.

Mr. Z. has been at Mohawk since literally the day it opened for business. Oh my God, I can't even imagine. He seems like a nice guy, 55 or so, & a little chubby with balding hair. At first blush it would appear he's lost the fire to teach, but how could you blame him. And he works for the State, so he'll be receiving a generous pension someday and lets face it, doesn't really have to bust his ass here.

My job description entails grading papers, quizzes, tests, and being available for anyone who needs assistance on a question during class. My desk is right along side Mr. Z's. The math questions seem to be the ones that most of the inmates have trouble with. I must admit, my math skills are a little rusty as well.

All the civilian teachers who work in the school building wear beepers around their necks or clipped to their belts in case any inmate gets pissed off and starts to cause trouble. All they have to do is push the button and the guards will come racing in.

Wednesday Sept 5th

Willie runs the dorm football pool. If you're interested (and I certainly am not) he'll give you a slip with all the games that particular weekend, and you try to pick the winners. Vegas comes to Mohawk. The entry fee is three stamps. From what I hear about 30 guys participate. So if you're lucky enough to win, thats 90 stamps coming your way. Which in prison is a major score, like winning the lottery. Stamps are king here.

Now there is a rule that you are only allowed to have 50 stamps on your possession at any one time (to prevent this very thing) so if you win, and get caught with 90 stamps in your pocket, or locker, well then you're going to the Box. Having stamps is very lucrative, for that is the currency we use. Need some coffee, sugar, pop-tarts, candy, or creamer? No problem, just show me the stamps!

For some reason Gordon is convinced he's going to win the pool this weekend. Not sure why, he must feel lucky. Having been down about 13 years so far, he knows his way around prison culture. Willie, for his efforts, takes a bit of the cut, his commission you could say. Considering he's served 30 years so far (for double murder) I'd say it's a wise decision to pay him off. Dino informs me (he always like to correct my prison naivete) that you don't say 'double-murderer' but rather he has 'two bodies.' Hmmm, yes, I suppose that has a better ring to it.

Thursday Sept. 6th

As I've written previously, from time to time I get pretty depressed. I think I might be too hard on myself, and maybe getting down is certainly a given. Maybe I should 'let it in' and wash over me, instead of fighting it all the time. I don't know, this whole thing is a work in progress, the answers aren't clear at this point.

What's made me more forgiving is I witnessed a scene last night that opened my eyes a bit. I looked over from my cube to the sight of Dino and "Country," two of the toughest guys I've come across, having served 13 and 8 years respectively, both with their heads buried in their pillows. Trust me, they weren't sleeping, they were crying, just like I do. It made me realize how the loneliness of the place affects even the hard core. So next time I see myself headed to that dark place, I won't anguish on how weak I am. It happens here, to the best of 'em. End of story.

Friday Sept 7th

During the week from 8-11:00 a.m., all the dorms are locked down. If you don't have a program, job, or school to attend, then it's off to the yard for mandatory recreation. Rain or shine! You should see the sight of 500 or so inmates fenced in; some playing sports, others walk around the perimeter, some sit at the benches and read or play cards, while others choose to sunbath when the weather is warm and sunny.

The flip side however, when it rains, you're trapped out there. Picture a dog in his cage, sitting outside in the pouring, cold rain.

I had been wondering what goes on in the dorms while the inmates were out and about. Earlier this morning I got my answer. Upon returning from school there were mattresses strewed upon the floor, pillows, towels, and magazines too. There are strict rules as to how one's cube area is expected to look, if something is out of place, the sergeant during morning inspection will simply wreck your world. Beds have to be perfectly made, shoes lined up single file beneath the bed, no books or magazines visible, everything placed inside your foot locker. As you can imagine, there are some real slobs walking around this place. It was their shit I found thrown around the dorm. First time it happens the Sgt. gives you a warning, but push his buttons a second time and you'll get a ticket with a possible trip to 'the box.' The other day I made a rookie mistake; I had left a small paperback on the foot of my bed. Sure enough it was there on the floor waiting for me when I returned. It won't happen again.

Saturday Sept 8th

At some point today I will receive a call from the mail room ordering me to come pick up my care package which Eileen has so kindly and generously sent. Each inmate is allowed 2 packages per month, with the total weight not to exceed 35 pounds. When you think of it, that's a lot of food. I doubt I'll come anywhere near that amount during my time here. A guy like Dino has his family send him the works; cans of tuna, cheese, deli meats, bread, even lemons & limes. For now I'm content with the basics staples; instant coffee, creamer, pop-tarts, Ritz crackers, and maybe a small amount of candy/sweets. I have to believe that Dino, who's been locked up so long, has to try and make his life inside these walls as comfortable as possible.

I ran out of coffee the other day and had to turn to Gordon for help until my package arrived. He was more than happy to help, but I just hate having to to go and ask for a single thing here, like a beggar. Being indebted to anyone can't be a good thing, payback will always be expected. In my package will also be peanut butter & jelly, not exactly the makings of a gourmet meal like Dino & Gordon, but good enough for me.

Sunday Sept 9th

I'm discovering that most of the inmates have their own private scams going on. Some are to help them survive, but others are simply a case of not being able to help themselves. How does that saying go, ya know the one about a tiger changing his stripes? I can only speak of the scams I see in the dorm, but I would suspect it goes on throughout the prison.

Fritz (Paul Newman look alike) is the laundry porter, and for a few extra stamps will sneak 'freshener' into your wash. Add another stamp or two and he'll fold your laundry and leave it at the foot of your bed. Then we have 'Country' (the neo-Nazi) who will remodel your cube and footlocker so as to utilize every available square inch of space. I must admit he has some real talent, call him the California Closet King of Mohawk. From his job on the painting crew he can smuggle in an extra shelf, (don't ask) along with the paint to spruce it all up. Oh, and if you desire some porno magazines, he's your man for that as well. Of course this all comes at a price. Either stamps, food, or "two bricks," which is prison lingo for cigarettes, will do the trick. On a smaller scamming scale we have 'Tito' the little Mexican tailor who will tend to any sewing needs you might have. He gets paid in stamps only. Another guy (Johnny Starfish) will custom design greeting cards for any occasion. Lets say you want to send something special to your Mom or girlfriend, for Valentine's day or Mother's Day, he'll take care of it. Depending on the size of the card and how much glitter you want sprinkled about, Johnny will charge you between o 1 or 2 bricks. He's a big smoker.

I suppose I could eventually have a scam of my own; I seem to have become the go-to-guy when an inmate needs help writing a letter back home. Whether it be his wife, baby-momma, girlfriend, or all of the above. They observe me at the writing table (actually just an old card table) in the dorm day after day and figure I know what I'm doing. The other day I helped a nice older man named Benjamin compose a letter to his girlfriend. Since then three other dudes have come over asking for help. I've yet to charge for my services, I'm happy to be of help. But that might have to change down the road as I have a feeling I'm going to be busy.

Monday Sept 10th

Guess who won the football pool? That's right, Willie the guy running the darn thing. I guess it was legit, no one appears to be grumbling as far as I can tell, but a bit of a coincidence don't you think. And hey, really, who is going to get in the face of a double murderer?

Peter (diamond thief) has been under the weather as of late. He thinks it is a combination of nerves along with something he ate in the mess hall. No surprise there! My stomach is in a constant state of flux. You're on egg shells all the time, cameras and barbed wire everywhere, C.O.'s watching you non-stop. There is not a single door available to inmates, that closes anywhere within the facility. Privacy does not exist. And don't even think about getting sick. From what I've been told you could be on your deathbed and you'll be lucky enough to get two measly aspirin.

Tuesday Sept 11th

One of my responsibilities as a Teacher's Aide is to correct papers. Mr. Z will usually give a test every other day just to keep these guys on their toes. As much as that's possible. After they finish they'll come up to my tiny desk and and stand there while I correct them. I sit with my red marker (Mr. Z insists I use red) ready to go to work. Just like a regular school we have a few guys who know what they're doing, finish the test early, and rush up to see their almost perfect grade. But it's the inmates who come sauntering (the pimp-roll they call it) up at the very end of class you have to watch out for. We have one such inmate nicknamed "little Shaq" as in Shaquille O'neill the huge basketball player. This guy is almost just as large.

This afternoon, with his enormous hands he threw down his test in front of me, beads of sweat dripping off his forehead, and a permeant scowl. "I think I did well" he says to me. I begin thinking to myself, ' Oh please let little shaq get a good score, I hope he got 100%.' But I knew that was a long shot. I picked up the red pen and went to work. The very first answer was wrong, not a good sign. The second & third as well. Oh shit! With each slash of my pen little shaq leaned in closer & closer, his scowl more menacing. I could almost smell his rancid breath. Finally he got one correct, the 5th answer. 4 out of 5 incorrect so far though, these are not good odds. I had to make a choice, do I continue marking them wrong, or look the other way and make Shaq happy and me safe? "Let's see how the next few go I decided. Wrong....wrong... wrong. He's now 1 out of 8.....and I'm about to be throttled. "Oh c'mon man, what is this shit," Shaq blurts out. I glance over at Mr. Z hoping for some support, but he was oblivious to my plight. Screw it I decided, I'm not ready to die yet. I proceeded to mark the remaining 12 answers ALL correct. No matter that they were ALL wrong, I didn't care. As I began to place a "c" (for correct) on the remaining questions, little shaq started to beam. He was happy, he was going to pass. Finally tally, 13 out of 20 correct. "You finished strong" I tell him. With that, his meaty hands pick up the test and he rumbles back to his desk. Oh geez, I think to myself, it's going to be a long semester.

Wednesday Sept 12th

One thing I've learned is you can never let your guard down, don't ever forget where you are. You can walk the straightest of lines 8 days a week, then one little slip up, and you're done. Before you know it you have yourself a Tier 1 ticket & a possible trip to the box. It happened to Dino last night; a guy with 13 years under his belt who should have known better. Here's what took place. The dorm didn't have it's usual night guard on duty, so when that happens you have to be extra cautious as you don't know what certain quirks this new C.O. might have. Maybe he's a real hard ass and lets nothing by, or perhaps he's easy going, wants to put in an easy 8 hours, no messy paper work or hassle, and cruise back home. With a guy like that you can get away with stuff.

There is only one dorm here where you are allowed to cook eggs, it's restricted to the honor dorm only! Strict rule. Now this being prison, rules are made to be broken, right. Plus knowing how Dino loves to

67

eat, nothing, not even a new guard was going to keep him from scarfing down an egg sandwich. See, Dino scored some eggs today from a dude he knows from the honor dorm. "I made some moves Mo" is how he describes it to me. So there's Dino last night cooking up a 4 egg sandwich in the toaster oven, when all of a sudden the new C.O. catches wind (or a whiff) of it. "What the hell are you doing, you're not allowed to have eggs in this dorm," he yells. Just like that, not only is Dino's tasty egg sandwich gone, but he might be gone as well.....to the Box.

Thursday Sept. 13th

Willie is gearing up for the weekly football pool, but given that he cleaned up with 72 stamps last week, some of the guys are a bit hesitant thinking that perhaps the fix is in. I doubt that however. In just a short time I've actually come to view him as one of the straightest shooters in this place. He is a hard worker, the hardest in the dorm; up each morning buffing the floors to a bright shine at 5:30. He keeps to himself, asks nothing of anyone, and expects nothing. His credo which he told me early on was this; " You do you, and I do me." He's been down 30 years now, truly hard to fathom. Willie continues to be kind to me. Having his stamp of approval so to speak, has been a boost, given me some "cred" in the dorm. Hey, around here I need all the "cred" I can get, I'll gladly take it.

Another week is drawing to a close. In spite of the sadness and depression that engulfs me from time to time, the weeks are moving at a rapid clip; half way through the month already. I felt sickish earlier in the week, nerves & anxiety no doubt, but I'm feeling a little better now. Maybe because today was a 3 letter day! Nothing like mail call to boost your spirits.

Friday Sept 14th

When it's time to go someplace, like say to class, meals or the yard, you go as a group. There's no such thing as saying independently, "ok, see you guys later, I'm going to Rec now." No, it doesn't happen that way. With approximately 1000 inmates at Mohawk the movements on the walkways need to be staggered, otherwise you'd have pure bedlam. So the prison is broken up into 'groups,' and then each group moves separately, within 10 minutes of each other. For example this morning at 8:00, Group 1 had the first movement. At that hour the dorm doors are unlocked and out comes spilling a sea of green, and off we go. It's quite a scene. You have the cigarettes immediately being lit up (no smoking allowed in the dorms) by a majority of the crowds. Guys seeing their buds from adjacent dorms, high-fiving each other like it's a homecoming. Guards are watching our every move, to be sure no contraband is being passed off, and also to look out for any stabbings or slashings. It's also amusing to observe the tortoise-like pace of some of these guys; there in no rush to get anywhere. Throw in a pimp-roll or two, the pants hanging down below the cracks of their butts (what's that all about?) and the chatter you overhear, well it certainly makes for an interesting way to start your day.

I like to be one of the first out the door when it opens, this way I get out ahead of the crowd and can walk at a brisk pace. More importantly though, according to Country, you don't want to get trapped off in the middle of the pack, where most of the crowd is, for this is where the majority of slashings will usually occur. I have no doubts Country knows what he's talking about, I take his advice seriously.

Let me pass on a small gem overheard this morning, this is typical of the conversation on the walkways and in the dorms:
Inmate # 1: 'yo, son'
Inmate #2 'what's up son.'
Inmate #1 'you see that new superman joint son?'
Inmate # 2 ' no, son'
Inmate # 1 ' he be up there in space looking down at earth, just chillin'
Inmate #2 ' that some shit son'

Can't make it up. At times like this I continue to think I've been transported to an alien planet.

Saturday-Sunday, Sept 15-16th

The inmates take their TV watching very seriously, hence each dorm has a three man TV committee consisting of an African-American, Caucasian, and a Hispanic. A few days ago, for whatever reason Fritz decided to resign from the committee. But really I can't blame him, it's a thankless job. I've read where more fights & stabbings occur in the over the TV and someone switching channels, than for any other reason in prison. So this 3 man group meets on Saturday mornings and maps out the schedule for the week. It's then posted and the channels and shows are programmed in, so there can be no switching. So far I have tended to avoid that room, but on occasion I'll venture in on occasion, out of pure boredom. There are a few regular shows that are always on the list; "Prison Break" is one of them, along with "24," "CSI" and "COPS." Throw in a few 'gangsta' movies, a few horror films, and you have your weekly schedule. You're never going to see National Geographic or a PBS show up there.

For some of these dudes, the night revolves around the TV and what show they'll want to watch. They have their favorite spots in the TV room (like Dino who always is in the back row, next to the window ledge so he can place his food there) mostly right up in front. Dino lives for his TV. It's kind of sad, I see him do nothing to rehabilitate himself (he doesn't read books, only People magazines) but he'll never miss a night in the TV room. I've got his routine down pat; he heats up the popcorn, chills his soda, and walks in with a look on his face that says 'there is no other place I'd rather be.' A lot seem to behave this way. The room (surrounded by plexiglass, so the guards can always see in) holds about 20, but on some nights (like Saturday) when a new HBO movie is being shown, you'll find about 30 squeezed in. You can imagine the germs floating around in there. Plus the temps have been very warm lately, so they've been outside playing sports all afternoon, and come right in without the thought of a shower!

Officer B, who is our day officer and works the all important 6:30 am to 2:30 p.m. shift, asked me to take Fritz's place on the TV committee. His shift is considered the most important in that he has a lot of direct contact with the inmates during those hours. Basically he is there when they wake up, sees to it that the cubes are clean, the beds made. He then is there when we come back from morning programs, he takes the 11:15

count, he dismisses us for lunch, and patrols the dorm until it's time for him to leave at 2:30. But back to the TV committee, oh man, do I really need this? I don't think I can say no to him though.

Monday Sept 17th

In spite of his never ending stories, ones in which I am unable to get a word in edgewise (he doesn't listen, he waits to talk) Dino continues to guide me through the intricacies of prison life. Plus he seems to have my back. I may tease him, but I'm grateful for that. Last night for example I was headed towards the wash room to brush my teeth and get ready for bed. But as I walked in Willie (double-murder) and another guy were in a heated exchange. Punched could be thrown any moment. Not knowing what to do I continued to head in, when all of sudden Dino appears (he seems to be everywhere) and spins me around. "You can't go in there Mo (he calls just about everyone Mo) what if a fight starts and you get knocked down by accident?" He then continued, "The C.O. won't ask any questions, he'll see you involved and you could be off to 'the box' for 30 days." He was right. It's not like back home when you might witness a fight on the street corner and then go on your merry way. The consequences here are vastly different. I don't have the right instincts yet, I have to keep checking myself as to where I am and the new rules I must survive by. This place is a world unto itself, one I am not familiar with.

Dino with his 13 years of 'being down' possesses that gut feel. For all his crazy quirks I am grateful for his insight. At least once a day he'll come over to my cube and say "You're only here for a hop & a skip Mo, a hop & a skip. Gotta take care of you."

Tuesday-Wednesday Sept 18-19th

There was a stabbing in the gym yesterday. I didn't get all the details as the administration understandably likes to keep a lid on shit like that, but apparently it involved two rival gang members. I overheard Country

71

saying one guy was just working out, when all of a sudden another dude came up from behind and slashed across his throat. The weapon of choice for this, and most of the stabbings, is a tuna can top, folded over to create a double-edged blade. Not only is it easier to hide & handle, but I guess it makes for a pretty potent weapon.

Besides the slashing news, I also found the following curious. Now of course I am way below the curve when it comes to insider knowledge of prison news/gossip, which is fine by me, but veteran guys like Gordon, Dino & Country are not. They're dialed in. They seem to know when a fight or slashing will occur days or hours before it happens. Like this evening (on the 6:00 movement) I was going to head to the yard and get a run in, but before I left the dorm, Country pulls me aside and sternly says, " Make sure you're out in front of the line." Now I don't think he knew exactly when something was going down, but knew enough so as to warn me that it could very well be happening that night. And he was right!! As it was time to leave the yard & head back to the dorm at 8:30, I remembered his advice and was sure to be out in front of the pack, "avoid the middle" Country said. About half way back (it's about a 12 minute walk) to the dorm, I heard this commotion coming from way behind, followed by a swarm of guards who patrol the walkways swooping in to prevent further blood loss. Someone had indeed been stabbed, and any inmate in that general vicinity has to come to a complete halt and separation. They are frisked, patted down, and even though most of them are completely innocent, in this case they will be suspected of being involved and the burden of proof is now on them. Meanwhile I kept a brisk pace and got back to the dorm with no involvement at all. Thanks Country.

Thursday Sept 20th

The 'blahs' continue to haunt me, I can't shake them. It's been a day of barely existing; ever so slowly I went through my paces with little or no energy. The stomach is in a constant state of acidity, a sickish feeling that won't go away. The only bright spot was entering Mr. Z's class this afternoon seeing he had the TV all set up to watch "A Beautiful Mind," one of my favorite movies. Most of the guys seemed to enjoy the respite, but not all, about 8 dudes were sound asleep in the back row. For me it brought back memories of happier days, as I recall I originally watched this with my girlfriend at the time.

At mail call I receive the NY Times, (thanks to Eileen who got me a subscription) each issue is a couple of days behind schedule, but that's okay, it's something to read and lets me keep tabs on what's happening in the real world. But for some reason the past few days I hadn't gotten it, so when the mail was being passed out there were 4 papers that had accumulated. The CO on duty that afternoon (not the regular guy) when it came time to pass everything out screamed at me, "Byrne if you think I'm going to haul your newspapers around everyday you got another thing coming." With that he threw them all to the floor. That movie moment from earlier today was now a distant memory. God I hate this place.

Friday Sept 21st

Fall is only a few days away, but the beautiful late Summer weather lingers on. With not a cloud in the sky, and school being cancelled, it brought me out to the yard on 3 separate occasions. (9:00 am, 11:00 am, and 6:00pm). Besides the perfect weather, I just can't stand to be trapped back in the dorms. Every chance I get I yearn to be outside. The air in the dorm is dank, stale, and at times, smelly. The site of grown men sleeping the day away (when school & programs are closed you can stay in the dorm and fall asleep.....but you are not allowed to actually get 'in' your bed, just on top of it during the day) depresses me to no end. It seems many have given up, resigned themselves to being institutionalized. They lie around talking about rappers, drugs, women & guns.

The coming weekend will be my last free one for awhile, possibly right into November. Next weekend my folks are coming up, along with two of my sisters. I can't wait to see them. The following weekend brings a Catholic Retreat I am taking part in, it's being run by the Deacon who works here, a really nice man. He'll be bringing in a group of civilians who give up their weekends for prison retreats such as this. Supposed to be quite moving and spiritual and will run from Friday afternoon until Sunday afternoon. Then the week after that, my brother Jack is coming up. I continue to wrestle with the idea of my sons coming to visit, for

73

as much as I ache to see them, right now I'm not sure I want them to have a memory of their Dad in a place like this. My biggest fear is it'll be a memory they won't shake for a long time. The three of us have too many happy memories, I'd rather they cling to those instead. For now at least.

Saturday-Sunday Sept 22nd-23rd

Unlike the real world, weekends here continue to be so very difficult. There is simply way too much time to sit & stare at the four walls. But then again, I understand thats what prison is supposed to be. I get it. On the rare occasion when I'm not reading or writing, I have time to look back on all those wonderful, happy memories of long ago. The BP (before prison) years. For the time being however, they are a thing of the past.

I'm looking forward to saturday night (6:00) Mass in a few hours. Since arriving almost 2 months ago, I have yet to miss a service. Besides the spiritual aspect, it brings me a tiny sense of normalcy. Plus I think Deacon C. give a wonderful sermon; it's message always along the lines of prison/survival/hope appropriate. For some reason however the services are poorly attended. On average only about 30 or so show up, this out of 1000 inmates.

Slowly but surely, my hair is growing back. One of these days I might actually need a comb. I remember so vividly that day at Downstate when it was all shaved off, about 2 months ago. I don't like being bald.

As it turns out Dino did not end up going to 'the box' for his egg cooking incident, but he did lose all Rec privileges for the next 2 weeks. Considering his doesn't venture out to the yard to exercise, no biggie. But what is a major blow to him will be the loss of TV watching. That's as big a hit as Dino feared, TV watching for him is serious business. He lives for his shows. Just a few minutes ago (as I was busy writing, it matters not however) he came over, " Mo, can you watch CSI for me and tell me what happens?" I'm like, " Dino, I don't want to watch that shit. Why don't you read a book, I'd be happy to lend you one." But he's not interested in books, just the latest 'People' magazine. I won't press it, I think it's perhaps he doesn't read very well and might be embarrassed.

The TV committee met this morning (Sat), for an hour no less. Ugh, why did I agree to sign on for this again? I'm beginning to think my, " I can make a difference mantra" is a big waste of energy. Plus who knows, it can only lead to frustration, and worse, possible trouble. Speaking of frustration, recently my family sent me a bunch of magazines, they sit in the package room, but guess what, I can't get a hold on them for at least 2 weeks.....yes, that's right, there is something here called the "media review" department. Whatever the hell that is. I can see if we were talking hard core porno, but these are main stream magazines, ones such as Time, Newsweek, Vanity Fair, and Sports Illustrated.

Monday-Tuesday September 24-25th

Well so much for the TV committee! I lasted all of two days. What a nightmare. Let me tell you what happened. Last night (sunday), literally just a day after putting up the schedule, a fellow inmate named James comes up to me. Now James is a dude that spends every available minute in the TV room, sitting there at his usual spot (yes, one of those guys) with a big dumb look on his face. His arms are literally the size of my calves, he's black as a piece of coal, and wears a green do-rag, along with one of those muscle t-shirts to show off his massive chest and arms. One mean looking guy. Prior to last night I had thought we were getting along okay, there had never been any sort of incident, I'd see him in the dorm, nod politely hello, and even a few days ago he asked me to help him with his math homework.

So as I was sitting down last night, minding my own business, James approaches demanding to know "Who picked this fucking show" that was now on the TV. To fill the 5-6:00 p.m. time slot I had made just about the only suggestion while on the committee, I thought the HBO show called 'Nine innings from Ground Zero' would be interesting. It's all about 9/11 and how the NY Yankees lifted the spirits and hope of the city when they reached the World Series that year. When James came up to me I happened to be sitting in the TV room with about 15 other guys, all of whom seemed to be enjoying the show. At first I wasn't really sure if James wanted to thank the person who picked the show, if he had a question about it, or was simply not liking it. So I readily offered " I picked this show." " Well it fucking sucks," James countered.

Now on those brief occasions when I do go in the TV room I have never heard anybody flat out disparage a show, or worse, seek out the member of the committee who picked it. In spite of James gargantuan size I felt a bit emboldened, still thinking that perhaps maybe maybe he was just busting my chops a bit. I looked at James and said, "Well then don't watch it." Oops, wrong thing to say. " Are you fucking disrespecting me?" he said. (James likes to use the 'F' word.) All of a sudden I was getting in the middle of something I hadn't bargained for. He proceeded to get right up into my face, but still I wasn't afraid. Besides, the day Officer on duty was Officer B, who I get along with well enough, plus I knew he was in the bubble, and could see right into the room. " No I'm not disrespecting you, just saying that if you don't like it, you don't have to watch it." Again James took this as a slight, but I wasn't backing down as the other guys in the room began to sense this might just bubble over.

Luckily for me one of the guys in the room also happened to be on the TV committee; Skeeter, a tough Spanish dude who has been down for awhile, currently on either his 2nd or 3rd prison bid. Also luckily for me I had helped 'Skeets' compose a letter to his girlfriend just a few days ago. Unbeknownst to me James & Skeets had had a run in previously. Quickly my involvement came to an end and this disagreement took on a whole new meaning. Skeets got up in front of James, "Let's take this to the yard mother-fucker." Not at that very moment, but next time Rec was called (tomorrow) these two would square off in the yard, possibly in the bathroom that is somewhat protected from the sight of the guards. This just shows how quickly a situation can explode here. And what fuels it is the prison code of "no one can be seen as backing down."

"I don't need no fucking yard to settle this, let's do it right now," James countered with. All of us were now wondering how far this was going to go. Geez, why isn't Officer B coming in to settle this down, I wondered. Well no sooner had I thought that when all of a sudden I saw Officer B coming down from his guard perch/desk, walking towards the TV room. Now fighting is automatic 60 minimum day trip to 'the box.' And as much as these two wanted to square off, neither was stupid enough to sign on for 60 days in the hole, this could be continued someplace where the guards might not catch wind. All it took were the words, "knock it off, don't even think about it," from the C.O. Just like that, for now at least, the fight was put to bed. I have no doubts these two will find a time and a place to continue what they started.

And as for me, I'm learning that perhaps 'making a difference' isn't all what it's cracked up to be, or at the very least, not possible here. I have to keep repeating Willie's credo, after all it's worked for him these past 30 years in prison, , "You do you, and I'll do me."

Wednesday Sept 26th

As Dino likes to say, "You're only here for a hop & a skip Mo." And relative to his 13 years so far, he's absolutely right! Do I really need the aggravation of the TV committee, what the hell was I thinking? My gosh, I don't even watch the stupid thing. Again I was under the delusion that I could make a contribution within these walls. Should've listened to Gordon. Ok, so let's call it what it is; a rookie mistake, won't happen again. I must continue to check myself, I'm not in Suburbia anymore, but rather in a world where I know very little. I have never encountered something like this before. Remaining under the radar and staying within my boundaries is the only sensible road for me. Let's just read books, write letters, and stay camped in my 7x7 cube for now.

Thursday Sept 27th

For some reason classes have been cancelled the past two days. I'm assuming Mr. Z is sick or using up some unclaimed sick days, and taking advantage of the beautiful Fall weather we're having. One thing for certain, the students/inmates could not be happier.

This morning at 8:00 I took advantage of the free day and went out to the yard. On any given weekday there will be about 400 inmates in the yard at that time. They can be found lifting weights, running/walking, playing handball (very popular), playing bacci, or playing basketball. The rest will be lying on the grass, shirts off, pants rolled up, or wearing gym shorts, and sunbathing away. My point is, here you have an abundance of able bodied men, strong and full of energy. Wouldn't you think the State could find something more constructive for them to be doing instead of getting a suntan? Perhaps day work such as painting or picking up trash at the local community centers, parks, or along the highways? Ok sure, you don't want to let all these psychos running through your streets, but I can tell you, at least half of them (the non-violent, 1st time offenders) out there in the yard would be more than capable of doing excellent work, practically for free. I often think to myself, ' If the taxpayers of New York could witness this scene in the yard.' Especially when you hear the prohibitive cost of housing just one inmate per year, now stands at $42,000. There are millions being wasted within the system. With each passing day it dawns on me more & more; prison means big business!!

Friday Sept 28th

Dino has four more days without TV privileges, the shutout is driving him crazy. And tonight his favorite show is on, ' Bounty Girls of Miami.' To compensate that loss, he's been doing double time in the eating department. As I glance over to his cube I can see a huge bowl on his lap, overflowing with potato chips and popcorn. His familiar refrain is " I'm going to start my diet next week Mo. Next week for sure." I can guarantee you there will be no diet next week. nor the week after.

Even though he's not in my dorm, I keep running into 'Jimmy Waldorf.' James is serving a 7 year sentence for robbing on more than one occasion, you guessed it, the Waldorf Astoria Hotel in New York City. Usually I spot him in the library, and with his slicked back hair, tortoise shell glasses, and handsome face, he could easily be mistaken for a Wall St investment banker. Except for the green polyester prison garb. When I do get the chance to catch up, we have normal conversations, discuss current events, talk about politics, and can usually finish a sentence without using the 'F' word. A rarity at this place.

Saturday, Sept. 29th

It's 9:00 on a Saturday morning, and I'm waiting for the call to head up to the visitors room to meet my parents, along with two of my sisters, Liz & Virginia. They arrived in Rome last evening and will head back home immediately after our visit. On one hand I can't wait to be together, all of us laughing, sharing, and probably as they are getting up to leave, crying. On the other, having Mom & Dad come here at all, subjecting them to witness their youngest son in prison, well, it just tears me up inside. How can I subject them to this sadness? I'm heartbroken, even though they have already seen me behind bars, this is different; this is my new home, a NY State Medium prison, for God knows how long. Did they ever foresee a day like this? No, and neither did I.

Here I was, given every tool to succeed in life, the right path always directly in front of me, the love to keep me there, and the assistance if I ever strayed. But instead, in a matter of minutes, I will throw myself into their arms, and as I have many times before, tell them both how sorry I am for the pain I have caused. My Mother is like a living Saint, really, she is. I have never seen anyone with such faith, love & devotion. I can just hear the words she will speak upon seeing me, "Jerry dear, if only I could do this time for you, I would." And she means every word of it.

So it's now five hours later, I'm back from the visit, and it was everything I expected it to be. My father and mother, 85 and 82 respectively, looked fantastic, at least ten years younger. So dapper in their attire, such stiff upper lips. My sisters, well they always look beautiful, no matter what the setting, even a dump like this. Since the weather was nice and sunny, we were able to sit outside. The prison has about 6 cement benches and tables, uncomfortable yes, but it sure beats the depressing visitors room. They are not allowed to sit next to me, so here we were, them on one side, me on the other, facing the CO who keeps watch.

After a few hours it was time to say our goodbyes, sure enough, it was gut wrenching for all of us. I stress to them that in spite of it all, I am safe, I will stay strong, and God willing return home in the not too distant future. They would all head to their exit, and eventually me to mine. Catholic Services begins shortly, I can't wait to thank God for continuing to look over me.

Sunday Sept. 30th

Today has been quiet, went to the yard after breakfast, and ran/ walked the entire two hours. Alone with my thoughts on this sunny Fall like day. In the afternoon I went back to the yard and met up with Peter and Joe. Most of the guys in the dorm remained inside to watch the NFL games. That's not for me, ugh, depressing to be in that shit hole of a dorm on a beautiful day like this.

It's been kind of a mellow day, much of it spent rehashing the wonderful visit I had yesterday. As with most days here, I simply want it to end. Lights are out at 10:00pm, a few hours from now. I'll sit in my cube and read until then.

Monday October 1st

Oh what a feeling to rip the month of September off the calendar! That's what it's all about here; as the lifers continue to remind me, "You do the time, don't let the time do you." Unfortunately though I have been suffering from a bout of depression at the moment. The "black dog" as the great Winston Churchill described it. I'm not exactly sure what triggered it, but I guess just being here is enough reason. Perhaps the letdown after seeing my parents and sister over the weekend, knowing it will be awhile before I see them all again. Or perhaps it was, after speaking with my son Brooks, who was telling me all about his H.S. football game the other day, how helpless and alone I felt. I miss terribly the satisfactions and heartbreak of everyday parenting.

It's late, I'm sad and lonely, and I don't feel like writing anymore.

Tuesday Oct. 2nd

Another sunny day. Off in the distance I can see the tree lines, the colors of the leaves ever so slightly beginning to turn. I promise not to harp on my sadness, hopefully I will snap out of it today. Last week I was recruited by the Officer who runs the Fire & Safety office to join his 2 man crew of inmates, to work there. From what I'm told, the job actually feels like a real job. It involves computer work, writing, filing, and movement throughout the facility.....in the State F&S pickup truck. It will mean leaving Mr. Z's morning GED class, but that's fine with me, I wasn't making any headway there. So this morning I started and it's off to a smooth beginning. My co-worker is Dee (serving a 5 year sentence for carrying a loaded weapon) a good guy who seems pretty in control of himself & surroundings. He's got a wife, two daughters, and talks about them constantly.

Part of the job description is to visit the other dorms, check the fire extinguishers, emergency lights, etc......we then head back to the office and file reams of paperwork about all we did. The CO who is the F&S chief, accompanies us on the rounds. Basically we do all his work while he bullshits with the other guards. In the tiny office (yes, can you believe, we have our own office) I have access to a non-internet computer, radio, and an occasional cup of instant coffee the chief will throw our way.

My first real laugh in weeks was provided by an inmate in the afternoon GED class where I remain a TA. (teachers assistant). Mr Z. was attempting to drive home a point on the importance of the topic sentence in every bit of writing. For five solid minutes he stressed how critical it is, and the inmates seemed to actually be listening, as opposed to sleeping. All of a sudden a hand shoots up, an actual question is being asked, kind of a rarity around here. Could someone really care enough to inquire about the topic sentence? "Yo, Mr Z, I'd like to ask when our next day off is?" The look on Mr. Z's face was priceless; here he thought he was breaking through. Not a chance.

Wednesday Oct. 3rd

The "blahs" refuse to go away, another day of simply existing, going through the paces. Marking time, nothing more than that. Stomach seems to be acting up again.

Gordon to the rescue though, he has whipped up one of his special pasta, garlic and sausage dinners. I'll shut down early after eating, read the papers a bit, and call it a day.

Thursday Oct. 4th

Just can"t bare to write anything today.

Friday Oct. 5th

Catholic Services Retreat began this morning at 9:00 and ended for the day a short time ago. I'm back in the dorm, and it's 10:00pm. There are about 40 inmates participating with ten civilians running the weekend program, which is called, Residents Encounter Christ. It's held in the chapel room (basically a glorified large classroom) and we get to talk about anything troubling us. We sing, share, and pray. Outside the chapel is a picnic area where we are able to eat our meals. At dinner, Peter, Gordon, and I were all so enjoying the moment; the sun was setting and it's almost like we were at a cookout back in the suburbs, surrounded by a white picket fence, our children laughing in the yard. We began to dream about when we might just experience a setting as that, again. The day when this place will be nothing but a distant, unpleasant memory. Someday, someday.

Saturday/Sunday, Oct 6th & 7th

Well it's Sunday night, the retreat has come and gone, and I'm back in the dorm. I can't say enough about my ten new friends; those people who gave up their weekends and came into the prison to run the retreat. The 40 of us were split into groups, mine was run by Nick, who has participated in this program for 17 years now. Each morning as we entered the chapel, the entire cast of civilians were there to greet us, and then literally hug us.

Some of the inmates who attended the retreat I have never once laid eyes on at Mass. Now I don't want to judge , but it was clear to most (especially our leader, Deacon C.) that they signed on strictly for morning donuts, afternoon cookies, and evening candy. There was one dude who wore sweat pants under his regular clothes, so he could smuggle as much as back to the dorm as possible. There is no escaping the madness of this place.

I've received some books from Mom & Dad, along with magazines that Eileen sent, so thankfully I have ample reading to keep me busy and distracted. I am blessed to have such love & support on the outside.

Monday Oct. 8th

It's Columbus Day, a holiday here at Mohawk. School is closed and there will be no programs. This all adds up to a long day, no way around it. I had been hoping for a continuation of the nice weather, but the day has brought cloudy, drizzly skies instead. No matter, I'll catch up on my reading and writing. This afternoon, if the rain stops, I will head out to the yard for a run.

Coming from a big Irish-Catholic family, it should be no surprise that I have quite a few first and second cousins. But as time rolls on, and people get married & have children, families tend to drift apart. One silver lining of my incarceration is that I have become reunited with so many of my cousins who have heard what happened. Their letters arrive and I am overwhelmed with gratitude. They want to know how I'm holding up, what can they send, how can they help. Just knowing how many people are rooting for me lends a great deal of strength to my day.

Tuesday Oct. 9th

Well Gordon received some good news, he won the weekly football pool. For his efforts Gordon collected 105 stamps (remember stamps are king, there is no such thing as cash here) even after Profit took his cut off the top. Rarely do I see Gordon write a letter, so he has no use for stamps on that front, but he can (and will) barter them for many other uses. Such as food, candy, coffee, or cigarettes.

An A.A. program is offered, but what they really need is a G.A. program. Next time I see my counselor I will inquire about this, even offer to assist in anyway I can. I certainly know a thing or two about addictions to gambling. I see guys getting in over their heads on these football games. Trust me, this is not the place you want to fall behind on your debts!

I am all too familiar with the destruction and heartache this insidious disease can cause. It's why despite every advantage I had at my disposal, given every tool to succeed; I am writing this story behind a giant fence, lined with barbed wire. A marriage of 14 years, torn asunder thanks to me. No longer would I be hugging my boys each night, putting them to bed. And they were so young, 7 and 4. This guilt haunts me to this very day. Ashamed and disgusted by choices I have made with my life. But I've come to recognize forgiveness for myself. For the past 8 years I have been All-American at rehashing my many mistakes. Flogged on a daily basis. I can't do it anymore though. To one day get out of this place, I have to be strong. I simply won't make it without that inner strength. In just my brief time of being incarcerated, I can see that clearly.

Wednesday Oct. 10th

Returning to the dorm after finishing up my program, Fritz (the laundry porter who bares a close resemblance to Paul Newman) cornered me and asked, "did you hear what happened?" No I replied, all I really wanted was to make myself a cup of coffee. "Gordon got hauled off to the box," Fritz said. I was stunned. Gordon, my closest friend in all of Mohawk, now banished from this dorm. In fact as I write his locker and cube are being emptied out, his belongings thrown into Hefty garbage bags.

'What the heck happened" I asked Fritz. At first I thought Gordon had been involved in a fight out in the yard; Gordon is powerfully built, a strong sense of prison right and wrong (coming from the 18 years he's spent behind the wall so far) and possesses a bit of a temper. But Fritz didn't know anymore than I did, except it wasn't a fight. It was looking more like a failed urine test. But could that really be it? Having spent the past three days (the Retreat) with Gordon, we became even closer. He opened up emotionally to the group how this bid was going to be his last, the desire to turn his life around, get back home with his family, and get back to his landscaping business. He only had 8 months left to serve on his current parole violation.

So for now I don't know what is going on. I do know however I have lost the guy I ate every meal with (eating together in prison on a constant basis is a tight bond) and the guy I went to when I found myself sinking. We ran together in the yard & talked about the two of us playing golf together one day. Gordon had my back. Now I'll most likely never lay eyes on him again. For once you go to the box, no matter how long, you get moved to another dorm. And in some cases, transfered to another facility. Hard to believe it was just a few days ago he was singing "Amazing Grace" at the retreat, his face beaming, so proud. Now as I write, he sits alone in "the box."

Thursday Oct. 11th

I find myself simply going through the motions ever since hearing the news about Gordon. Rumors abound, but still no official word on what happened. It was quiet last night, not having him around the dorm. Gordon was usually front and center, either playing cards or offering to cook up a little something. He had a certain spark, difficult enough to come across in the real world, much less a place like this. Now there's not a sign of him anywhere; his cube already occupied by another inmate.

Friday Oct. 12th

I spoke with my ex-wife last night. We get along pretty well & she's been supportive of my ordeal, especially when it comes to the boys. Abby wanted to let me know that our oldest, Brooks, a senior in High School, has just finished his college application essay. She will be sending along a copy of it. The question was, "what event has impacted your life the most?" Apparently, Brooks, completely on his own, has chosen to write about his dad being in prison, the effect it's had on him so far, along with the unforgettable day I broke the news to the boys that their dad was going away, possibly for a long time.

Abby has praised the writing; it's emotional, honest, straight from the heart, and powerful. Part of me dreads reading it. I'm so very proud of my son.

Saturday Oct. 13th

Fall seems to have arrived; the weather these past few days has been cold and blustery. The leaves have changed colors practically overnight. I keep hearing about the massive amounts of snow Rome, NY gets during the Winter. I'm hoping for a strong dose of global warming. Ugh, the thought of trudging through the snow to make it over to the mess hall by 6:30 a.m. depresses me.

I have visitors this weekend. An old friend from Short Hills, NJ has driven up to see me. Tom had heard about a month ago what had happened, found out where I was being held, and just decided to get in the car for the 5 hour drive. As simple as that. He is so full of life, not once in the 20 years I have known him has he not had an uplifting word, a smile, or a witty one-liner to elicit a laugh. He can only stay until 1:00 p.m., but will be quickly followed by Eileen who has driven up as well.

Sunday Oct. 14th

The visitor's room here at Mohawk is about the size of half a football field. Filled with cheap formica tables, steel chairs, and vending machines (which the inmates are not allowed to go near) it's kind of like a High School cafeteria. On a weekend, let me tell you, it's loud. When the weather is nice, there is a much nicer, quieter portion outside, where you can bring your family and actually feel somewhat civilized. Thank God the day my parents were here that was the case. Similarly it was pleasant weather when Tom & Eileen came to visit.

The only negative thing about having visitors; the letdown when they get up from the table and prepare to leave. You're allowed one quick hug, the eyes of the guards burning down on you. You don't want to let go, the thought of them simply walking out to their car, driving off like a normal human being. The rest of the inmates exiting through a separate door where we prepare to be strip-searched.

It's now late Sunday, about to call it a night. I'll do a little more reading, say a prayer of thanks for this wonderful weekend, put on headphones and listen to my radio. Another day down.

Monday Oct. 15th

I'm really getting to like this morning job @ Fire & Safety. I didn't realize it when Chief R. hired me, but this position is considered one of the best in the facility. It offers a lot of variety; driving around the grounds in the truck (only the chief drives) to inspect various buildings. It's especially cool when we head to the mess hall where I can pick up an extra piece of coffee cake. The F&S office, located in the Tier Building (where they hold disciplinary hearings) always has a bunch of CO's around, Lieutenants, and Sergeants. Not bad to get exposure to those guys, although I keep my distance. I just have to be careful not to get too close, as the other inmates see me constantly interacting with the CO's. I can't have them thinking I'm a snitch or something.

Still no word on Gordon, he remains in the box, that's all I know. In his brief absence from the dorm I have come to realize (once again) you are just a number here & how quickly you can be forgotten. No one even mentions his name now. Gordon went out of his way to share with many of the other inmates, whether it be scoops of coffee, stamps, or food, it didn't matter. If he had it, he would almost always lend it to you. 99% of the dudes here wouldn't give you the time of day much less a precious stamp. And when you tried to thank Gordon, he produced his standard reply, "It's not that serious." I'm pissed how all these pieces of shit have forgotten him. But then I get a grip and remember where I am, I should expect nothing less. Remembering Willie's (the double murderer) popular saying when anyone would approach him for something, he would shake his head and say, "You do you, and I do me." Simple but profound.

Tuesday Oct. 16th

When I speak on the phone with anyone in my family, especially my sons, I always try to come across strong and determined. It's paramount that I let them at least think I am surviving here, without all the negativity I could heap on them. After all though, what good would that do? Besides depressing the shit out of everyone.

There are however three days I will be hard pressed to stay strong for; Thanksgiving, Christmas, and today......my son Brooks 18th birthday. Just look at me, his dad, locked up in prison. I would give anything to be there, to hug him, let him know how proud I am. I can't dwell, I can't. If I go 'there' I will make this day so much harder than it already is. I almost have to block it from my mind, like it's not happening. I don't know another way to deal with it.

Wednesday Oct. 17th

As the weather turns colder, the popular item of clothing around here is the "hoodie." It's a large sweatshirt with deep front pockets, and of course the pull over hood. They are especially prevalent at breakfast where most of these guys will attempt to smuggle out half-pints of milk & bring them back to the dorm. Technically, nothing is allowed out of the mess hall except if there is some kind of fruit (which is rare) given out at lunch or dinner, and of course the 4 slices of bread.

At the exits there are at least 3 CO's and 1 Sergeant standing by. To try and take anything out is a risk. You get caught and it's a ticket with possible loss of privileges. You get caught a couple of times, and you're going to the box. But this being prison, well some guys just can't help themselves. A few steps in front of me earlier was some cat trying to smuggle out milks. he didn't make it. All of a sudden I hear, "Hands up on the wall." It was frisk time. No back talk, no questions asked. That's the absolute last thing you want to do. What does this guy do.... he talks back. "Hey man, don't hassle me, I didn't do nothing." Before you knew the CO's were in his face. I wasn't able to stick around, no stopping allowed, so I don't know what happened, but my guess is a trip to the box was probably in order.

Thursday Oct. 18th

For the first time since starting this diary I'm having a hard time getting motivated. I can't really put my finger on why exactly, as my writing usually provides such relief, but I'm very low at the moment. If I had to guess what ails me, it would be the news about Gordon. I learned earlier he will be locked in the box for 120 days! Of course this also means he'll be transfered to another prison. Not to be overly dramatic here, but chances are our paths will never cross again. I keep harking back to the Retreat, just 2 short weeks ago, how hopeful he was to be heading home this Spring, to start his life over again. He spoke of this only minutes before he picked up the microphone and belted out, "Amazing Grace."

Friday Oct. 19th

My depression continues, sitting down to write is a chore. I hate this place. There is so much I miss, the boys at the top of that list. But I've lost my freedom, the freedom to do even the simplest of things. My stomach (nerves) are on continuous alert, only when you're sleeping (in a room with 38 other men) can you somewhat relax. The minute I wake up I find the need to be on point, watching my every step, making sure I don't get trapped off in some way. You look at some of these inmates strangely and next thing you know they're in your face, "You got a problem with me white boy." And you have to answer them, otherwise it's disrespectful, and you can't cave, you have to come back respectfully, but forcibly. There is a real fine line there. Most often I walk around with my head down, trying not to make eye contact with anybody. I continue on a pace of reading a book a day. It's my escape.

Sat/Sun Oct 20th 21st

The weekend is here, and with no visits, not much to look forward to. The first thing to do will be the mandatory saturday chores. Breakfast at 8:00 (Rice Krispies & toast) then back to the dorm for clean up of our individual 7x7 cubes. Your supposed to have your living area pretty much spotless anyway, so this doesn't really take all that long. I sweep, then mob. Tidy up the bed, which always has to be neatly made.

You can set your watch by Willie's waxing/buffing of the main floor, 6:00 a.m. Seven days a week he's at it. It's quiet right now, one or two guys called to the Visitor's Room earlier. Or as Dino refers to it as; the Dance Floor. A few dudes playing cards, some watching TV, and the rest have gone back to lying on their beds, trying to fall asleep. I made a vow, at Rikers, when I saw all these guys sleeping the day away, that I would never succumb to that! I just won't allow myself to take a nap here, I must keep busy, either by reading or writing letters.

There was a funny and telling moment the other night. I popped my head into the smelly TV room just to see what was going on. About 15 inmates were in there watching the show "Cops." On the screen was a car chase taking place; two dudes had robbed a bank and were trying to escape from the police. Well the action got pretty crazy, it was quite a chase, all of a sudden the police car crashes. As soon as that happened, everyone in the room started hollering, clapping, and high-fiving each other. You'd think they were all just pardoned. But no, the cops were hurt, they crashed, the bad guys had gotten away. Good grief, what a place this is.

The warm Fall weather continues, so I look forward to heading out for afternoon recreation, starting at 1:00 p.m. The only thing I'll do is walk/run around the track, allowing my mind to drift to the places I cannot. Tonight we have Catholic Services which I never miss. Not a very high attendance, over 1000 inmates at Mohawk, and only about 30 or so go to Mass. My Mother sent me the new John Grisham book the other day, which I finished immediately. I've since lent it to Officer B, who from the first day I arrived here, has treated me fairly. He's one of the real decent CO's I've encountered. Even though he's been at this job for over 20 years, he still has a heart. Don't get me wrong, he kicks ass when he has to, but I find he'll only give you the rope, so if you hang yourself, it's on you. Officer B is the one who recommended me for the Fire & Safety job, which I continue to like.

Dino has been prowling about the dorm the past few days. Apparently his brother didn't send him a food package this month, so he is extremely out of sorts with the prospect of no treats to consume on a saturday night. Considering he's about 50lbs overweight, you would think he would be happy to lay low for a weekend or two, but Dino doesn't want to hear it. Feeling bad for him I offered him a microwavable bag of popcorn, which he happily accepted. He's already planning (8 hours ahead) at what point during the movie tonight he'll fire it up. I like Dino, but he has some serious food issues. I imagine 13 years behind bars will create an issue or two.

Monday Oct. 22nd

I suppose there are all sorts of ways to end up in prison, but for the third time during my brief stay, I've met another guy in for DUI. Greg entered our dorm last night (you can always spot the new guys, they have "that look" about them, just like I did three months ago) and after he unpacked his draft bag, containing everything you own in prison, I walked over to introduce myself. Why you ask? Well it's always something I wish guys had done for me, he was white, about my age, and he looked approachable. I wondered if Greg needed anything, a cup of coffee perhaps. I know he appreciated the gesture, and we made a plan to have breakfast together in the morning.

Greg was a Lieutenant Colonel in the Army for 19 years, spent 10 months in Afghanistan, and up to 6 months ago, was preparing to deploy to Iraq. He's the father of two girls, and his wife teaches first grade at a school not far from here. Perfect life, right. Well not too long ago Greg was driving home from work, had had a few beers, and proceeded to hit a car, pushing the other driver into the other lane where she got hurt badly, but not killed. It was his 2nd DUI. As a result the Judge sentenced Greg to 2 1/2 years flat, and in addition he faces a huge civil suit.

We got to talking how doing the time here was. While quite difficult, the real heartache came from being apart from our families, those moments we're missing, never to get reclaim. He seems like a real decent guy, someone I can relate to; we made mistakes in our life, and are paying dearly for it. And it's funny, I'm not the new guy in the dorm anymore. Moving up the prison ladder!

Tuesday Oct. 23rd

Out of the blue, a major case of nerves has struck, along with something bad I ate, which have combined to knock me down. I don't feel like doing anything, even my precious writing.

Wednesday Oct. 24th

Thankfully I'm feeling better. Not being up for mess hall food last night, I haven't eaten much. I find myself sipping quite a bit of green tea. I have to learn to settle my nerves more. Still missing Gordon for many reasons, one of them being these delicious (for prison) salads he made.

Mr. Z (the teacher I'm a TA for) announced that after 18 years of teaching at Mohawk, is set to retire. He'll leave here in the next week or so. I'll be sorry to see him go, he has always treated me well, and he had a respectful rapport with the inmates. Oh, and one other thing, he has a ton of patience. You'd have to for sure, working in a place like this. Given that Mr Z. is leaving, he's kind of on cruise control, today he allowed us to watch the movie, " Pursuit of Happyness." About thirty minutes into it, I counted 9 guys asleep.

Thursday Oct. 25th

As I've mentioned, the weekends are long & boring, but this one will be a little different; yes I have a visit!! My brother's Joe and Jack will be here. Jack is in from Honduras for about a week, they'll drive up Friday night, spend the evening at a local Hotel, and spend most of saturday (visiting hours are from, 9:00-3:00) with me. I can't wait to hug them. One visit provides me with weeks of happy memories.

Quiet day otherwise, the usual madness taking place in the dorms. I look forward to one thing;; lights out at 10:00 p.m. Another day down.

Friday Oct. 26th

For the second time since I've been at Mohawk, "Country" has forewarned me of an event that is going to take place. Specifically, a stabbing or slashing. He knows I don't have a clue about all this, that I'm a fish out of water, and looks out for me. He tells me when it's time to head out on morning or afternoon movement, to get out in front of the pack, not getting caught up in the middle, where these things tend to happen.

Sure enough, he was right again. There was a slashing on the walkway this afternoon, as we returned back to the dorm after school for some, and Rec for others. Apparently it was all gang related (the less I know the better) and this dude got slashed across the face with a tuna can lid, folded over, to inflict twice the damage. Thanks to Country I was indeed in front of the line & didn't even know about it until guys came back in the dorm. Country has been in and out of prisons most of his young (he's about about 22 years old) life. He's tuned in and prison savvy. I'm grateful he looks out for me. Maybe his being a white supremacist probably has something to do with it, he seems to keep most all the white guys in check. I notice him and Dino are good friends. Country has no one writing or sending him a blessed thing, so I'm happy to repay the favor by giving him coffee, candy, a stamp, whatever. He also has a six year old daughter whom he hasn't seen since she was 2 months old. He'll be leaving Mohawk in about a month, but not for freedom. The day he gets out of here, the State of Pennsylvania will be outside the gates waiting to extradite him for a burglary charge. A 2 year sentence.

Back to the slashing, it was the 8th one (that I know of) in the three months I've been here. No one seems overly alarmed by that number. When I mention to some guys the horror of getting your face slashed, it's met with a shrug, not an ounce of sympathy or outrage. What a fucking place this is, I can't get out of here soon enough.

Saturday & Sunday Oct. 27 & 28th

After being frisked, I walked into the visitors room on a rainy Saturday morning. Who do I see at the lead table but my brother's, Joe and Jack. In an instant I'm overwhelmed with emotion. We hugged, I cried, and from there we had a glorious three hour visit.

As a family we've always been close, but inevitably life gets in the way, children come along, work takes hold, and before you know it you've drifted away from each other with only limited contact. If I was to search for a silver lining in my being held here (I'm always in search of those silver linings) it would be, now more than ever, the bond I have reestablished with my brothers & sisters. I am so grateful for their love and support. It's true what they say, if you don't have family, what do you have?

The three of us talked non-stop for those three hours. Joe and Jack looking like aliens in the visitors room, with their khaki pants, loafers, and button down shirts. It's funny, not long ago when my parents came to see me, all dressed to the nines, the Guards in the processing center, before you gain access to visit, asked, "Um, excuse me folks, are you sure you're in the right place?"

When it was time for them to leave we set a date for their next visit (Christmas), hugged once more, and proceeded to our separate exits. How I wanted to get in the car with them.

Monday Oct. 29th

For weeks now Dino has been gearing up for the Thanksgiving meal he wants to prepare. And it's still nearly a month away! 3-4 times a day he'll come over to my cube (I'm directly across from him), and not caring if he's bothering me, will ask what I like in my salad, my favorite dressing, and how pissed he his at his brother because he won't send him a small tin of caviar. Yes, caviar.

When I tell Dino I'm not much of a foodie, that I really don't care what I eat (hey, it's prison after all, it's not like I'm going to be with my family) he gets a bit testy. "Listen Mo, when you've been locked up as long as I have, you need to at least try to make an attempt at being civilized, not all of us are here for a skip & a hop like you are." And then I think to myself, ya know, he's right. For him, food is his only outlet. After 13 years and counting, it's literally what's keeping him going.

Tuesday Oct. 30th

Just as I was getting to know Greg (who came in last week, 2 1/2 year sentence for DUI) and enjoy his intelligent company, he receives word he's being shipped over to Marcy CF, right next door from here. He's being sent over there to enroll in the 6 month ASAT (Alcohol Substance Abuse Treatment) program. DUI offenders are mandated to take this. I'll be sorry to see him go. I found Greg refreshingly honest with his feelings, smart, new to the prison world, and one of the very few 'normal' guys walking around here.

This afternoon I met with the new teacher I'll be working for, Mrs. D. She seems nice enough, but on the meek and mild side however. Almost like she should be working in a library. I foresee some of these dudes really pushing her buttons, just waiting to make their move, they can smell weakness.

Wednesday Oct. 31st

As another month draws to a close, despite these depressing surroundings, time is moving along quickly. I have found an important key is to stay as busy as you possibly can. Maybe it's that I have 2 programs (TA and F & S) or it's all the writing and reading I do. I don't know, but I do know I try to prevent my mind from wandering back to Short Hills, NJ where my sons are. As soon as I let myself drift there, the depression hits. Could it be that I have to forget they exist? Is that the answer for my survival? Oh God I can't do that.

I signed up for a Bible study class that begins tomorrow night from 6:00-8:00. It's run by two civilians I met at the Retreat, they couldn't be nicer, a husband and wife, probably in their early 60's. Anything that gets me out of that dorm for a few hours.

Before leaving the Mess Hall each inmate has to show the guards their fork and spoon, and then drop them in a bucket.

My 7x7 cube where I spent so much of my time. Here I read a book a day & did the bulk of my writing. On my left lived Willie P., serving a life sentence for double murder, and across was Dino, serving 18 years for kidnapping.

I lived for my visits to the yard. Here I would run/walk around this track non-stop, for the entire 2 hours. There were also numerous push-up stations. I left Mohawk in the best shape of my life.

REQUEST FOR INTERVIEW OR INFORMATION

From: 8/18   No. _____   Date _____

Block _____ Co. _____ Cell _____ Shop _____

To: The Road Home

Subject: (State exactly what you want. Do not ask for an interview without stating your question.)

Weekends continue to drag on, especially rainy ones like this. I've come to be sure I make a visit to the library on Thursday or FRIDAY, and stock up on books. My family is great also, in keeping the ~~books~~ reading material coming.

As I've stressed, for me anyway too much idle time allows my mind to wander & think about all that I am missing, plus ~~and~~ how sad and lonly it is here. My thoughts immediatly (sp?) go to the boys and what activites are they partaking in this weekend. which Friends

are they hanging out with and

REQUEST FOR INTERVIEW OR INFORMATION

From: _____ No. _____ Date _____

Block _____ Co. _____ Cell _____ Shop _____

To: The R. ng Home   8 / 8

Subject: (State exactly what you want. Do not ask for an interview without stating your question.)

I have been setteling (sp?) into my dorm, my routine here at Mohawk. As the new kid on the block I go by the old adage, "be seen and not heard". Three of us came into this house last week and already one of them has alienated himself by trying to "be the man." The old timers here (guys like Dino & Profit) don't take kindly to that, and made him AWARE IN NO UNcertain terms. I haven't mentioned Profit before. He his kind of like the House Porter, who

BW285   Continue on back

sees and hears everything. He's

Early on I had no access to writing paper, so I grabbed whatever I could. I tore pages out of my Bible, and wrote on the back of envelopes.

99

I am reunited with Brooks and Phil in New York City. 13 months have passed since I saw them last. They have grown up so. My story ends here.

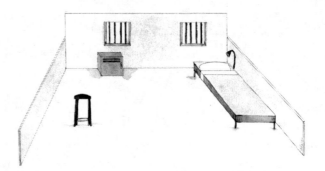

Another look at my cube, # 25 in Dorm 74-D. It always had to be this neat, otherwise you'd be written up and receive a disciplinary ticket.

November, 2007

Thursday November 1st

I have come to love the phrase 'the 1st of the month.' It has an entirely different meaning in prison, with each passing one all of us here (except for those doing 'life') get closer and closer to an end date.

I'm looking forward to this evening Bible study. Just simply being able to converse with two outsiders, civilians who have no agenda other than to help us cope with our surroundings. What a wonderful and kind gesture on their part.

I've pretty much grown accustomed to the food here, but dinner tonight was basically uneatable. Some kind of brown mystery meat they had the nerve to call 'salisbury steak.' The same rotation of food is served every week, they just mix up the days/nights it's served on. I'll be sure to make myself a peanut butter & jelly sandwich next time this is offered.

Friday Nov. 2nd

Bible study was terrific! Run by a local husband & wife, each about 65 years old. There were 8 of us in the class. We recite the rosary, all of us taking turns with the readings. This is followed by discussion and starting next week about 30 minutes of a current religious themed movie. A regular 'movie night.' As I said, any slice of normalcy you can find here is a must. Those 'slices' are far & few between.

Saturday Nov. 3rd

Not only is it the weekend, which you know by now are long and lonely, but I am drained emotionally. I try to write on average, 2-3 letters per day, and in each one I really put it out there. I don't think there is any other option. Hey, it's prison and it sucks, so I can't go about trying to sugar coat them. I avoid from making them come across as a 'poor me' letter, but rather talk about what I'm seeing & experiencing. Nonetheless they are draining to write, but ya know what, it's all part of the bid. When it's all said and done, whenever that is, I'll be a better person for it. And that is what counts.

Sunday Nov 4th

To put it simply, I'm not in the mood today. 9:30 on a Sunday morning (turned the clocks back last night, ugh, just what I want, an extra hour here) and 80% of the dorm is sound asleep, and will be until the 11:00 AM count. It's cold (35 degrees) and gray outside, time to dive into one of the several books my mother sent me. I will head over to the mess hall for lunch, but skip dinner; mystery meat is on the menu. Tonight I'll be living large, will whip up a peanut butter & jelly. Lights out at 10:00 p.m, listen to my transistor radio for a half hour, say my prayers, and then call it a day. Another weekend down.

Monday Nov 5th

Chris from my dorm (he's the poor man's George Clooney, doing 7 years for armed robbery) learned the other day he was being sent to Marcy C. F. (5 miles down the road) so he could take the ASAT program, which in his case, was court ordered. It's a six month alcohol treatment course. He's quite the character, never without a wisecrack, always seems to be the one pushing the envelope. About every other week he'll rearrange his bulletin board with different pictures of partially nude women, the ones you get out of maxim magazine, or the Sports Illustrated swim suit issue. (you're not allowed to have totally nude pictures on your bulletin board) I mean he'll literally spend a couple of hours getting every picture at just the right angle!

After hearing about his upcoming move, he figured he had to leave for ASAT in style. Chris proceeded to set in motion mixing together a quick batch of hooch… homemade alcohol. The ingredients are all readily available, bread for the yeast, lots of sugar, and pineapple juice. I had no intention of tasting it, but quite a few guys bellied up to Chris's cube last night for a glass or two, and they swore it had a "kick to it." Chris himself seemed satisfied with his brew. He left for Marcy the next morning however complaining of an upset stomach & looking a bit hungover.

Tuesday Nov 6th

The weather has really turned cold; the sky is a continuous shade of gray. We had our first blast of snow yesterday, a 15 minute squall. So it looks like I'll have to bite the bullet and start to wear the state issued, hideous shade of green, winter jacket. Up until now the turtle necks, corduroy shirts and cotton sweaters (all which were bought by Eileen) have done the trick, but when that wind blows, it's chilling. Fashion be dammed, I need that ugly jacket. It's also one of the items you can't substitute with something from say L.L. Bean or Brooks Bros., it's that or nothing. No jackets come in through the package room. Wearing my own clothes allows me to retain my dignity and myself. From day one I've felt very strongly about this. Yeah that's me, wearing a Ralph Lauren canvas belt, sure I'm probably the only person here to do so, and yes I stand out. But damm it, I don't care, this is who I am, and you're not taking that away from me.

Wednesday Nov 7th

It doesn't look like I'll continue being a Teacher's Aide for much longer. For the most part I've enjoyed the challenge of working with these guys, teaching them in a way where I don't come across as "better" than. But rather simply trying to be as helpful as possible. I must say though, the experience hasn't been as rewarding as I naively expected it to be.

The old adage, "You can't help someone who won't help themselves," applies here just like anywhere else.

I'll never forget my 1st week as a T/A, when I was correcting the test paper for Lil Shaq, as he lurched over me, scowling each time I had to place a red check mark to one of his incorrect answers, too funny.

So it's a combination of my wanting to work full time at Fire and Safety, where I really enjoy the variety of the day, and have come to realize what a plum job it is. It's certainly the safest; I work just a few doors away from the Lieutenant's and Sergeant's office.

Thursday Nov 8th

Dino continues to annoy with his non- stop planning for our Thanksgiving meal. Okay yes, he means well but his mindset is light years away from mine. He could prepare one of the finest meals ever made, but we're still in prison, away from our families. I just can't get on the same page, but I guess given this will be his 13th Thanksgiving here (can you imagine) and he's reached a place mentally where the significance of the day is simply not the same. He can block out the sadness, I can't.

Friday Nov 9th

Friday, another week down! We have a 3 day weekend ahead, thankfully the weather is supposed to warm up and by Monday could reach 60 degrees. I need to catch up on my running, haven't been out to the yard all week. It's tough to get motivated for the 6:00 P.M. movement like I used to, as not only is it so cold, but the folks in charge have changed the nightly rec. hours to extend until 8:00, rather than 7:30. I can't get worked up to be outside, in freezing temperatures, for that long. As a result, my evenings (other than Thursday when I have Bible Study/ Rosary) are spent doing a lot of reading in my cube, that is when I'm not being interrupted by Dino. Not ten minutes ago he came over, "Mo, do you like sweet potatoes?" "Yes Dino," I said. "Ok, ok, I need to make a few moves, see if I can get my hands on some brown sugar and we can have them for Thanksgiving." Good grief.

Saturday Nov 10th

Gordon is officially gone from Mohawk. I've learned that he was transported up to Lakeview C.F. which is outside of Buffalo. Apparently he also had six months added to his sentence. Remember, he was back in prison on a parole violation, which if everything had gone according to plan, would have had him out of here in April of 2008. He's now facing time until late '08 or even into '09. Plus as I write this, he's been in the box for a month with three more to go. I can't even imagine.

Sunday Nov 11th

Beautiful Fall sunny day, temperatures might reach close to 60 degrees tomorrow, which is a holiday, so, no school or programs. I will plan on getting out to the yard twice so I can get some running in. I feel like I haven't had any fresh air for awhile.

Eileen visited me this weekend, as always it was wonderful to see her. She never fails to bring along a gift or two, an article of clothing, food, whatever. This time she dropped off 2 sweaters, mouthwash, a stack of People Magazines (mostly for Dino who refers to them as "Gold") and Dove soap. I am very, very grateful.

Wednesday Nov 14th

When I arrived here, one of the first things I did was to read up on the requirements for getting into the Honor Dorm. You had to have been at Mohawk four months, along with a spotless record, i.e., no tickets, no infractions, no nothing! Honor dorm, honor dorm, that's all I kept saying to myself in those early weeks. Well, now I'm eligible and guess what, I don't feel like going anymore. In this dorm I've been lucky to meet a few nice guys (easier said than done) to hang with, talk and share with. I have a good relationship with two C.O.'s who run the dorm. One of them is Officer B who treats me very decently. "Good morning, Byrnsie!" is the usual greeting (9 out of 10 inmates here don't get a word, much less a greeting). He was also instrumental in my getting the F&S job. The other C.O. who is here for the 2:30- 10:30 p.m. shift, officer D, brought me (and a few other inmates) homemade pasta and a brownie the other day. I mean that's like unheard of, yes, I'm very lucky. The other inmates were like "What the hell?!" I tried to downplay it as best I could. Plus, my new cube (finally, a single) which I got last week when Chris went to ASAT, has 2 windows (with bars of course) that actually open! Ok this isn't the Plaza, but for prison, it's about as good as it gets. Someone is watching over me. Hence, I have abandoned any notions of moving to another dorm.

Thursday-Friday Nov 15-16th

Besides Dino, the two guys I'm closest with here are Peter and Joe. But, since they're in different dorms I only get to catch up with them either at meals or the yard on weekends. Joe I've known since we met at Down State, remember he ended up here by drinking a few beers, getting in his pickup truck, and hitting a man riding a bicycle on a dark, deserted road, late at night. Plus he left the scene of the accident. The man died and Joe is serving 2 1/3 – 7. In that blink of an eye, two lives would never be the same. Joe holds up pretty well, but understandably, not a day goes by when he doesn't think "what if?" He's also being sued for a million dollars. I did run into him at dinner tonight, he looked downcast. "What happened?" I asked. As it turns out, Joe who is the friendly, outgoing type, simply talks with the C.O.'s too much (in the dorm he'll go up to their desk and try to engage them) got sort of roughed around a bit by the guys in his dorm. They thought he was a snitch with all the talking to the C.O.'s he partakes in. I told him to cool it, otherwise he was asking for real trouble.

Saturday-Sunday Nov 17-18th

At school yesterday afternoon, apparently there was a brief scuffle between two inmates as they were entering the building. My friend, Peter, was right there to witness it. Two quick punches were thrown but basically it didn't amount to much. Well, the C.O.'s got wind of it and were determined to find out who was involved. Normally, when we break for recess (because 99% of the guys are like school children) everyone piles out of class at the same time. However, there was an announcement that we were to leave our classrooms one at a time. At the door of every room there was a guard who ordered us to exit with hands extended so he could check for scratches, cuts or bruises on the knuckles and fingers. I was thinking thank God I hadn't accidently cut my hand earlier. From what I heard they did indeed catch the two guys involved, you can bet they're sitting in the box at this very moment.

No visits this weekend, so it's slow moving. Read the entire new John Sanford book, went to church, got out to the yard both days to run, and did my best not to be cornered by Dino who needed to vent, as his brother hasn't mailed his food package yet. Dino's not happy.

Monday Nov 19th

After 4 years, this is 'Country's' last week at Mohawk. Apparently, he is being released this Friday, day after Thanksgiving. (Don't you think they could let him out the day before Thanksgiving?) There are a few reasons why he's not very excited to be leaving. While he has a six year old daughter, he hasn't seen her since she was two months old, so he's not sure at all how that might work out. His wife divorced him and doesn't want him back; he has no real family as he was raised mostly in foster homes. Worst of all, he owes 18 months to the State of Pennsylvania, for a crime (burglary) he committed years ago. There is a very good chance they'll be waiting for him as he walks out the gates come Friday.

He's had a hard life without too many lucky breaks. Yes, Country has been a career criminal, now paying for those crimes, but in my limited time of observing him, I've seen a good heart, a hard worker and a guy who wants a chance to start over. I think for the most part his white supremacy label (all the tattoos, the shaved head, the Nazi swastika on his stomach) is an act, prison bravado he was forced to adopt to appear tough and be part of a gang. I see him all the time talking and joking with the black guys in the dorm.

Eventually, he'll have to shed his prison skin, if he can. Personally I think he might make it, I hope he finally does. I'm in the minority though; most of the guys think it's a matter of time until he returns to the only life he's ever known.

Tuesday Nov 20th

All's quiet as this is the second to last day of the week; programs and school tomorrow, then we have Thanksgiving. Friday everything is closed. Luckily I have many books to escape with, and I'll get out to the yard as much as possible.......anything to keep myself from dwelling on the holiday.

I will however have a special visit; Eileen is coming on Thanksgiving morning. I begged her not to as I'd rather she enjoy the day with her family, but Eileen insists, and will be here for a few hours before heading back. I'm very grateful, however, and can't thank her enough for wanting to spend the day with me; especially in a place like this.

Wednesday Nov 21st

Other than the home- cooked meal Officer D brought me a couple of weeks ago, at lunch today I had my first taste of non- state food in five months! My boss in fire and safety, Officer R treated my co- worker (his name is Dee, great guy, who's been very welcoming and helpful towards me) and I to a pre-holiday lunch... pizza, turkey sandwiches and pumpkin pie. Yes, okay, strange combination, I'll grant you that, but to me, we might as well have been dinning at The Four Seasons. It tasted that good! I guess that gives you an idea how bad the food has been, oh how I can't wait to eat home cooked food once again.

That was a very kind gesture by the Chief (he likes to be called that) to order in the food and share with us. Dee and I just sat there at our desks munching away, nothing needed to be said, our jaws and the smile on our faces did all the talking.

I didn't have the heart to tell Dino what I had for lunch, it truly might have sent him over the edge.

Thursday Nov 22nd

Happy Thanksgiving! I've already (probably too often) touched on the somber mood that prevails on a day like this, it sucks, there is no other way around it. I was one of the lucky ones who had a visit this morning. As I mentioned, Eileen drove up to see me. What a treat It was and how thoughtful of her to do so. She was here for about three hours. I headed back to the dorm to help the guys prepare our meal. Country, who organized it, had each of us (the six white guys) got about $5.00 worth of food from the commissary. We pooled it together, and at 4:00 p.m. (right after the count) sat down for our Thanksgiving dinner. The setting was one I never, ever imagined myself in, but I must admit, it was touching in its own unique way. Six men from all walks of life, running the spectrum of time served, from Dino's 13th year to my 5th month. Here we all were, brought together by various circumstances, connected for at least this moment, as a family.

Friday Nov 23rd

No school, no programs today, which makes for a long Friday. That's okay, I plan to keep busy. After breakfast I'll read for awhile, and then head out to the yard to work off some of that big meal from yesterday. The sun is out; it's brisk and cold, perfect running weather. In spite of my being here, I have much to be thankful for. If that doesn't always come across on these pages, I apologize. I never take all my blessings for granted; I think God everyday for them. Yes, I'm in prison and I hate it, but things could be so much worse.

Saturday-Sunday Nov 24-25th

Due to the very cold weather, I didn't get out to the yard as much as I like to on a weekend. I was able to get a run in this afternoon (Sunday) with the rest of my time spent reading a new novel, ("Rhett Butler's People"), going to Saturday night church, and writing a few letters. I tried hard not to think of Thanksgiving's past and present, but concentrated on and imagined the wonderful holidays of the future.

Here's a clue as to what kind of asinine sentences are (all too often) uttered in the dorm, I heard this earlier today... "I ain't know nobody who do that." It doesn't shock me anymore; sadly I guess I'm getting accustomed to that kind of chatter. As Peter and I will say jokingly (but getting truer by the day) to each other, "not only do we have to get out of here, but we have to get out of here without losing our minds."

Monday Nov 26th

Every two weeks, the taxpayers of New York make a deposit to my account in gratitude for the work I do here. Both my jobs are considered to be a level 4 (the highest pay grade) which translates to $2.50 per week, per job. Yes, that's right; I work for one dollar a day. To break it down even further, my six hours a day spent working pays out to a little over 16 cents an hour. Geez, what do those guys at level 1 make?

I'm not trying to make a statement here, not looking for sympathy, it is what it is. I just thought you would find it interesting, funny, or sad. Perhaps all of the above. Considering it costs the State $42,000 a year to house an inmate, we know that money isn't being spent on our salaries.

Tuesday Nov 27th

Country has left Mohawk, but what happened to him when he walked through the gates is unclear. Whether or not the PA state police

110

were there waiting for him, I don't know, he seemed to think they would be. I imagine we'll hear some news of his fate eventually.

Taking his place in the dorm (it's like a revolving door, the beds are never vacant for long) is John, mid 40's, white, mild mannered, father of 5. I've had a few chats with him so far, he's an ex- lawyer, polite as could be, who fed his cocaine habit by pulling off some burglary jobs on the side. Well, he was caught, "Jerry, I'm a knucklehead" he mockingly said. He already knows his exact release date, Valentine's Day, 2011. His children range from 2 through 14, and I happened to be in the visitor's room thanksgiving morning when his wife arrived along with his 6 year old daughter. To see the smile on her face as she went running into John's arms, well, if you have a pulse, it would have brought a tear to your eye.

Why do we hurt the ones we love the most? I'll be sorry for my actions every single day, for the rest of my life.

Wednesday Nov 28th

The cold weather continues, I guess that shouldn't be so noteworthy anymore. But the day has been a slow one with not a whole lot taking place. Dee and I have been busy at work however. Chief R. has us painting the Ready Room (storage room for extinguishers, hoses, the tool cabinet, as well as accumulated junk from over the years) and it's all okay, we have the radio on, the snow outside is falling, we're shooting the bull and I feel at ease.

Thursday Nov 29th

The day began like so many others. Breakfast at 6:30 followed by coffee back in my room, where I read the Bible, a serenity book, and then listened to the radio for 15 minutes before I headed over to work at 8:00. About halfway into my paper work I heard Chief R. yell out "Byrne" a bit more gruffly than usual. That's his way of letting Dee and I know he wants us for something, screaming out our last names. As I hurried to his office, he was standing at the door, "come with me," he said. Immediately I knew something was off kilter as I was lead deeper into the building, areas which were normally off- limits to inmates. We stopped, the Chief opened an office door and there sitting was the #2 man in all of Mohawk, the Deputy Superintendent of Security himself, the Prince of Darkness, Deputy M. He's a big burly Irishman, ruddy complexion; think white mustache, ex- football line backer, and a lifer in the corrections business. "Oh my God, why am I here," I said to myself.

The Chief closed the door leaving just the two of us. The Dep engaged me in small talk, asked how I was faring, how I liked Mohawk, etc... I tried to catch my breath, slow my speaking down as I answered his questions. His next one was the reason I was summoned, "So, I've been reading your Blog, for the past 3 months to be exact, what the hell do you think you're doing?" The air went out of the room; I sat and tried to compose myself. I knew with the Blog I wasn't doing anything wrong. I hadn't broken any rules, so in spite of a case of the jitters, I was somewhat relieved to know the Dep wasn't about to throw me in the box.

I explained to him how the Blog was initially a vehicle for my family and loved ones to keep track of me, to know I was safe, a way for me to express my sadness and remorse with the direction my life had taken. Also, to educate people about the destruction of addiction, and give others a look inside what State Prison is like.

"You're a smart guy, one we don't see around here very often, but Mr. Byrne, you are very naïve about prison," the Dep said. "I don't deny that I'm behind the curve on prison life, I've never been before," hoping this didn't come across as a flip answer. He was right though, he pointed out how my writing about Willie winning and running the football betting pool had put him at risk, or the story of Dino cooking eggs that one night, his getting caught having them in our dorm, where eggs are not allowed, does the fact that this particular C.O. did his job by ticketing him, meant that other C.O.'s are over- looking petty infractions? And as a result they're getting "soft" and looking away from infractions? I began to realize I might have done more damage recording my blog towards the three men (Officers B, D, and R) I was trying to thank the most. The ones I wanted my family to know who were decent, treated me fairly, engaged in conversation with me, and went that extra yard to look out for me. I wrote about them because I had come to appreciate their kindness so. I suppose that's where the problem is. The Deputy doesn't want the C.O.'s to show "kindness" to an inmate, in any way, shape or form. While I always made a point to refer to them by their initials only, it was easy to trace who they really were. As a C.O., "soft" is a label you don't want attached.

The Deputy knew he couldn't make me put an end to the Blog, but in a not so subtle attempt, hinted that my stay here at Mohawk would become a lot different (uncomfortable). He was tempted to transfer me to PCU (Protective Custody Unit) and in fact made me sign a waiver saying that I had refused. I believe this to be a scare tactic; I don't for a second think I'm in any kind of danger.

Our 20 minutes together ended with a handshake and my promise to stop writing anything further on the Internet. Later that day, my locker was searched (most of my mail was read, along with a daily diary I keep) as they were convinced I was in possession of a wireless device. How else could I be turning around my entries onto "My Road Home" so quickly? Never mind that I had already explained to the Deputy about my wonderful girlfriend, Eileen, who after I mailed each day's activities promptly typed them onto the Blog for all to read. They're trained not to believe anybody, of course. They found nothing in my locker. This day has shaken me as much as any I have encountered so far. The Dep has the power to squash me like a bug. So much for staying below the radar.

Friday Nov 30th

The bulk of the fallout from my blog has come down on three men (C.O.'s) who I've come to know and respect. My hope is that they came to know and respect me as well. Since I wrote about their acts of kindness, they've come under scrutiny, which I now feel responsible for. They will be spoken to because they treated an inmate like a human being, they went too far I suppose in making me feel decent. For this they will catch shit. And it's absolutely the last thing I ever wanted to happen. Two of the three C.O.'s have assured me since, that things would work out okay. They know where I was coming from. I simply wanted my family to be aware there were decent, caring men here, treating their son and brother well.

December

Saturday-Sunday December 1st & 2nd

Except for an incident which took place Saturday night, the weekend played to form. I'm embarrassed to say, other than heading out to eat, and church Saturday evening, I didn't leave the dorm. This kills me as I love to get a run in, but the weather was bitterly cold, and you have to be out for the entire two hour movement. There's no such thing as just heading out for a quick jog. Once you're out, the dorms are locked, and you don't come back until the entire movement does.

I was jolted awake Saturday night (Sunday morning) around 1:00, by some violent threats and screaming. Two inmates going at it, "F you, and F that," back and forth. The distance between them continued to get smaller, I was convinced punchers were about to be thrown. The yelling went on for about five minutes, where the heck was the C.O. on duty I wondered. Sometimes on the night shift the guard on duty falls sound asleep. One black inmate and one Spanish, going at it, a lethal combination. Finally, the C.O. came running into the dorm, "Knock it the fuck off, give me your ID's, both of you." What ignited the fuse was the black guy felt like having a cigarette (smoking is forbidden in the dorm, but that matters little, just don't get caught, otherwise it's a ticket) at 1:00 a.m. of all times! The Spanish guy, usually mild mannered and quiet, took exception to this, and one thing led to another. Perhaps he was simply having a bad night and the smoking set him off. Ironically, the smoker, all he received was loss of recreation for two weeks. The other guy, the one awakened, who wasn't bothering anyone, was sent packing that very night. He received a total of 90 days in the box!

Monday Dec 3rd

The snow continues to fall and accumulate. Officer B still hasn't spoken to me since the blog surfaced & he learned I had made a point of writing about my loaning him the new John Grisham book a couple months ago. Seems kind of minor doesn't? Nonetheless, I'm on the receiving end of the freeze out. I do my best to avoid his line of vision, but that's almost impossible as this desk is front and center. I just keep my head down and hope he'll eventually realize I had the best of intentions and wanted to reflect his acts of kindness.

Tuesday Dec 4th

Officer B finally had a word with me this afternoon, although they were not quite the ones I had in mind. "Byrne, you're an early riser aren't you?" he asked. Hmm, not really sure where he was going with this, but I was just happy he was speaking to me again. "Yes, officer B, I get up earlier than most." He replied, "Well, that's good because I'm designating you my new guy in charge of shoveling the walkway." Gulp, we get snow every night here. Boy did he sandbag me, picked me right off. "Byrnsie I want this path cleaned by the time I arrive, throw a little salt down as well." He shows up at 6:30, this means I have to be out the door by 6:00 a.m. or so, earlier if we get a ton of snow. Wouldn't you know it, we've been getting snow all day and should continue though the evening, 6-8 inches! The path isn't all that long, about 20 yards, but the idea of getting bundled up every morning, stepping out into freezing weather, then shoveling, doesn't put a big smile on my face.

This is a test, that's all. I understand where he's coming from, he's getting the upper hand back, slapping me down in the process. I don't have much of a choice, do I?

Wednesday Dec 5th

So every morning now, at 5:45, Willie will stop by my cube to make sure I'm awake. To be ready at that hour, I lay all the warm clothes I'll need out the night before, because the last thing I want right now is for officer B to arrive before I'm finished! And wouldn't you know it, the snow has been falling non- stop since I was assigned this job, with no let up in sight.

Thursday Dec 6th

I haven't been able to get out to the yard for close to 2 weeks now. As much as I enjoy hunkering down in my room to read and write (staying under the radar), I really miss going on that 2-3 mile run, along with stretching and push- ups. With the onset of winter weather, in order for the yard to be open, you need at least ten people ready at the gate. Otherwise, it's a no- go, which has been the case. I've always felt one of the keys to mental survival (which is the most important) is to maintain the desire to get outside, away from the dorm where trouble lurks and lethargy seeps in.

Either I have to pray for a heat wave or come up with a new exercise routine. I think the latter is probably more doable.

Friday Dec 7th

Another week down! Sorry, but there's no other way to look at it. As just about all the weeks seem to do, this one went quickly. Thankfully there were no repercussions from the events of the past 7 days. Although, don't think for a second my mind wasn't conjuring up images of being thrown out of this dorm (still no real dialogue with officer B) or finding myself transferred to another facility, which still could happen. I have a real gut feeling it just might. Two reasons lead me to thinking this way. My time remaining is literally getting shorter by the day, as that happens my classification should drop to a minimum facility (a camp). The other reason is, that I've become a potential nuisance or headache to Mohawk. I could easily make this blog public again at any time, legally there is nothing they can do to stop me. Of course, they could seriously clamp down with regard to my dorm and job, but if I'm willing to endure this, then they can't hurt me. But I can sure embarrass them by letting everyone know what a joke this place is, how horrible it is, the amount of waste (taxpayers) that goes on, and how the administration is clueless to stop it.

While I'm far from being a trouble maker (in fact, the Deputy, when we spoke last week, said "I bet you'll make history here, the first guy to come through without getting a single ticket.") I do have a bit of leverage, and that is 100%, the last thing, the administration wants an inmate to have. I think they are going to get me moved.

Saturday-Sunday Dec 8-9th

Normally, when it's time to write about what goes on here I have to hold back a little. There is so much material to share; I could fill pages with what takes place on any single day or night. However, this morning (Sunday, 10:45) I've been staring at this paper for 30 minutes and still don't know what to say. Do I write about how sad I've been the past couple of days? How lonely and depressing the weekends are? Or how for the first time in my life I am dreading the arrival of Christmas? Perhaps I could write about how all I want to do is have a good cry by myself. But, there is no place where that can be accomplished. There are always people around, no such thing as privacy. Yes the "black dog" (depression) has returned and is deep inside me at the moment. About every three weeks, it rears its ugly head and stays for a couple of days or so. It's times like this when I wonder why I can't adapt better. I mean, you see guys laughing and joking all the time. They approach each day with seemingly not a care in the world, like the time spent here is more of a homecoming with old friends, a vacation perhaps. Why do I carry this shame and guilt with me constantly? Why do I tread so lightly, afraid of every step I take, thinking one false move could lead me straight to the box? With some inmates, time spent in the box is simply the cost of doing business. They could care less.

But you know what; I'll never get to that line of thought, never! I won't reach a level of disrespect and the prevailing rally cry of so many here, "I'm the victim" mantra. Hopefully, I will shake my depression in a day or so, in order to feel better physically at least.

117

Monday Dec 10th

When I first learned of the mind- blowing recidivism rate of 83%, I thought for sure there has to be a mistake, how can that be so high?! Is it possible for that many people to return to the awful life that is prison? Guess what, I don't think that way anymore. I hear more stories of inmates serving their full sentences (maxing out) because they either refused to take programs assigned to them, or they were on the receiving end of numerous tickets for fighting, drugs, contraband, etc...

As I've mentioned before, hard as it is to fathom, they seem to really like it here. Even Fritz, who I've become close to, confided to me the other day that after 10 years of prison, he's scared of re- entering society and at times "is not really sure if he wants to" when his sentence expires in a couple of years. I was stunned when he said this to me.

Tuesday Dec 11th

Too depressed to write & not feeling well.

Wednesday Dec 12th

About a week ago, Jon (serving a 7 year sentence for robbery) moved in the cube right next to mine. What a pleasure it has been to have intelligent conversation, a rarity here. John is the father of five young children- he is only 32- who was a successful business man. A hard-working, devoted Dad, who unfortunately had a severe cocaine habit. The addiction led to his business falling off the cliff, but the bills and mortgage still had to be paid. A scheme was hatched with friend to break into a warehouse and make off with $200, 000 worth of cigarettes. Sadly for John's sake, things didn't work out as planned. There were six people inside the building who weren't expected to be there, and even worse his partner stupidly pulled out a gun. Now all of the sudden you're looking at armed robbery which carries a maximum 15 year sentence!

Jon and his friend took off empty handed. Six days later, while he was at home reading a story to his daughter, the police broke down the front door, guns drawn. Jon's life would never be the same. He's already completed 3 years of his term at another prison, and was moved to Mohawk a couple weeks ago.

Like me, he's content to stay put and read, could care less about watching TV or getting involved with the lunatics that dominate. He won't have a blank look on his face if I use a 3 syllable word and if I mention current events, he doesn't think I'm talking about today's menu. Eventually he'll need to take the ASAT program and they will move him out of the dorm, I hope that won't happen for quite some time.

Thursday Dec 13th

Earlier this evening (it's now 10:00pm) as I was reading the paper, the decibel level all of a sudden began to rise. Usually a sure signal that two inmates are about to go at it. This time it was "knucks" (short for knuckles I suppose, I've never said a word to him so I wouldn't know) a young black kid with too much attitude and strut, who apparently rubbed "Star" the wrong way. That's all it takes, a look, a smirk, an off-handed comment, it could be anything at all taken as a slight. Before you know it, you have two guys, neither who can afford to back down (or be reasonable) or lose face. Especially now that the whole dorm is watching and the inmates are riveted, ready to see someone go down. For if you carry a tag as an untouchable, you just can't be seen walking away from a challenge, not here anyway. Your stature would never be the same. Star is Puerto Rican, usually keeps to himself, but if cornered, becomes volatile. He's also part of a gang, so he can't afford to yield to threats, especially from a young punk like Knucks.

My money would have been on Star if it had come to blows (and it still might) but just as "let's do this" was uttered, the C.O. on duty came into the room and everyone went ducking back to their cubes. To be continued, I'm sure.

Friday Dec 14th

The lull in falling snow came to an abrupt halt today; we're getting hit with a big storm (8 inches so far) that is expected to continue off and on throughout the weekend. Of course with snow comes my breaking out the shovel. I'm trying to stay on top of this mess. I've been out twice so far, but waging a losing battle. To make matters worse, it's windy and cold.

Officer B continues to keep me at arm's length, but I did get a nod from him the other day. I've hinted (a very tiny hint given my shaky footing) at some possible relief or assistance with the shoveling, but it was met with no reply. Eileen is scheduled to come for a visit this weekend, but I'm worried she might not be able to make it with this wintery weather. I'm so looking forward to spending time together, but not at the expense of her getting into a jam, or worse, an accident. I will call her later on to see how she wants to play it.

Saturday-Sunday Dec 15-16th

The 1st big storm of the winter hit this weekend. As a result, Eileen was unable to make it up for our visit. This made for a combination of events, primarily one of a long, boring two days, interspersed with my shoveling at 6:00 am Sunday, going back to bed (freezing) at 6:45. I was awoken a half hour later by the ranting of an inmate named "Butter," who felt disrespected by someone turning on the fan which jolted him out of a deep, Sunday morning slumber. Butter is a black convicted murderer on about his 22nd year of a 25 year sentence. He came into our dorm a few months ago from a maximum facility as his classification was down- graded to medium. I've actually found him (until today) pleasant and easy to deal with. In fact, I was touched by something he did on my behalf early on in meeting him. Before I got my single cube, I shared a bunk. As you can imagine, space was tight, but it's prison, so you learn to deal with it. On this day I was opening mail in the afternoon, and had received a sweet, sad and encouraging letter from my 17 year old niece, Kyle. Her words hit me and I began to gently cry. Butter, who was across the way, saw this unfold. Out of the corner of my eye I saw him stand up and whisper something in my bunkie's ear. My bunkie immediately stood up and left, leaving me be to shed my tears in privacy. I didn't really know Butter then, but I've never forgotten this story and decided to share it with Dino (who's not very sentimental). All he said was "that's old- school Mo, old- school."

The tirade I witnessed today, however, was from a man down for 22 years! Think of everything you've done in those years, then imagine being in a cell, maximum security all that time. Not that I'm condoning what he did, but I guess I can picture how he might just go psycho every now and then.

Monday-Tuesday Dec 17-18th

From the vantage point of my cube, often times I will sit back, seeming to be staring off in space, while in actuality I take in the dynamics of the dorm. If TV cameras were allowed inside a prison, trust me, there has not been a reality show invented that could hold a candle to what goes on here! On a nightly basis one episode that takes place disturbs me. There is absolutely nothing I can do, but watch it unfold. It's prison in its rottenest form, plain and simple. I believe it to be a sort of end result as to why so many young black (and white, hispanic, spanish, etc) men return to prison again and again.

I mentioned "Butter" yesterday, that he's been down for twenty- two years so far (murder). Well there's also another inmate, my friend Jon has already dubbed him "Sammy Six- bid," who is in prison once again, for, you guessed it, the 6th time. Every night Sammy & Butter share their war stories with an impressionable young black man (a boy really), 19 years old, named Tommy. Well Tommy has become so enthralled with the tales of prison life, the gangs these two have been a part of, both on the street and inside, and listening in awe about the various guns used by Sammy Six- bid during his many crime sprees. You can see the look in Tom's eye, one of "Wow, these brothers are where it's at, I wanna be down with them." He thinks it a glamorous life. They are taking his soul, twisting his thinking, glorifying both crime and prison! Night after night! Now Tom is a 1st time offender (drugs of course) and goes home in about a year. But really, what chance does he have? He's been so brain- washed into thinking pushing dope is the thing to do it you have to rob (or kill) someone along the way, not a problem. And if you happen to get caught, well then prison is simple the cost of doing business. And Butter, along with Sammy Six- bid, will be there waiting to greet you.

Wednesday Dec 19th

Following up on my rant from yesterday (not much Christmas cheer in these postings) Jon shared with me some truly eye- opening statistics regarding prison. These are taken directly from the NY State Bar Assn. 2006 Executive Summary.

- One in 3 New Yorkers will go through the Criminal Justice system at some point in their lifetime.
- Every year, there are well over a half million arrests in NY.
- More than 71 million people in the U.S. have a criminal record. If the current incarceration rates continue, an estimated 1 in 15 persons born in 2001 will serve time, and for African- American males, that likelihood rises to 1 in 3.   Countless families are affected: over 10 million children have parents who were imprisoned at some point in their children's lives.
- In 2004, there were 519,590 arrests in NY State, 105,429 that resulted in some term of incarceration.
- In 2005, NYC jails averaged a daily population of 13,576. On any given day in NY State, the total prison and jail population in '05 exceed 93,000.
- And lastly, 2/3 of the entire state prison population is from NYC.

Thursday-Friday Dec 20th-21st

Can you imagine going to "the box" (the prison within the prison) for taking extra grilled- cheese sandwiches? No, I can't either, but that's what happened to "Little Jay," a baby- faced, hapless, twenty- one year old kid who lasted in our dorm not quite a month. I'm not sure what crime brought him to Mohawk, but other than his walkman, which he treasured, he didn't have a pot to piss in.

My friend Jon- whose company I enjoy more each day- out of the goodness of his heart (something you don't see in prison too often) decided to take Jay under his wing and guide him through the minefield that is prison life. Whenever Jay seemed to be on the verge of doing something stupid- which was practically every day- Jon would quickly put him straight. You could almost set your watch every night, waiting for the inevitable "you moron, you can't be smoking in your cube, 20 feet away from the C.O." Jon would yell. I'd chuckle to myself and think, "That poor kid is never going to make it." But Jon stuck with it, hammering away, getting him to see the light a little bit." They had meals together and Jay, walkman in hand, would shuffle over to Jon's cube at night, like a lost puppy, begging for a cigarette afraid to make a move without his input. Jon was breaking the #1 rule they explain to you upon coming to prison… don't stick your neck out for anybody!

But guess what, it seemed to be working. Sure, Jay hadn't become a model inmate, he still messed up, but there was a resemblance of hope that he could complete his 2 year sentence without any major infractions. Jon was feeling somewhat proud of his, okay a bit of a stretch here considering what he was working with, dare I say it, protégé.

Then this past Tuesday, as quickly as you can say "I'm hungry," Jon's project came to a crashing halt. Because this kid thought taking a few extra grilled- cheese sandwiches from the mess hall was a good thing to do, he'll now be waking up Christmas morning in the box. He was sent there minutes after getting caught, (lying to the C.O. didn't help matters) all his belongings (within the hour) were packed up and shipped out of our dorm, and he's looking at probably 30 days in the box. Was it worth being strip- searched (videotaped while it's performed), thrown into the showers- the last one he'll have for a week, no phone calls, no walkman or books, and being alone in a cold cell, where they keep the light on 24 hours a day, was this all worth a grilled cheese?

This being a cruel place, no one has sympathy for him, just ridicule. How could you be so stupid, of all the things to end up in the box for?

Of course, Jon feels bad for him; feels somewhat responsible but I know that shouldn't be the case. He did as much as he could, more than anyone here ever would have done.

Saturday-Sunday Dec 22nd-23rd

As I've said before, there's nothing like a visit, especially when it's you mother and father, along with one of your 3 sisters and 2 brothers. They arrived Friday night, spending the evening in Rome, NY. I got the call yesterday morning at 10:00 to head up to the visitor's room. Being three days before Christmas, the place was packed. We lucked out though and were given a table all the way at the end, removed from the throng of humanity. You could spot my family a mile away, dad never without his blazer and tie, mom even at age 82 looking so refined, elegant and attractive. My sister, Liz, causing all the C.O.'s heads to turn with her good looks, and Jack, who has never had a bad hair day in his life, just off the plane from the dregs of Honduras, appeared looking like he has been held up at a $800 per day spa.

Our three hour visit went faster than Lindsay Lohan in rehab. So many laughs, memories, positive thoughts for my future, and then of course when it was time to say good bye, a few tears. That wonderful visit will carry me through the Holidays. For the 1st time ever I'll be relieved when Christmas day has come and gone. That being said, I do know I'm much more prepared emotionally to face the day than I was only a month ago for Thanksgiving.

Today (Sunday) has been quiet, other than walking over to the mess hall for breakfast and lunch (I skipped dinner) I've been confined to the dorm and my cube, where I have been reading. Family and friends have reached out to me this Christmas with all sorts of new books to keep my mind occupied. You have no idea how grateful I am.

Monday Dec 24th

I was glad to have work this morning, the Chief kept me busy from 7- 11. Being busy means there is less time to focus on the realization I'm here, and that this will be the 1st Christmas ever apart from the boys.

Church was at 1:00 p.m. and brought in about twenty new faces for a total of 50 or so inmates. Back to the dorm by 3:30 p.m., where eight Christmas Cards awaited me at mail call. I'm blessed to have that much love and support coming my way. Sadly to say, many of the guys in the dorm won't get that much mail in a year. I try to downplay it, and will hide seven letters under the pillow while I open and read one. Mainly I feel bad, but I also don't want anyone to get jealous and then pissed off. I can just hear it, "Hey man, you think you're better than me with all that mail?" Good grief, I don't need that.

Quiet night in the cube, read the paper, part of the new book Eileen gave me, said my prayers, shed a tear or two right around midnight, then off to sleep.

Tuesday Dec 25th

Christmas day! Earlier this morning, I overheard this exchange that I think best sums up the day. One of the new guys in the dorm went up to a 22 year veteran (in for murder) and asked, "how do you handle being in prison on Christmas?" He answered, "You can end up in the box just as easily today, as you can any other day."

If you take away the roast beef that was served for lunch, it truly is like any other day. And that's the way I approached it as well. In speaking with the boys mid- morning, who were just about to attack the presents Santa left, I cut our conversation short as I knew my emotions were about to get the better of me. Once off the phone it was a day of reading, writing, listening to music and at the end of it all, praying to God that this will be my last Christmas at Mohawk.

Wednesday Dec 26th

The majority of the facility is closed until after the New Year. Fire and Safety is open however, and I'm grateful for that. I go to the office at my usual time, 8:00 (although this morning Chief R. called for me an hour earlier) and take care of whatever needs to be done. Before you know it's 11:00 and time to go back to the dorm for the count. Pretty much everyone else isn't working but instead just hanging out which makes for a very long day. I work in the afternoon as well.

I find that when inmates are cooped up like that, playing cards (gambling for stamps) and such, tensions are much more likely to reach a breaking point. It wouldn't shock me at all to see a fight erupt at some point during the next week or so.

I've been saying for some time now the two hardest days will be Thanksgiving and Christmas, and they were. But you know what? I'm proud to say I faced them and got through them! I now await and pray for happier times in '08.

Thursday Dec 27th

The long days haven't dimmed Dino's obsession with food, if anything they've accelerated his hunger. He came bolting (his eyes literally bulging, Jon witnessed this as well) over to my cube first thing this morning, "Mo, I'm going to cook a pasta dish today, now if you fix the noodles, I'll prepare my special sauce, etc." I was like "Dino, it's 7:00 a.m., I haven't even had my coffee yet, let me think about it." At first he looked a little hurt, but he wouldn't be swayed for long, "Ok Mo, let me know because I want to get going on this right away," as he retreated back to his cube.

I've spoken to Jon about Dino (he gets a kick out of him) and his single minded focus on food. Jon, who is very level- headed and whom you can tell just "gets it." When I ask this question, he simply looks at me and says "Jerry, the guys done 13 years, think about it, he's fried." And I have no retort to this, there is nothing you can say other than it's sad. Like so many before, prison has broken him. Nonetheless, he's one of my closest confidants and the source of much amusement. He puts a smile on my face and for that alone, I will always be grateful for his friendship.

Friday Dec 28th

Every night, around 7:00 there is a random cube search. The call comes into the C.O.'s desk from the Admin. Building, the officer then slips on the rubber gloves, saunters over to the lucky winners cube, tells him to step outside while he proceeds to rifle through, looking for contraband or something of the sort. Normally nothing turns up, but last night we had a guy caught with 'unprescribed' medicine (basically, someone else's pain killers). This is a big time no- no! He'll have his hearing in the next day of two, but there's no way he can avoid a trip to the box... for 90 days! The guy ("Achbar") didn't bat an eyelash, and why should he? He's been down 27 years for murder (came to Mohawk 3 years ago when his classification dropped) and was just denied parole, which means at least two more years here. The box won't faze a guy like that one bit and since he's obviously not eligible for a good time, he doesn't forfeit any months like I would. He could give a rat's Ass!

My locker has been searched three times, so far so good. I'm still here writing!

Saturday-Sunday Dec 29-30th

Eileen drove up to visit this weekend. Believe it or not, it was her 27th trip to a correctional facility since I was sentenced a little over six months ago! As expected, given the holidays, the visitors' room (the dance floor as Dino calls it) was packed. We had the particular misfortune to be seated next to a Puerto Rican mother, her 2 young children, whom she swatted at liberty, and the father/inmate, whose main concern was consuming as much vending machine junk food, as possible.

After the visit Saturday, Eileen went back to her hotel in town. I of course, back to the dorm where it was surprisingly subdued... men mostly lying on their beds, reading or listening to music. Thankfully, Sammy Six- bid was in the TV room watching a gangsta movie, giving us a respite from his nightly rants, war stories, and insights on the best guns to use when committing a crime.

Sunday morning (10:15) it was back to the visitors' room to see Eileen for a few hours before she headed home to NJ. She leaves around 1:00 to get ahead of the ski traffic coming out of the Catskills, so that the 5 hour drive brings her home at a reasonable hour. I'm tired and drained, it's been a long weekend. Lights are out in a couple of hours. At

10:00 p.m. I will say my prayers and listen to my radio for a bit before putting an end to the day.

Monday Dec 31st

After speaking with my parents this afternoon, trying to stay strong, wishing them a Happy New Year, and all of us agreeing that '08 will be a year of happiness and joy, Dino came running over asking Jon and I, "Hey, are you guys going to watch the ball drop at midnight?" We answered him with a collective "no." He had a hurt look on his face so I explained to him my (Jon is on the exact same page) reasoning. "Dino, by looking at all the happy, smiling, carefree faces in Times Square its only going to make me feel that much worse knowing I'm stuck here. If I stay in my cube and read, I can at least try to prevent those wonderful New Year's Eve memories from taking hold." Dino got a little indignant and said "Well Mo, if you've been down for 13 years, you have to grab on to happy scenes, so I'm going to watch." Which is fine, I guess I can understand his thinking. Everyone handles their doing time differently, the key seems to be identifying what works best, what will keep you in a positive frame of mind, and don't let any of these career criminals knock you off course.

As predicted, I was in bed by 11:00 p.m.. Before that, Jon and I shook hands, wished each other the best. Just prior, I pulled Dino away from the TV to give him a hug and thanked him for all his counsel these past 6 months.

I then went to sleep trying not to think about my sons and family and how I live for the day when we can all be together again. The ball dropped on 2007, but I was nowhere to be seen, I was sound asleep.

January, 2008

Tuesday Jan 1st

Everyday I hear or see something at this mad, mad place called Mohawk that truly astonishes me. Today's incident, which actually Jon overheard, took place in the mess hall, on the line for lunch. The conversation drives home my point regarding those inmates who view spending time in prison merely the cost of doing business, a badge of honor, if you will.

Inmate #1: Leon, where you been man?
Inmate #2: Yo son, I just got transferred from Groveland prison.
#1: Oh man, I love that place, the way they had it set up was official! I'd go back there in a heartbeat.

When Jon laughingly relayed this exchange, we were both speechless. This guy actually used the word "love" and prison in the same sentence? He'd go back there in a heartbeat? Gives you pause doesn't it. Is it any mystery why the NY state budget allots more money to prison than education?

Wednesday Jan 2nd

Just about every night you can find Sammy Six- bid holding court, his gold teeth shining off the reflection from the overhead lights. Jon actually witnessed Sammy cleaning his teeth with a washcloth the other day like he was waxing a car or something. Anyway, there he was talking with his "man's," informing them he has just spoken with "my nigger Reggie" who had recently maxed out (served a full sentence) and was already back on the streets. I normally tune Sammy out but had a feeling this might be the makings of a hidden gem if you will, so I listened in......

Sammy: I'm so proud of Reggie, he told me he's got a whole block locked up already. Out only 3 months and he's scoring all kinds of shit.T ommy: That is mad crazy son, that nigger be making some moves. Sammy: Yeah man, Reggie is official! I can't wait to party down with him.

They say there are no "sure things" in life, but there's one. Tommy, the youthful 1st time offender serving a 2 year sentence, who looks up to Sammy and Butter as if they're a couple of role models, will be back behind bars for a least a second and probably a third bid. The poor kind doesn't stand a chance, sure thing, just like death and taxes. The State is going to fail him.

Thursday Jan 3rd

I've been lucky with the lack of heavy snow the past couple of weeks. That doesn't mean it hasn't been cold... 2 degrees this morning. And cloudy every day, I swear it seems like the sun never shines up here. One thing the frigid weather is good for, it seems the number of gang related slashings has really fallen off. Doesn't mean they aren't happening now and then, but I definitely don't hear guys speaking of them as much.

Eileen sent a food/ care package today. Items such as coffee, creamer, cookies, cheddar cheese with Ritz crackers, along with other assorted treats to help the days be a bit more bearable.

The only downside of a package is when you enter the dorm with that big bag in your hand, well the "have- nots" begin to swarm on you like a pack of wolves. You don't even have time to unpack before they're leaning over your cube, "Hey Jerry, man can I get a cup of coffee?" "Jerry I'm mad hungry, can I get a pop- tart?" etc.,etc., etc... Ya know what, I've gotten real good at saying no! Enough already, go ask someone else. Geez, guess I'm getting hardened.

Friday Jan 4th

While the past few days have brought single digit temperatures, I heard the forecast this morning that by Tuesday of next week it will be close to 60! Yes, it'll be just a tease, but a welcome relief nonetheless.

Quiet day at fire and safety, my boss (Chief R.) was off, so in his place was a substitute, which means other than a little paper work, we did nothing but take turns playing solitaire on the computer in our tiny office. Hey, for 24 cents an hour what do you expect.

I've talked about it before, the weekends, especially in the winter, are long and boring. The tedious factor kicks in and there is no escaping from your surroundings. You're in prison, it's beyond depression, and it sucks being here.

Saturday-Sunday Jan 5-6th

Saturday mornings are one meant for cleaning your 7x7 cube, sweeping and mopping. It doesn't require much effort to keep this tiny space clean, but you'd be surprised how some of the inmates can't even manage that. Be a lazy mess in this dorm though and you have a few key rules, none of them too difficult. First and foremost he'll announce, "I don't like slobs!" When he inspects the cubes your floor should be spotless, no dust anywhere, no food bowls lying underneath the bed. If he likes you maybe you'll get some slack cut one time. Disrespect him more than that and you can almost guarantee you'll be hearing those three dreaded words; "pack your bags." This means you have about an hour to collect your entire world, put it all in 'draft bags,' which are nothing more than heavy duty Glad garbage bags. Throw your mattress on your shoulders, pray it's not raining or snowing out, and trudge on over to whatever new dorm you've been assigned. Say another prayer that it's not the 22- Dorms, otherwise known as 'the projects.' There you will find the paint chipping off the walls, floors that are rarely polished much less swept, bathrooms and showers where germs infest and dominate every square inch. Living there are all the dregs, the lowest of the low who populate Mohawk.

All this awaits you if you can't follow a few simple rules. You would think avoiding a stay at the projects was pretty easy wouldn't you. Well guess what, it's the biggest dorm in the prison.

Monday Jan 7th

Spring fever arrived in Rome, NY, today. Record warm temperatures; 70 degrees. While you can't exactly "enjoy" it, by taking a stroll, or sitting on a bench reading the paper, nonetheless it's welcome. The jackets were put away and you saw guys shuffling along the walkway, wearing t- shirts like they were back in the hood. Fritz (laundry porter, 12 years for robbery) even managed to get in a few games of handball at Rec this morning. It's just a tease though I'm afraid no doubt winter will return shortly

Tuesday-Wednesday Jan 8-9th

I received a letter from a friend the other day and he wanted to know "if I had any privacy here." Hmm, that's an easy one to answer, NO! Private moments do not exist, whenever you turn there are bound to be a pair of eyes watching. Even the shower and bathroom stalls are only separated from view by an ultra- thin sheet of plastic. There is no such thing as a door, if you do manage to find one, it certainly doesn't lock. While today brings even more spring like weather; wanna take a walk and enjoy the day? Forget about it, not happening. Receive a sad letter from a loved one that touches at your heart strings requiring you to have a good cry? Yeah sure, go right ahead, but just know a lot of these dudes will be watching. Have a bad day and you just want to be alone? Alone, what's that? Don't go there, not going to happen.

How's this for alone, last night I asked my friend Travis to cut my hair. He (Travis is serving a 10- 20 year sentence for armed robbery/ attempted murder) quoted me his usual price, 4 stamps, which I agreed to. He told me to be in the bathroom (his barber shop) at 9:15 p.m. Now we all know how peaceful and relaxing a haircut can be, you just sit in the chair, close your eyes, and contemplate the day. But here was the scene; all five shower stalls in full use, with every sort of inane, obscene and asinine comments being spewed back and forth. Just my luck, Sammy Six- bid happened to be one of them. He was screaming about his "bitch" (that would be his wife) who had forgotten to do something for him. My quiet, relaxing haircut continued on in spite of his shower talk, as well as three out of three toilet stalls in overdrive. I kid you not! All I could do was close my eyes and tell myself, "There will be better days." Quieter haircuts too.

Travis finished up after about 20 minutes and he does a pretty good job, especially considering it only cost $1.64, plus brilliant jail- house conversation brought to you by Sammy Six- bid. As I was headed back to my cube. I thought about my friend's "private moments" question. You have to smile, laugh, grin and bear it, whatever, because if you don't, you'll go crazy.

Thursday Jan 10th

A tiny sliver of normalcy comes my way each Thursday night from 6-8:00. I'm part of a Bible Study/ Rosary group that is run by 2 civilians, a husband and wife, who graciously give of their time. It's a small gathering- about 6 of us- where for the 1st hour we say the rosary together, and then the 2nd half we watch a movie which always tends to have a spiritual bent to it. Tonight after 3 weeks, we finally finished up with "Schindler's List."

It's so kind of Bill and Duff to come and spend their evenings with us. As we walk in the door, they are always ready to greet all with a hug. Consider yourself lucky if you get so much as a grunt from 95% of the C.O.'s, so you can imagine how a hug makes you feel.….just like a human being as a matter of fact.

How is it that only six inmates take advantage of this civilized evening? I don't understand. Fine with me though, it makes for a much more relaxed and intimate setting.

Friday Jan 11th

It's Friday, another week down. Ho- hum. That's right, no "T.G.I.F.," just simply ho- hum. That's because unlike back home in the real world, Friday's have a totally different meaning here. They herald the start of a tedious 48 hours, where being in prison sinks in loud and clear; your freedom to come and go is nothing but a distant memory.

Tomorrow morning I'll tidy up my 7x 7 cube (mandatory Saturday cleanup) receive new supplies, including my razor which immediately gets hidden away in a sock in the back of my locker. Not that you would ever encounter someone who would steal from you here.

Saturday-Sunday Jan 12-13th

No sooner had I mentioned "the projects," a.k.a. 22- dorm, and the reasons for being banished there (sloppy and lazy get your ticket punched) did Sammy Six- bid find himself headed in that direction. Yes, Sammy got the word yesterday, good riddance to bad rubbish I say. He has truly been the biggest dirt-ball and low- life that I have come across at Mohawk. And that's saying something! He has no regard for human dignity, sentiment or values and considering this is his 6th stay in a NY state prison. He has o remorse either.

From a selfish standpoint (literary and entertainment) though, I will miss Sammy's distorted outlook on life. His nightly commentary on everything from his favorite guns, the cheapest way to produce crack cocaine, and the collection of bitches he's gone through over the years, including wives, girlfriends, whores and mistresses, was certainly an eye-opener.

As a result of Sammy's sudden departure, the dorm has gotten much quieter. Okay yes, many of the guys were glued to the NFL Playoff games, but still, it seems to be as quiet as it has ever been. "Enjoy it while you can," says my friend Jon, "no doubt there is another Sammy Six- bid not far behind; another prisoner with a record that began in the womb."

Monday Jan 14th

On more than one occasion I had said to myself "Geez, how lucky that out of 39 guys in this dorm, there seem to be no snorers." Well, that was the case up until a few days ago when Cee Cee arrived. Think of the loudest snoring you've even encountered, okay now double it and you'll begin to get an idea of Cee Cee's decibel level. A league of his own. But then again, you might be too if you were pushing 400 pounds! To complete this nightmare, he happens to be just across the way from me. Upon seeing Jon this morning, we looked at each other shaking our heads. "Did he wake you?" I said. Jon could hardly contain his anger and simply held up 3 fingers and uttered, "three times Jerry, can you believe this guy?" Oh, and while it doesn't have anything to do with his awful snoring, Cee Cee is on a fourth bid. Another poster child for a prison system that's broken.

Hmm, maybe ear plugs might do the trick. No, guess what, you can't have them... not allowed. Oh that makes sense; you can have full access to a razor, tuna can lids as sharp as knives, but earplugs, no way, too dangerous.

Tuesday Jan 15th

Think of a moment when your stomach knots up. Perhaps at night you're all alone and you hear a strange voice, or driving along the highway when all of a sudden flashing red and blue lights come up behind you. You know that feeling you get, the sudden bout of fear that seeps through your entire body. Well imagine for a second having those same emotions right beside you every waking moment. Okay, welcome to a typical day in prison. For me anyway.

Knowing that one false move, something you wouldn't think twice about on the outside; like asking for an aspirin from the guy next to you, or looking at a C.O. the wrong way, who will proceed to spread eagle you up against the wall. That knot in your stomach, it's always there, affecting your eating habits, nerves and digestive system. Even as I'm writing this, 2:30 in the afternoon I feel a bit twisted. You never get a sense of relief because you're always being watched, from the minute

135

you wake up, until the time you call it quits. And even then you could be in jeopardy if someone has a grudge and decides to pay you a visit while you're sleeping.

My first four months in prison caused my digestive system to be totally out of sync. Quite simply my stomach was a nervous wreck and I'm afraid it will continue to be until the day I walk out of here.

Wednesday Jan 16th

Ever since Officer D left (now working at a facility closer to his home) Mohawk we haven't had a permanent (2:30- 10:30) afternoon/evening C.O. Instead we get a rotation of new ones (male and female) about every night. This might not sound like a big deal, oh but it is. You see each officer has his or her own style of running (patrolling) the dorm. Some of these guys come in and will do the bare minimum for the entire eight hours (an "easy eight" they call it). Even to ask them a simple question is more than they want to be bothered with. You tip-toe up to their desk (in case they might be sleeping, don't laugh, one officer we've nicknamed "sleepy" because that's all he does) and it will go something like this. "Hmm, excuse me officer, do you have and such and such forms?" He then proceeds to look at you as if you just asked him for his 1st born. Ten seconds pass and then he pushes (I swear a prerequisite for being a C.O. is to carry at least an extra 100 pounds) himself up in the chair, you now get the "sigh" which translates to "can you believe this good- for- nothing convict wants me to actually do some work." Finally, he'll speak, and you can pretty much count on the answer going something like this, "No, I don't think I have any forms, there might be, but I'm not sure." You stand there dumbfounded while he sinks his (or her) 300 pound frame back into the swivel chair!

I've worked in NYC for the past 25 years, around and with all sorts of people, in and associated with the financial services sector. Never have I come across a group who do as little as possible for their paycheck than these guys. And I mean no malice here, I really like a few of the C.O.'s, and have been treated fairly well by most of them. It's simply the way it is.

Thursday Jan 17th

With Sammy Six- bid no longer with us, the dorm is a much quieter place, especially in the evenings which was usually his time to hold court. A few of the baby- faced, wannabe gangsters seem to be picking up where he left off however. Tonight there was a heated (yes, heated) discussion amongst them as to where in NYC the largest drug trafficking occurs.

Think of a debate you've had with a friend over let's say, who's better, the Yankees or Mets, or should we have gone into Iraq or not. Well, these psychos were screaming back and forth, "Harlem or Brooklyn as to the best place for dealing cocaine." If you're looking at the bright side, I guess you could say, "Well, at least they're passionate about something." Both these cats are around 20 – 21 years old, on their 1st bids. Oh yeah, they'll be back.

Friday Jan 18th

I know I must sound like a broken record, but it is Friday again, another week down. Monday to Friday flew; unfortunately the next 48 hours will seem twice that long. I've gotten better at preparing for them and knowing what to expect. I line up a book or two, catch up on the New York Times that have begun to accumulate, crank out some letters, get to church, set aside time for push- ups, and hopefully this all leads me to around 9:00 p.m. Sunday.

Not everyone hates the weekends, take Dino for instance. A weekend means the TV room is open until 2:30 AM both nights. He'll bring his chair in around 6:00 PM, plant it in the usually spot (back row, by the window), work around the commercial breaks for optimum food consumption, and just be as happy as you could be. Ugh, I swear, you do over 10 years (he has 13 so far) in prison, and your mind can't ever be the same. Jon simply says, "Jerry, he's shot."

Saturday-Sunday Jan 19-20th

For every 10 C.O.'s like the ones I wrote about the other day (lazy, burnt out, do the bare minimum) there is 1 overzealous, gung- ho, screaming redneck. He obviously was a total loser growing up, beaten on a regular basis by his classmates and probably family as well. Now that he works as a Corrections Officer, it's payback time. No doubt he has a miserable home life, probably can't stand his wife, and uses the 8 hours here to intoxicate himself with a shot of power. We have such an officer on duty this Saturday morning. I've learned to spot these cats right off. They're the ones carrying the night- sticks (which are optional and most C.O.'s don't carry), and invariably are all short in stature. "Officer Shorty" is in the house. Go ahead; make his day by not having your cube cleaned, looking at him the wrong way, or even worse, talking back to him. He'll then get his jollies by humiliating you verbally (and you can't say a word) in an attempt to degrade you as much as possible. Secretly he's hoping you come back at him in some way, and then the fun can really begin. That club will come down on your head faster than Britney Spears in and out of rehab.

Personally I don't have a problem with any of them. I give them no reason to even look at me. It's the career criminals that generally run afoul, along with the young **turks** who come in, guns a blazing, looking to make their mark.

Monday Jan 21st

Monday, Martin Luther King Day, which means no programs or work, which also means it's going to be a long one. Willie P. woke me at 5:50 AM as we were greeted with about 5 inches of snow overnight. Even though I'm half way out of Officer B's doghouse, I'm still the designated shoveler. So, I bundled up and went outside to make sure the walkway was clear for him and the other officer's arrival at 6:25.

On a holiday the lights in the dorm remain off until the 11:00 AM count. So, it's a given 3/4's of the guys will be asleep until then. I don't know, maybe it's me, but I find it very depressing to witness 25 or so able bodied men sound asleep on a Monday morning, holiday or not.

Wouldn't you want to be up and about, reading a book, or writing a letter to your family?

I'll never forget when I was made aware of the astonishing recidivism rate which stands at 83%. I was stunned. You know what, the more time I spend here, I'm not quite as stunned.

Tuesday Jan 22nd

Seven months ago today marks the worst day of my life. No check that, the worst day by far was when I sat the boys down to inform them their Dad was going to have to spend time in prison. Anyway, 7 months ago Judge Michael Obus sentenced me to prison for a minimum 2 1/3rd years. Led away in tears, I was in the dark as to how I would survive, how could I possibly muster up the strength and willpower to last in the environment. The first couple of days I felt the sentence might as well of been ten years. I mean what was the difference, my life was over anyway. I'll never recover from the shame of a live changing event such as prison.

But as the days turned into weeks, and the weeks to months, I grew to feel proud of what I was accomplishing. Yes, there were set backs from time to time, days that I felt I wouldn't get through, but I started to find something within me. I found a sense of calm and inner peace. I began to pray more; please God walk beside me on this journey. I came to realize how blessed I truly am, with not only the loving support I received on a daily basis from my family, friends and, of course, Eileen, but, I also came to believe that God really did have a plan for me, and he felt I needed to come to Mohawk. On the outside the past few years I had lost my way, taking life's blessings for granted, short tempered, and rarely did I stop to look around so I could soak up all of the beauty I was constantly surrounded by.

So, perhaps seven months ago wasn't the worst day of my life. Maybe, in fact, it represented a whole new beginning, initially beset with sadness and hardship, but in time, the realization of how precious and incredible life is!

Wednesday Jan 23rd

The bitter cold greeted us again this Wednesday morning, snowing on and off throughout the day. For some strange reason, my boss, Chief R. thought today would be a good time to do outside work. Two hours later I could barely feel my fingers and toes, all for 24 cents per hour! Outside work today?? It was 5 degrees.

As I was reading in my cube last night, here's a snippet from a conversation overheard. "Yo son, you still be reading that trash?" "Yeah my nigger, I read 2 pages and close the book, this shit gets me tired." There you have it, another enlightening moment in the dorm.

Thursday Jan 24th

Just as I was walking out of the fire and safety office this afternoon, the NY State D.O.C. bus came rolling down the service road. No doubt it was filled with a fresh batch of "New Jacks," some coming to prison for the first time, others making a return appearance. My boss (Chief R.) happened to be with me and uttered what I thought to be an insensitive (but accurate) comment. "Here comes my job security, new product every day." I usually force a chuckle at his silly jokes, but in this case I simply looked at him, disappointed.

Yes, okay, on that bus are men who did indeed commit crimes, but now they're here, paying their debt to society, some of them trying to move forward in a positive light. I don't see the need to mock them or make fun of the sadness and hardships their sons, daughters, and wives will now have to endure. Perhaps though, until you've been on that bus, in handcuffs and leg shackles, you'll just never be able to relate to the anxiety and fear that you're about to face. Some of them, I'm sure, for a very long time.

Friday Jan 25th

It's Friday, so you know what that means… another week down! Some of the inmates think they are still on the street so they **equate** a Friday with getting rowdy, loud and obnoxious. I have to laugh, I mean it's not like you'll be stepping out tonight, hooking up with your homeboys and getting wasted. No, you're in prison stupid, tonight is like any other, locked up with nowhere to go, lights out at 10:00 PM.

That won't stop a few of these cats, they'll get worked up, maybe smoke a little grass, and laugh like there's no tomorrow. I'll be in my cube observing the scene, wondering why they aren't more somber, why they won't pick up a book, maybe even improve their mind, who knows. I'll glance over at Jon, we'll shake our heads and vie a look which says it all… "yup, they'll be back again."

Saturday-Sunday Jan 26-27th

I have something to look forward to this weekend; Eileen will be here for a visit. It'll be great to see her, catch up on life back home, what's happening in NYC, and generally just have a very pleasant time; civilized, along with intelligent conversation. Of course I will crash back to reality when our visit is over, Eileen will head towards the "exit" door that actually means something, and I will go through the "Inmates Only" door where the strip search proceeds to take place; most likely given by an overweight, red- neck C.O. who becomes gleeful as he screams "spread 'em." Yeah, that's reality all right! Not a day or night passes that I don't pray to God, asking to walk through that other door someday soon.

On Saturday evenings the TV room remains open until 2:30 AM. I couldn't tell you how many inmates are there at that hour, but I imagine it's a fair amount. Beginning at 8:00 PM the 1st movie comes on, it's usually somewhat tame, quality acting, well known stars, and was probably a Box Office hit when released. When that's finished, it's now gangsta movie time. You won't see Tom Hanks staring in any of these. Guns, drugs, and women with big tits are the order of the day. These guys love that stuff, just love it.

At this point in the evening, I'm either in my cube reading, or sounds asleep, dreaming of someday being back home.

Monday-Tuesday Jan 28-29th

I've broken one of the prison commandments by feeling sorry for someone in our dorm. His name is Jake, who arrived a few weeks ago, and is a big "Baby Hooey" type of guy. I'm not sure what he's in for (I'll find our eventually) but you can tell he has family support, as in the short time that I've observed him, he's been the recipient of two large food packages. Normally when you walk in with a bag of food the goal is to get it tucked away in your locker as fast as possible. There are vultures lurking everywhere, ready to pounce on the weak, someone like Jake. But Jake wants to be accepted and seems eager to almost buy his friends. As a result he's been sucked into a cooking group by three lowest of the lows. I've watched him contribute all the ingredients (cheese, chicken, ham, noodles, etc.), prepare the dinner, and then hand it all over in the belief this is one big happy family. I want to scream "No, Jake it's not, you're getting taken."

This group of three has promised him "Sure, we'll get you next time, I'm expecting a big package myself." These guys don't have a pot to piss in, now Jake's food has been all used up, and they don't have the time of day for him.

Even though I saw this coming from a mile away, and wanted to help, I couldn't. I mentioned my dilemma to Jon. "Jerry, don't get involved, this is prison and you can't stick your neck out for anybody." Sure, Jake created some of this mess himself, but mentally he's child-like and doesn't know any better. I hope he learned a lesson this time around, but I doubt it. We'll know soon enough though, it's almost a new month and he'll be eligible for 35 pounds of food his family can send. The three vultures are waiting in the wings.

Wednesday Jan 30th

As a non- violent, 1st time offender, I'm a candidate for work release. Besides those criteria, you must amass 32 points based on mostly good behavior, and programs completed. I've actually appeared before the Temporary Release Committee, back in October, only four months into my sentence. They called me in because I had tallied up 34 points already. Given that short amount of time served, I knew I wouldn't get it… and sure enough, I was denied. No worries, I carried on, and as you know by reading this, I have maintained a spotless disciplinary record, and am now allowed to reapply.

Now it becomes a bit more serious, I have been here nearly 8 months, almost halfway through my sentence, and am allowing my mind (and heart) to actually believe I have a chance this time of being granted work release. The thought of walking out these gates is hard to describe, my stomach and nervous system push up against each other and I begin to feel giddy, light- headed. I have to quickly reign these forces in, I can't allow them to run amok within me. In order to accomplish this I tell myself "Jerry, it's not going to happen." And just like that, wham, I've sobered up and come back down where I need to be. Can't get ahead of myself, it will only bring pain.

Thursday-Friday Jan 31st-Feb 1st

I've played the following potential work release scenario out in my mind for the past few weeks. I know I'm supposed to stay "in the now," but this can't be helped, not when we're talking about walking out of here, and never looking back.

I will stand in front of two people on the committee at Mohawk. They won't know me from a hold- in- the- wall, but they have the power to literally control my life. Unfortunately, these two have become so jaded as to the prospect of someone actually being rehabilitated; they are programmed to rubber stamp; DENIED! I believe another reason they continue to deny non- violent, 1st time offenders is job security. That's right; NY State is looking to reduce the hemorrhaging D.O.C. budget, best way to do that, close a few prisons. Now do you think for a second these civilians on the committee want a half- empty prison? Hell no they don't! **We're full Albany, you can't close Mohawk, go find another facility to shutter**. Thankfully for me there is the appeal process. The day after my meeting I will learn my fate. Fully expecting to be shot down, I will gather my wits and write to Albany where I believe they are more open- minded, less jaded. I plan to accompany my appeal letter with a few letters of support from family.

This avenue doesn't have a 1 day turnaround time; from what Jon tells me, it'll take about a month. Now that's going to be a long thirty days! One last note of optimism is that if Albany says no, I can re- apply in about two months. Maybe eventually they will simply get sick of me and decide to let me go home.

Saturday Feb 2nd

As I move closer to the realm of possibility that I'm granted work release, not only do I obsess on how glorious and wonderful it will be to be near my family, beginning my new life, but I can't help but think of the many aspects of Mohawk that I will never, ever miss.

Below is a list that comes to mind right away.
- Receiving mail that hasn't already been opened
- Sleeping with a pillow that's thicker than let's say, a washcloth.
- Having to wear shower shoes when taking a shower.
- Sleeping in a room with 38 other men and dealing with 38 various, and sometimes violent, personalities.
- Wearing polyester, sans-a-belt green state ordered pants.
- Standing at the sink, brushing my teeth, when along comes some dirt ball who proceeds to spit and regurgitate non-stop in the sink next to me.
- Sleeping on a mattress thicker than a few pieces of cardboard.
- Eating all my meals out of a plastic tray, along with using a dull and dirty spoon and fork.
- Waking up 7 feet away from a psychopath, back in prison for a 5th time, all for violent felonies.

- Having to listen to the most childish, imbecilic conversations. For example, who is richer? Beyonce or Eddie Murphy? To some of these idiots here, that is actually important. Or something like this on the walkway: "Yo Leon, holla at Quame for me, tell him I learn-d that shit he be telling me."

Sunday Feb 3rd

Super Bowl Sunday! For obvious reasons, I can't get overly worked up about it. Seeing all those happy, carefree, cheering spectators in the stands, will only reinforce that I am currently not any of those things. Looking at the TV, witnessing the high- fives, the laughter of all the people- whom I was once like- will make the end of a long, sad weekend even that much more difficult.

In addition, watching the big game with about 20 screaming inmates, never shutting up for a second, well, that doesn't do it for me either. I think I'll sit in my cube and listen to it on the radio.

Monday Feb 4th

My request for a meeting with the TRC committee went out this morning, hopefully within a couple of weeks they'll set up an interview… what a different outlook prison provides, it's a Monday morning, thank God the weekend is over. I don't think I ever uttered those words in my previous life.

Just as an aside, every every time I see Barack Obama on TV, I'm more and more convinced I'm looking at our next President.

My spirits are low, I've been in the valley the past few days, I hope I come out of it soon……. maybe it's the winter doldrums. Dino seems to be in a serious depressive state, in fact I haven't spoken to him in a week. I'm going to leave him be, hopefully he snaps out of it, but truth be known, it's a blessing. While for the most part I've enjoyed his company, these past months, I've come to see what a user and a con he is. In his 13 years of prison he's developed serious "game." And ya know what, if it works for him, that's fine, buyer beware. It doesn't work for me though, I don't like the way he operates, he's been down too long I guess. I do my time in a completely different fashion, reading, praying, reflecting, not "making moves or going onto the street" as Dino refers to it when he is about to pull off a scam. So I welcome the silence and separation that has developed. With each passing day I become more self-sufficient, I'm doing me, and I've come to learn that is the way it works best.

Tuesday Feb 5th

Jon and I were talking the other night about support and faith shown our way by family and friends. How important and helpful it is towards surviving this place. He then asked me a question which I've previously reflected on, but I suppose I have blocked from my mind, "Jerry, have any friends abandoned you while you've been here?" Well I think to myself, I suppose one or two have let me down in terms of staying in touch, writing me back after I had sent out a flurry of letters. But then I think, 'hey, listen, I have so much damm support here, how could I possibly expect anything more?' Perhaps it's simply too hard for these one or two friends to write, maybe they don't know what to say. It could be legit, I'm in no position to judge or cast dispersions. So I'm not going to get negative on anyone I perceive as letting me down, it is what it is. I know I'm loved by many, and will carry that thought along the road with me. Getting upset about a few who have chosen to look the other way is not productive, and more importantly, something I have no control over.

Wednesday-Thursday Feb 6-7th

Just like anywhere else, you have cliques in prison, but unlike anywhere else, they are usually formed in a much different manner than they would be in the real world. When guys come together here and eventually become more at ease with each other, a decision is made to validate the clique. What that means is you agree to meet at a table out in the yard, rap sheets in hand. Yes that's right, you bring the piece of paper the DOC gives you on your first day, outlining your crime(s), what you did and then length of your sentence. Inside these walls, there is only one reason for this, and that is so a sexual predator, rapist, or child molester doesn't present himself falsely. Hmm, you wouldn't think that would be necessary? Wrong, think again. Statistically, 55% of white men are locked up for some sort of sexual offense.

Over the past few months, I've become part of a clique; Jon, whom I've written about, and Mike, a married father of two young boys. We've eaten a lot of meals in the mess hall together. However, the three of us never had one of those 'rap sheet in hand' types of meeting, never even considered it. After all we were three white guys, successful at one time in our careers, married, children at home who love and miss us, and loyal families at our side. Sure we made a stupid mistake by ending up here, but certainly we weren't any type of sexual deviant. Well, as the old saying goes "appearances can be deceptive," I guess we should have had that rap sheet meeting.

Knowing the beans were about to be spilled and he was about to be outed, Mike informed Jon and I last night that as a result of a "huge mistake" he made four years ago, he is a Class 3, registered sexual offender!!

To say I was shocked is an understatement. This news has also potentially placed me (and Jon) in a dangerous line of fire… we have openly been hanging out with the lowest class of prisoner there is. Are people automatically associating us with Mike, do they think we condone this sort of deviant behavior? Some of these inmates will settle things in a hurry, act first, ask questions later.

I remember when Mike came into the dorm, immediately the pictures of the family went up on the bulletin board, you couldn't get more Norman Rockwell. As I got to know him better I learned he worked successfully in the family electrical business, had a nice house on Long Island, and was here due to drug possession. Okay, sure, perhaps a little vague, but I didn't press him on it.

He broke the news because he knows Jon and I would've found out shortly. Mike was court ordered to attend, for lack of a better word, sex offender's class, starting this morning. This class is offered in the main school building, so I mean now everybody knows who these cats are; so much for remaining anonymous. By this afternoon, everyone in my dorm knew, it went something like this, "Hey, I saw Mike in the rape- o class, that dirt ball." Or perhaps this: "Another child molester, he better not come near me, I'll cut him." Already, the news only hours old, someone has approached Jon. "Hey, you're not one of those, are you?" No doubt I will get the same type of interrogation.

Obviously I am sickened by what Mike has done (I'll go into that further in my next couple of postings) and now I have to figure out which direction this news leads me. Do I write him off? Or stick by him? Especially now that he needs a friend more than ever. Am I pissed? Yes, I most certainly am.

Willie P.'s words of advice to prison rookies begins to ring truer and truer, "You do you, and I do me."

Friday Feb 8th

As I have more time to reflect on the shocking news about Mike, I grow increasingly disgusted. Initially upon hearing this news my knee-jerk reaction was akin to "on my God you're kidding, not Mike." But I didn't have a chance to fully absorb it all, and I hesitated to rush to judgment.

So I don't have to tell him to his face, I hope my continuing efforts at avoiding Mike will have the desired effect. Only an hour ago he came over to me, "Hey Jerry, are you going to join Jon and I for dinner?" I replied with a terse "no, not hungry." Jon has made the decision not to abandon Mike at this moment. I understand of course, Jon has a kind heart and is willing to let the jury remain on stand- by for the time being. Also, as he explained, "Jerry, I've seen this shit and much worse during my 3 years at Gowanda CF. I'm more hardened than you right now." Okay, I'll buy that.

Jon is a model inmate, generally keeps to himself, is self- sufficient and knows what works best in terms of doing his time. As this tale unfolds, I'll be surprised if he doesn't eventually throw Mike to the curb as well. The peer pressure alone might force his hand. I do know our small clique is a thing of the past. Jon and I will of course remain friends, but with Mike, I need to step back. He was not a particularly endearing type of guy to the members of the dorm to begin with. Now, with this news out of the bag, the knives were drawn. The only question remaining is, how long until someone beats the shit out of him. Stay tuned, I give it a couple of weeks at the most.

Saturday-Sunday Feb 9-10th

Reflecting on the week just passed, leaves my head spinning. The big news obviously was Mike, and all of us learning about his sickness, but there were other pockets of intrigue which took place. I'm still not speaking with Dino who has viewed my friendship with Jon as a personal affront towards him. He had been trying to feed me a ton of negativity in regard to Jon. I asked him politely to refrain, questioned his loyalty to friends, and we haven't spoken since. Dino is too much of a "con" for my liking, and while maybe he has had to develop that kind of temperament to survive 13 years in prison; I don't and I won't. I'm leaving someday soon, and cannot have a person instilling "prison acceptable" behavior in my mind. I've worked damn hard at preserving my heart and soul while in prison, I'm proud of that, it's not an easy thing to do. I refuse to let anyone here pollute it.

Around 10:00 last night I observed one of the New Jack's, a fresh '08 number stamped on his green state clothes, bringing his food package (which I'm sure his Mother had lovingly sent to him) over to one of the card shark's in our dorm. About four of these guys make a small fortune hustling the new fresh meat on the poker table. The only time they lose is when they feel a shred of compassion for their victims and let them win a hand or two, other than that it seems to be a steady flow of food and stamps coming their way, courtesy of the New Jacks.

Monday Feb 11th

TGIM! No, that's' not a misprint, "Thank God it's Monday." As I've written many times, the weekdays fly by like the speed of light, the weekends slower than a three wheeled ox- cart. I'm hoping this is the week I hear about my meeting with the Temporary Release Committee.

Knowing how rotten these people are however, they'll probably wait until the last day of the month to schedule me.

Work (Fire & Safety office) continues to go well, my co- worker and I get along nicely, we have our own little office (practically unheard of in prison) with a radio and computer, (no Internet) fully loaded with Windows XP, not to mention solitaire and pinball. Half the day is spent doing paperwork, the other half driving around the facility with Chief R. We have an entrée where few others can venture, along with exposure to all the other C.O.'s, Sergeants, Lieutenant's and even the occasional run in with "The Prince of Darkness" himself, Deputy Superintendent M. We have an opening for one more on the crew, I've been able to get Jon an interview with the Chief and it looks like he has a good shot to come on board.

Tuesday Feb 12th

I'm not sure if it's a coincidence, deliberate, or something else entirely, but as of last night, Mike is no longer in our dorm. It's been a tumultuous week for him and so last night Jon and I helped Mike carry his three draft bags full of clothes, books, pictures and all his prison belongings, along with his mattress. As we began our walk over to the 22 Dorms, a light snow began to fall & I actually felt sorry for Mike. Apparently, on top of everything else, he is court ordered to enroll in A.S.A.T. (Alcohol Substance Abuse Treatment) which is a sex month program. When you take A.S.A.T. you move to the 22 Dorm, otherwise known as "the projects." Besides being filthy, you have some real bad apples over there, just look at some of those dudes the wrong way and you'll find yourself in a fistful of trouble.

So Mike has a long road ahead of him, not just the next 6 months surviving the projects, but in reality, a lifetime sentence as a result of his Class 3 designation. Any town he ever moves into will be notified of his presence, he can never life within a mile of a school, and if he rents an apartment, his landlord is required to notify all the tenants. It'll never end for him.

Wednesday Feb 13th

The dullness of the morning routine was interrupted by Officer B calling for a rare early count at 7:30. This can't be good I thought to myself, he's definitely pissed about something. Once the count is announced you have about sixty seconds to get inside your cube. It was funny to watch three guys come running out of the shower, shampoo on their heads, still literally soaking wet.

Officer B sees to it that this dorm remains one of the cleanest in the entire facility. No let up, day in and day out. He continuously stays on top of us. And you know what, he has to. Some of these guys are such dirty slobs ; spitting or blowing their nose in the sink then simply leaving it. Underwear left hanging in the showers, toilets un-flushed, filled to the brim with crap and toilet paper. The other night we had a dude removed from this dorm down to the projects, at the time I didn't understand what he had done. Today I found out. Officer B had placed a dirty piece of paper on the floor, this poor guy just happened to be at the wrong place at the wrong time, he walked right past it, Officer B watched it unfold. Busted, game over, pack your bags.

Anyway, this morning was a not- so- gentle reminder of how he expects us to conduct ourselves. Like I said, I welcome the crackdown, get the slobs out of here, put 'em on notice. I keep hearing the refrain from some of these guys, "hey man, you wanna get respect, you gotta give respect." Well let me tell you, Officer B is giving them more respect than they deserve, but I guarantee you he won't get it in return.

Thursday Feb 14th

I received notice to appear before the Temporary Release Committee tomorrow morning at 9:00. I'm a nervous wreck just thinking about it. I have a pretty good idea regarding the scene; 3 civilians sitting around a table in a small room, ready to pounce, and skeptical as hell on any inmate appearing before them. Hopefully they haven't already prejudged me, when I get the opportunity to speak they will listen, hear my words, and feel the utmost sincerity behind them.

I imagine the opening question will be along the lines of, "So, Mr. Byrne, tell us how you're doing," followed by "Why should the committee consider you a candidate for work release."

I will pray this evening, asking the Lord to prepare me, give me strength to do what I have to do.

Friday Feb 15th

I arrived on time for the 8:00 am TRC meeting, my stomach in knots and bowels way out of sync. The C.O. on duty took my ID card and told me to go wait on the bench. I had been preparing for this moment quite awhile, I knew there were certain points I wanted to touch on, even if denied I had to exit that room knowing I had spoken from the heart, kept composure, and put forth my best effort. As jaded as these committee members are, I wanted more than anything for them to believe what I was saying, to feel my anguish, the depth of remorse, and a solemn vow that I will never return to prison. Did I accomplish this? Well, you know what, I really think I did. Whether they thought so or not is a different story, one in which I'll have an answer for tomorrow afternoon, when the mail arrives. While red tape and ass dragging are the norm here, one thing they don't waste time on is letting you know their decision, thumbs up or down. I'll do my best to stay occupied the next 24 hours. As I've been saying all along however, I don't expect Mohawk to grant me work release, most likely tomorrow at this time I will be reading a sheet of paper listing the reason I've been denied.

Within days I will have the appeal ready to be sent to Albany where a fairer assessment hopefully awaits. In the appeal will be two letters of support; one from my ex- father- in- law, retired federal District Court Judge. Along with one from another family friend, the just retired Chief Justice of N.J. So yes, a bit of muscle is attached to the appeal, and that's okay, I'll need all the help I can get. Thank God I'm so blessed to receive the support I have. I beg for Albany to really <u>read</u> these letters; please capture the sincerity and love flowing from them. Whether they will or not remains to be seen.

Saturday-Sunday Feb 16-17th

As I wait for the mail to arrive it brings me back to the days of my youth, peering out the window, awaiting the mailman's truck to pull in the driveway, my final exam grades buried somewhere in his satchel. This scene is quite a bit different however, a Corrections Officer will be carrying the mail, in a locked canvas bag, I'm looking through windows with <u>bars</u> attached, and most of all, the stakes are a whole lot higher than a final grade in Algebra. We're talking about a letter possibly placing me on the road back to freedom. Or the letter says I have another year here, at the least.

Well, the letter has arrived and I just finished reading the decision of the TRC.......DENIED!!! I can't tell you how deflated I feel right now, if only there was some place I could go to have a meaningful cry, let it all out, but there is no such place here. As much as I wasn't expecting a positive result, my mind in the past 24 hours slowly took over and began to let me think there was a change. I wanted to see signs, and the mind was happy to oblige. Sitting here I feel a sense of hopelessness once again. Will I ever leave? How much longer must I remain a prisoner? When will I see my sons again?

Jon stopped by to console me, I appreciate his honest concern. I need to bring my head back to a level place; these past 48 hours have played with my emotions, not to mention anxiety levels. I'm so sad right now, I would give anything to hug Brooks and Philip, be with my family, but instead I'm back to being in limbo. When will I ever walk out these gates? When will I be free again? Oh it's going to be a long weekend.

Monday-Tuesday Feb 18-19th

I try hard to maintain an even keel with my emotions. While I've never had to worry about getting too high, I'm currently struggling with the depths. Right now I hate this place more than I ever have. Besides the separation from my family, and sons, what I hate most about prison is having to live and co- exist with the multitude of despicable, truly moronic and psychotic individuals. On Wednesday of this week I'll watch "Cee- Cee" walk out the gates, (all 350 pounds of him!) currently

153

serving his 4th bid, all for drug dealing and possession. He somehow made his merit board and is being released early. I fucking guarantee you he'll be back within a year, not a doubt in my mind. With 5 years post release supervision, his world will consist of listening to rap music, getting his grimy hands on the latest issue of "ButtMan Magazine," and dealing drugs, most importantly, without the slightest desire to improve himself. One thing for certain, there will be a bed waiting for him back here at Mohawk.

But guess what, the esteemed TRC folks, none of who made it beyond high school, in all their wisdom, deem me to be more of a risk to society, a non- violent 1st time offender. Am I bitter right now? Ok, yes I am. I had a carrot dangled in front of me, I allowed my emotions to take the bait, and then they quickly pulled it away.

On top of everything else, I learned yesterday my mother is in the hospital with breathing problems. Never have I witnessed such love, faith, and compassion. She is everything to me, a living saint. How I wish I could be there with her, to hold her hand, tell mom how much she has meant to me. But I am here, trapped, helpless and alone! God forbid anything happened I would not be allowed to attend my mother's funeral, which would be in NJ, and the DOC doesn't let you cross over to another state. I'm not being morbid, simply realistic, the worst could happen. So all the events of the past 48 hours have placed me in a bad way. I need to center myself soon and most importantly regain the strength I had. It's too easy to give up, I can't allow that to occur, I just can't.

Wednesday Feb 20th

It's winter break time at Mohawk, yes that's right, even Prison closes for winter recess week. Well technically the prison is open, but all school and vocational programs are closed. I'm happy to say the Fire & Safety office is open though. Not only does that get me away from the depressing dorm (at least half of these guys will be sound asleep until the 11 am count) but more importantly, keeps the day and week moving along.

Now more than ever, am I trying to stay occupied. While I'm regaining some of the wind that's been knocked out of me the past few days, my mother is still in the hospital. I can't speak to her, see her, or hold her. Saying countless prayers is my only option.

Once again winter is in full gear, 6 degrees as I write, along with light snow. How I long to be able to spend more time outdoors, running, walking, whatever. It makes such a difference, especially for someone like me who has always been so active. My first few months, I spent every available free moment outdoors. Un- trapping myself from the confines of prison. These past few months I've felt more trapped than ever. I can't wait for some warmer weather, to be 'free' again, at least for a few hours.

Thursday Feb 21st

A fight broke out in our dorm this afternoon. Yes, punches thrown and landed, all over a 41 cent stamp. Two guys, who just the night before had been partners in crime at the poker table, now going at it. What's that old saying? "There is no honor among thieves." These (supposedly) grown men accusing each other of holding back on one stamp, which then led to the name calling (sounds like a couple of twelve- year- olds), which led to "You be disrespecting my name man, my name's Jay, no one disses Jay son" Countered brilliantly with this exchange, "Well I'm Cuba, no one gets over on Cuba, no one man, let's do this right now." That's all it takes, neither one willing to back down. The crowd in the dorm, after a long boring morning, smelled and wanted blood. There was not even a whiff of somebody attempting to bring reason into the mix. Cuba and Jay squared off, a couple of quick punches thrown by each. The noise level rose, the blood thirsty inmates wanted a knockout. Lucky for these two fighters the C.O. on duty was focused on either his crossword puzzle or his Sudoku book, I couldn't tell which. Normally, one punch thrown means at least 30 days in "the Box." But eventually the C.O. did finally stir, word quickly filtered to the dorm room, and the fighters separated.

Friday Feb 22nd

Each morning you'll see anywhere between 5- 15 inmates walk out of the reception dorm (75A), where every inmates spends his first and last night at Mohawk. These are the cats going home (for now anyway), mattress's slung over their shoulders, draft bags in hand, big shit- eating grins on their faces. I spotted Cee- Cee walking out this morning, just completed his 4th bid. He had made his merit board (good grief) and was back on his way home to Harlem where he'll wreak havoc once again. As I said good bye and wish him luck last night, I could tell that in the back of his mind, he just knew he was destined to return here. With five years of a Parole Officer on his ass, the chances of Cee- Cee staying clean are doubtful.

I take no glee in writing this, it's sad actually. I don't have all the answers, but the system is broken. With a recidivism rate of 83%, something is very wrong.

Saturday Feb 23rd

I notice the poker games are not only becoming more frequent and intense but starting earlier in the day. This morning after clean- up and supplies being given out, the first game of the day kicked off at 10:15. On weekdays, due to programs or school, they get underway at a more respectable 2:00 p.m. or so. I watch the "New- Jacks" belly up to the table, full of hope and attitude ready to make their mark, only to be turned away a few hours later, beaten and downcast. They will drop anywhere between 20 or 30 stamps (the primary currency here) and if they can't cover that, it's time to turn over your care package or worse yet, your commissary sheet.

This losing then festers bad blood that will seep through the dorm. Guys will stew about their loss, begin to imagine they're been cheated (uh, hello, look around you, you're in prison, do ya think?) and possibly seek retribution. Now that's when it gets ugly, just like a few days when punches were thrown all over a 41 cent stamp.

The mindset is so truly different here sometimes you can't help but laugh and shake your head in amazement. For example, last night, I was watching <u>Fox News</u> along with Benjamin (we're the only ones who watch the evening news), when they cut in with a live video report of a car chase that was underway out in California. Well, you had five police cars chasing this one dude driving a pickup, who was obviously wanted for something. As the chase ensued it attracted more inmates over to the TV, before you knew it there were about 20 gathered around Benjamin and me. Well, this went on for 10 minutes, the pursuit growing in intensity, when all of a sudden two of the police cars crashed into each other. In an instant, an ear- splitting cheer went up and high- fives were going around the room. You would have thought each and every one of these guys had just been pardoned by the Warden. Never mind that the cops might have been seriously hurt, or worse, this group had their nights made. What a place prison is!

Sunday Feb 24th

Nothing to say, don't feel like writing. Depressed. The only good news (and it's very good) is that my Mother left the hospital and is back home resting, doing a little better. This news gets me through the day.

Monday Feb 25th

Phew, I made it through another long weekend. T.G.I.M. I have something really special to look forward to this coming weekend however, two of my sisters, along with their husbands will be coming to visit. Other than Virginia who's been been here a couple of times, I have not seen any of them in over eight months. Throughout the week I will be trying to steady myself for the inevitable emotional outburst when I first spot them upon entering the visitor's room.

The last week of the month is always quiet at the Fire & Safety office. All the inspections and extinguishers have been checked, all the reports written up and filed. Chief R. will be sure to try and find some meaningless tasks for Dee (my co- worker) and I to do, I guess he feels we need to justify our hefty salaries of $1.50 per day.

Tuesday-Wednesday Feb 26-27th

For the past three months or so, thanks to the generosity of Eileen, I had been receiving the New York Times every day. While it would usually be at least a day or two behind schedule, and on some days I wouldn't get one at all- and then receive 3 the next day- nonetheless though, I can't describe to you what a treat it was. I always look back to my days on Rikers Island, when upon receiving a newspaper even 3- 4 weeks old, pages worn bare, articles torn out; I still savored it. But, a few weeks ago, I asked Eileen, much to her consternation, to cancel my subscription to 'The Times.'

Let me explain why I no longer wanted the paper. It wasn't because on occasion, the C.O., when having to carry three papers to the dorm at mail call, would proceed to throw them at me (that only happened a couple of times), but rather I had begun to feel too comfortable. Yes, that's right, I was feeling a little to 'at ease.' I considered the hour or two required to fully read a paper like 'The Times' was eating into my reflecting on the sorrow being of here, my spiritual growth, and most importantly, my writing. Not only this precious story I record each day, where I bare all, but also the letters I enjoy composing to family and friends.

Eileen couldn't make sense of this at first, thinking that I was just being too hard on myself. perhaps when I explained to her, I might have failed to articulate it well, but I know eventually she will understand, although she sometimes will say "Jerry, you don't have to punish yourself."

Unlike 95% of the inmates here, I want to make my hours count; I want them to mean something. When my knees hit the ground each night, to thank God for getting me through another day, I want to know I used those hours to better myself. Reading the NY Times, as much as I love it, and while I can't wait to one day reclaim the experience of plunking down $1.25 at the local newsstand, currently it isn't making me a better person while at Mohawk. All of my other activities are, and that is why I chose to cancel the subscription: to make the moments count!

Thursday Feb 28th

Even though I often speak about the importance of staying in "the now," I can't help but wonder what the outcome of my work release appeal will bring. I figure it is in the hands of the bureaucrats in Albany and most likely there will be no word forthcoming for at least 3-4 weeks. Nonetheless, with a decision as big as this, my brain (and emotions) take full command and I have to catch myself from daydream overload. The thought of not being behind bars anymore overwhelms me, makes me giddy and light- headed. And as much as I crave it, I am telling myself I won't be leaving here anytime soon. Mentally I need to be prepared for rejection, for if that indeed does occur; I must be ready to face it straight on. So when those thoughts of Work Release come marching in my head, quickly as I can I will try to send them on their way.

Friday Feb 29th

Well, here are those magic words once again, "another month down!" Three little words that mean and represent so much; at least to someone in prison. I have to say this month of February went faster than any of them so far. Yes I know it literally is the shortest month of the year, that's not what I mean. Plain and simple it flew by. And now with winter on its last legs, I will start spending more and more of my free time out in the yard. With all the snow we've gotten up here there have been few opportunities to get out and run, I really have missed that feeling a good run brings; the fresh air, the sweat trickling down your forehead. and most of all, I don't seem as 'locked up.'

As I write (4:00 p.m. Friday) two of my three sisters, along with their husbands are making the trek up the NY Thruway. They'll spend the evening at a local hotel and tomorrow morning we will visit. Other than Virginia, I haven't seen any of them for close to nine months. I can guarantee a few tears, but many more laughs and hugs. I'm beyond wishing this was under different circumstances, it's not, it is what it is, and we've all come to accept my sorrow for being here. Growing up in our privileged, rarefied, secluded world, setting foot in a Correctional Facility was never even a farfetched possibility. Never say "never."

March

Saturday-Sunday March 1st-2nd

Around 10:00 a.m., the C.O. on duty called out, "Byrne, head up to the visitors room." I must admit I was nervous, I knew I had to keep my emotions in check, while at the same time I was hoping that the table assigned for our visit would be in a good location, that is, far away from a lurking psycho, or an inmate that can't keep his groping hands and lips off his overweight girlfriend who is stuffed into an outfit three sizes too small for her. As I entered the room (after being frisked of course) I saw two hands shoot up like anxious school girls sitting in the 1st row of class hoping the teacher would call on them, my sisters Virginia and Susie, along with my brothers- in- law, Doug and Sarg. The five inches of snow we received the night before kept many from making the trip to Mohawk, so thankfully the decibel level was manageable for a change; and it appeared at a quick glance the tables surrounding ours were unoccupied. Phew, so far so good, no psychos sitting next to us. Before I even had the chance to say one word to my family the visit was off to a wonderful start. And it only got better from there. The three hours we spent together seemed more like five minutes. There was so much catching up to do; so immediately after the tears and hugs we picked up where we had left off nine months ago.

Of course the girls looked as pretty as ever- some things never change- and the guys rounded out the foursome of visitors this Correctional Facility doesn't see all too often. Trust me on this.

After many laughs, poignant moments, and heartfelt dialogue, it was time for them to get in the car and begin the four hour drive back to CT. They know I will continue to stay strong, keep the faith, and carry on. What I knew but choose not to tell them, is that I don't want them to ever come back here. We needed to see each other; we did, and got through it.....now it's over. We kept the stiff upper lip but I can't bear for my family to see me in state clothes, in an overcrowded visitors' room, any longer. Not to mention having a guard watch over us while we do so. Next time I hug my sister's it'll have to be when I'm wearing khaki pants, a blue button down shirt, and won't have to worry who's at the table next to us.

Monday Mar 3rd

The snow from the past few days and weeks is melting today.....the temperature rose to over 50 degrees! Do I dare say Spring is in the air? Hmm, that might be rushing things but we'll take what we can get. Tonight for the first time in months I'll head over to the yard where the track will be slushy. No matter though, with the warm weather and the fact that it is now March, this brings a sense of optimism that the worst is indeed over. The coming of Spring has always done that for me, instilling a feeling of fresh energy, an anything-is possible- outlook on life. Thank God I am able to possess that same sense even here, an aura of hope. I can't think of any place you need it more; without it you're lost, to be sucked into the misery and morass of prison life. I refuse to go there.

Tuesday-Wednesday Mar 4-5th

About two months ago a new guy came marching into the dorms; before I knew a single thing about him I whispered to Jon, "Uh oh, I think we have a psycho alert." Boy what a call that was. Brian (a.k.a. Irish) is white, 32 years old, and has spent 12 of those years behind bars. What first led me to peg him as a poster child for your classic psycho were his bulging eyes; picture Marty Feldman, now double that crazed stare and you have Irish. And wouldn't you know it, just my luck, guess which cube he moved right next to? That's right… mine.

Even though he annoyed me right off by calling me "Mr. Jerry," I felt mildly sorry for him, as you could tell he was one of those guys that didn't have a pot to piss in. So Jon and I would give an occasional cup of coffee to Irish who would immediately claim, "I'm waiting on a huge package, there will be plenty of coffee coming my way in a few days." Well, two months later, we're still waiting on that huge package. To survive he's managed to perfect the technique of begging. Hence, Jon and I have bestowed upon Irish our own nickname… Ollie, after the Charles Dickens's character, Oliver Twist, who was always in search and begging for food.

Now besides Ollie's saucer- like-eyes, he has some serious anger management issues as well; hence his already spending more than a 1/3 of his 32 years behind bars. He's the type of psycho that one day you might say to him "Good morning, Brian," and all of a sudden he'll freeze in his tracks, spin around towards you, get right in your space, eyes fully bulging and say, "What's so fucking good about it Mr. Jerry." Truly, he gives you at that moment the impression he would enjoy nothing more than killing you right then and there. However, a mere ten minutes later, someone could approach him with the exact same greeting, and this would be Ollie's response, "Yes, it is a nice morning, have a wonderful day."

So naturally, I, along with Jon, try to avoid him like the plague, especially when it comes time to head over to the mess hall. Since Ollie has not a single friend, he somehow believes he can latch onto us.

On the few occasions we were unable to ditch him fast enough, and he found his way to our table, it turned out to be torture spending even 10 minutes with him; for you just don't know what could trigger a psycho moment. Once as Jon reached across to grab a pitcher of water, Ollie stopped eating, looked at Jon and said, "When I was in prison in Alabama a few years ago, this dude put his hand on my plate, so I punched him in the face and broke his fucking nose, Mr. Johnny." At that moment I really thought Ollie was going to take his fork and plunge it through one of our necks.

It's gotten so bad, that now when the phone rings in the dorm signaling time to head over to the mess hall, Jon and I have to plot strategy to avoid Ollie's line of sight. Lately we've taken to a plan since labeled, the "Ollie Shuffle," whereas we let him go first over to chow, and once he's chosen a particular side of the mess hall to sit on, we go to the exact opposite. Mission accomplished, the Ollie Shuffle works again, and we can proceed to eat in peace. Lately however, we've glanced over only to see Ollie staring back at us, eyes bulging out of his head, a look that screams of "I'm going to fucking kill you Mr. Jerry and Mr. Johnny." Gulp.

There are three inmates in our dorm who are serving a sentence of murder, one here for double murder. However, none of these three scare me as much as Ollie does. He's textbook psycho and I have to really watch my step with him

Thursday Mar 6th

A quiet and calm afternoon was interrupted by the appearance of five C.O.'s who arrived to shake down the dorm. This entails a quick frisk of every one, we must stand at attention in front of our cubes, no talking. Then, about ten cubes are picked at random- at least they claim it's random- and basically torn upside down. The slightest bit of contraband will get you a ticket, the slightest backtalk gets you thirty days in the box. I'm not quite sure what prompts these searches, perhaps a tip, more likely though it's just a show of force, or plain old ball busting.

Thankfully my cube was not searched; while I have nothing to hide, it's just that they go in there and tear them upside down, a real pain- and mess- to put back together. The final tally for the dorm: no weapons found, but eight tickets written; from something as simple as having a container of milk taken from the mess hall- no milk is allowed out- to not having a permit for your transistor radio or lamp.

Friday Mar 7th

After you receive a ticket, you will be summoned to the Tier Office the very next day, where you will be given a hearing date, usually within a day or two. At the hearing you're given a chance to present your side of the story, versus what the Corrections Officer knows. The lieutenant on duty that morning is the moderator; how do you say, 'The deck is stacked against you.' You can spare yourself the trouble- and aggravation- and just plead guilty. I believe all of the tickets written from our dorm search were Tier 1, the lowest, with the highest being a Tier 3. The penalty for a 1 is usually loss of Rec. privileges for 14 days. If they don't like you and feel like busting chops, the loss can include packages and even telephone. Generally, there is no "box" time for a Tier 1, but they can hang a 60 day hold over you; which means if you so much as look at an officer the wrong way for the next sixty days, you're going to the box.

So, the losses of Rec. tickets out of my dorm ranged from ten days to twenty-one, and start to finish the shake down lasted 45 minutes. More importantly though it reaffirms how you can't ever let your guard down and (for me anyway) the fear and anxiety levels that are on constant alert. I mean, I'm not saying they would; but what is to prevent a rouge C.O., who had a certain dislike for some inmate, from planting weapon, or drugs into your locker. Has it happened? Hmmm, who knows.

Saturday-Sunday Mar 8-9th

The weekend has brought a stark reminder that winter refuses to simply fade away. We were lucky to receive a few days of Spring-like temperatures earlier in the week; now it's Sunday morning and there is close to a foot of snow on the ground. As I've said before, anywhere else that falling snow would be scenic and it's beauty appreciated: here it is snow, in no way can it be utilized (making or throwing a single snow ball will get you an immediate ticket) and is simply a messy obstacle.

On weekends breakfast begins at 8:00 a.m., as opposed to 6:30 on weekdays. Ollie, being the lazy, irresponsible, pathetic, loser that he is, will often ask either Jon or I to wake him around ten minutes prior to chow time. I want to shout out to him, "You're a grown man, are you really that inept that you can't wake yourself by 7:45 a.m.?" So as to keep peace- and not to get smothered by Ollie's pillow in the middle of the night- I will on occasion give his bed a very quick tap, a wake up call. Well, last night, Ollie did not ask to be awoken, and seeing him this morning, sound asleep at 8:00, the snow falling, I certainly wasn't going to assume he wanted to get up for breakfast. Especially since the clocks were turned forward one hour last night- yeah, one less hour at Mohawk. So Jon, Fritz (the laundry porter, Paul Newman look alike) and I braved the elements, thankful that we did not have to employ the Ollie Shuffle.

As we entered the dorm (74 D) twenty minutes later, who do we see but Ollie, rubbing the sleepers out of his eyes, a nasty scowl planted on his face, a look that screams... "I'm going to fucking kill you, Mr. Jerry and Mr. Johnny." No words were spoken, the look said it all, as Jon and

I averted his Charles Manson like stare. With that Ollie turned around and crawled back into bed, where he will remain until the 11:00 a.m. count. It's a standing count, so Ollie will get out of bed for all of five minutes, the count will clear, and immediately he will throw himself back down until 4:00 p.m.; the next count. God forbid he uses any of this time constructively, towards the slightest hint of rehabilitation. Not to pick on him as he is most definitely not alone; but very, very few of these guys make any attempt at using their stay here wisely, to better themselves. For most, it's what time does the Gym open, who's got the basketball, what's on TV later, when does the poker game start, or what's for dinner? That's it, that's all they care about. Recidivism rate of 83%; no, doesn't shock my anymore: it is what it is.

Monday Mar 10th

Thank God it's Monday! Back to work, the long tedious weekend is over. I can't stress enough how much quicker the weekdays go by; I love Mondays in prison! The chores within the Fire and Safety office keep my co- worker (Dee) and I busy until quitting time at 2:00 p.m. We do computer work, filing, paperwork, and without fail, there's always an extinguisher in one of the dorms or buildings that needs to be replaced, so we get into the truck with Chief R, and do that too.

Crazy weather; the foot of snow we received yesterday is now melting away in this afternoon's 50 degree temperatures. I'd be thrilled if we have indeed, seen the last of old man winter.

Tuesday Mar 11th

My father (who turned 86 today, another moment gone for me) sent an article from the front page of last week's NY Times: all about startling new facts regarding the prison population in America today.

Just released this week is the Pew Center on the States, ranking America the world's #1 incarcerator. I guess that's one thing we outrank China in. Yes, for the first time ever, one out of every 99 adults was in prison at the start of 2008. All told, the 50 states spent more than $49 <u>Billion</u> on corrections last year. The rate of increase for prison costs was 6 times greater than for education spending.

Drill down a little further and the numbers get even more depressing. One in nine black men between the ages of 20 and 34 is behind bars. This is how it looked when the ball dropped ringing in the New Year: 1,596,127 in State and Federal prisons, 723,131 in local jails.

Wednesday Mar 12th

Mid- week already! I can't tell you how much faster the weekdays fly by when you have a prison job to go to, or program to attend. Before you know it Wednesday night is staring you in the face, & the ladder two days are all downhill. As I've mentioned the weekends feel like they will never end.

The fact that it's winter and really been too cold to spend outdoors explains a little of it, but for me what is so aggravating is being stuck in the dorm and having no choice but to listen and endure the truly moronic chatter. The endless war stories, guys proud and boasting about their various crimes. They don't give a minutes thought to look back on what led them here, the majority simply make a promise to not get caught next time. Here is a refrain I just overheard, "Shit man, no mother fucking undercover cop is going to bust my ass again, that's some official shit there son." "I'll cap his ass!"

And as much as I attempt to bury myself in a book, there is no escaping.

Thursday Mar 13th

There are all sorts of ways to find yourself on the receiving end of a ticket; surely one of the strangest occurred in the dorm the other day. An older- about 60- Spanish inmate decided to wander over to the window and feed one of the squirrels peering through the bars, who occasionally surface, begging for food. On his best day this Spanish guy is clueless, constantly walking around in a daze along with the most annoying habit of coming to a complete stop, smack in the middle of the doorway, so as to light his cigarette.

Anyway, cracker in hand, he gestures to the squirrel who must have a grudge against prisoners; because not only does he grab the cracker, but before he runs away, the squirrel takes a bite out of the guy's finger. A bite big enough that he requires medical attention, which also means paperwork and an explanation to the officer on duty.

Well, one thing leads to another and the idiot is issued a ticket for feeding the animals. He went to his hearing yesterday and the Lieutenant hits him with a Tier 2: fourteen days loss of rec., Commissary privileges, and phone usage. Ouch, literally and figuratively.

Friday Mar 14th

I mentioned briefly the other day that I was missing my father's 86th birthday, which occurred three days ago. No matter how hard I try to insulate my mind from drifting home, back to the real world; I can't help but take pause when my dad is blessed enough to reach the age of eighty- six, a joyous celebration by any means, and his youngest son is behind bars. Sad no matter how you look at it, so I try not to, but I fail badly. I think of my parents and the sorrow I have inflicted on them. On end do I think of that. No parent, at any age, should have to endure the sight of their son being led away in handcuffs. Sadly mine have. I long to sit with them and just talk, no not in a crowded prison visitors rooms, or over a phone that is probably being monitored; but in person, their son sitting in front of them so we can catch up on not only the last 9 months, but everything else I've wanted to share.

I talk about the importance of 'staying in the now,' well THIS is a prime example of why I do, or at least try to. It is so damn painful to look back and I don't want to be punished and longer! To transport my brain outside these walls hurts, it takes a toll, one that has already worn me down enough. It's all a gigantic Catch- 22.

Saturday-Sunday Mar 15-16th

When going to the mess hall you're not allowed to having anything in your pockets except your I.D., and if you choose to smoke, cigarettes and a lighter. Sounds easy enough, right? Well actually, places like the mess hall and church are the most convenient spots to "pass off" contraband. There aren't many opportunities available to hook up with your home boys, so those venues are it. Movements are strictly watched, no stopping on the walkways, and certainly no passing along any material from one inmate to another. Get caught doing so and it's labeled an "illegal exchange," you're probably going to the box.

So when you go to chow it's one of your few chances to pass along stamps, betting slips, notes, or perhaps even drugs. If I know this, you can be the Administration knows it as well; therefore on occasion they will place guards at the entrance, ready to order you up against the wall so as to begin a frisk. Do they choose guys at random? No way, it's profiling at its best. They know who the bad apples are, the schemers, the dealers. You can get frisked coming in, or going out. In addition to the potential of sharing box time, or a ticket if caught smuggling contraband, it's also humiliating to be up against the wall, spread eagle, getting verbally abused. "You suck convict, ya know that," as everyone watches and mutters, "better you than me."

It's not as bad at church services, but you can tell the handful of guys who are there for the back row....... eyes darting, stamps either being collected or passed off, exchanged for cigarettes, even eggs. Yes, eggs going back and forth (remember, eggs are only allowed in the honor dorm, and are only available for purchase by guys in the honor dorm) in the middle of church. Only in prison.

Monday Mar 17th

When I was working on Wall Street, without fail, I always made it a point to break away for a few hours, jump on the subway, and head to Mid- town so I could catch some of the St. Patrick's Day Parade. Today, however, I am about as far removed from that celebration as a person could be. I am dressed in my 'state greens' though. Instead of watching marchers head down 5th Avenue, I'm watching murderers and child molesters stroll to their court ordered sex offender class.

In spite of having nine months of prison under my belt, I still at times catch myself; for a split second or two I actually think perhaps this is all a bad dream, a brief "am I really here?" moment. As you can probably guess I had one today. My heart and mind were back on 5th Avenue, unfortunately the rest of me was right here.

Tuesday Mar 18th

Spring is only two days away but you'd never know it here, as snow flurries are predicted for tonight. Still no word from Albany regarding work release, yes I know they've only had my application ten days now, but that doesn't prevent me from racing towards the mail each day. Not easy to block the emotions and expectations form my mind.

Yesterday I learned that my first "Bunkie," here at Mohawk, was sent to the box for failing a urine test. When you come into a new dorm you initially share a 7 by 7 cube, and sleep in a bunk bed. My first 6 weeks was on the top bunk and "Rome" was on the bottom. He's a nice, quiet guy, Jamaican. We got along well, he loved to talk about his three-year-old son, how much he missed him and how he couldn't wait to be with him again. I wasn't aware he liked to smoke dope as much as he apparently did, but somehow the Administration learned of it, called him in for a piss test, which he flunked. Hence an immediate trip to the box. Doing drugs is a serious offense here, Rome could possibly even acquire a new charge. He'll be in the box at least 90 days. All I can think about is his son, now potentially missing his dad perhaps even longer.

Wednesday Mar 19th

Just not up for writing today.

Thursday Mar 20th

At Holy Thursday services this evening, I saw my friend James (serving a 7 year sentence for robbery at the Waldorf- Astoria Hotel, NYC) as I often do at church. Like me, he's one of those guys you just look at and immediately say "what the hell is he doing here?" That's not to say we don't belong at Mohawk for what we did, we do, but simply that we look severely out of place. James had completed about half his sentence, scotch free from any tickets... until today! He received a Tier 1, which means he'll lose Rec. privileges for 13 days, as well as commissary and packages.

Okay, so what awful deed occurred to warrant such action? James dropped a tissue and failed to pick it up. He claims that when he pulled his knit hat out of his jacket the tissue came out along with the hat; and fell to the ground. The C.O. who for some particular reason has a major problem with James, didn't see it that way. He stated he dropped the tissue deliberately. I believe James 100%. Guess whose side the Lieutenant took; yeah, that's right, the officer. That's all it takes is one uptight officer with a grudge, who for no legitimate reason other than he doesn't like the way you look, wear your hair, or perhaps he had a fight with his wife the night before. It comes down to his word verses yours. An argument, unfortunately, he's going to win every time!

Friday Mar 21st

It's Good Friday, one of the holiest days for Catholics, of which I am one. We're lucky to have a devoted, long serving Deacon here. All of this Holy Week there have been services, most just simple opportunities to walk in the chapel door, and for an hour or two escape from this negative, miserable place. I believe this is the absolute extent of all the peace and solitude one is capable of receiving here.

The Catholic contingent is small; on average you won't see more than 30 of us at any given mass. As I left the dorm at 1:00 p.m. for the Passion Service, I couldn't help but look around: guys sound asleep, some gambling at cards, the others watching and cursing the latest "gangsta" movie. I want to scream out at their recalcitrant behavior. Yes, prison sucks, and I know I'm far from perfect, but this is your chance to at least try and rehabilitate yourself, make some sort of effort so that at the end of the day, before you place your head on the wafer- thin pillow, you at least feel like you made an attempt to improve yourself. C'mon man, you have to at least try.

Saturday-Sunday Mar 22nd-23rd

Now that I'm officially into month number ten, I was going over the numerous run of the mill, everyday, you never used to give a second thought about activities, that I so dearly miss. Yeah, the same ones I will never take for granted again. Never. Here are just a few, in no particular order.

My hands haven't touched one single coin or dollar bill, and I have yet to misplace my car keys for ten months. The only pair of pants I've worn are state- issued green polyester specials, boy do I miss my favorite pair of khakis. I would kill for a fresh cup of coffee, & for a latte or cappuccino I'd kill twice. My own bed and pillow, ugh, don't get me started. How about a steak, mashed potatoes, salad and a beer. Pulling up to the gas pump, geez what are gas prices these days? I miss taking a shower by myself (without having to wear shower shoes) and having a door to close when I go to the bathroom. Boy, will I feel human again when I sit down at the dinner table with more than eight minutes to eat. Go on a walk or run without being surrounded by fences or guard towers. It'll be really nice when I can walk up to my TV, change the channel and not be afraid that a chair is going to come crashing down over my head; yeah, that will be a good feeling. Or better yet, fall asleep without having to worry whether some psychopath decides to smother you with his pillow because he felt you looked at him funny earlier in the day.

Above all else however, what I have missed the most these past 10 months is being with my two sons. Just to simply watch and be with them, listen as they talk about their day, see them smile.

Yes, those 'daily chores' that you don't think twice about. Well trust me; I will never take them for granted again.

Monday Mar 24th

On the menu for dinner this evening were chicken legs, each inmate got two of them. Actually they weren't too bad. As Jon and I were eating he blurted out a few statements that really sent our minds reeling about the enormous size of the NY State prison population. "Jerry do you realize 70,000 chickens gave their lives for the inmates of NY to eat tonight." The scope of his question got me thinking. You see, there are 70 state prisons throughout New York, with approximately 1000 inmates in each. Being as quick in math as I am, this equals to 70,000 inmates that need to be fed 3 meals a day. Like I said, Jon and I had fun with the sheer size of the numbers. Here they are.

We get 12 slices of bread daily (4 with each meal), which would bring the total slices per day to a mind- numbing 840,000 pieces of bread doled out each and every day. I needed to break out the calculator to figure the weekly total.

In case you were wondering. Some more fun facts about a typical day within the NY State prison system:

- 140,000 4 oz. containers of milk consumed per day
- 420,000 pads of butter used per day
- 420,000 utensils that need to be washed each day
- 210,000 napkins handed out each day

I could go on & on, but you get the picture. Prison is big business, a big expensive business; the numbers are staggering! And if the taxpayers could see some of the waste; well let's just say I'm afraid to write about it until I'm safe at home. Stay tuned.

Tuesday Mar 25th

Still no word from Albany regarding my work release appeal. With each passing day however I know I'm getting closer to an answer. When the C.O. yells out "mail" each week day at 3:00 p.m., I delicately tread towards his desk, my stomach in a ball of knots, hoping for the best and expecting the worst.

When it does finally arrive I have already planned out my course of action. I want to be alone- as "alone" as you can possibly be here- in my cube. I will be stoic with either decision, although if I were truly alone, and the answer is no, I'd probably break down, a total mess. But you can't do that, no show of weakness allowed. And if the appeal is successful, I will not shout or jump up and down, but I can promise you a smile not witnessed since my first son was born... a smile from ear to ear. A smile that says "I'm a step closer to coming home."

Wednesday-Thursday Mar 26-27th

As of today there is one less psychopath residing at Mohawk!! Yes that's right, Ollie received word early this morning he is being transferred to Marcy C.F. so he can undertake his court ordered, 6 months Alcohol Substance Abuse Treatment (ASAT) program. When that call comes in (11:15 a.m.) you immediately pack your bags, everything must go, and bring it all down to the Draft building where it gets tagged and then loaded on the bus. Ollie, the psycho, will be out of my hair forever; I can now sleep with both eyes closed.

Tonight on the 6:00 movement he will carry his mattress over to the Reception dorm where he will spend his final evening at Mohawk. Good Riddance! As Ollie was packing his meager belongings (state issued clothes from head to toe, I guess that "huge package" never arrived) he leaned over towards me, eyes bugging, "maybe I'll be seeing you again Mr. Jerry." "Yes, maybe," I replied, knowing full well once I leave here I will never set foot in prison again. They say death and taxes are the only sure things in life, well let me add one more to that duo...... Ollie returning to prison at some point to being serving yet another bid; good 'ol number 5.

I will say though, Ollie was the source of much comic relief for Jon and I. Between our devising ingenious methods (the "Ollie Shuffle") to avoid his joining us for meal, to the laughs we got observing him sleep all day with his hat pulled below the eyes, wads of tissue paper stuffed into his nostrils, it was all quite amusing.

So while I won't go as far to say he'll be missed, I will say he had been one of the more interesting characters I've come across during my stay. But I do think Ollie represents a snap- shot view of how the recidivism rate holds steady at 83%. He's not being rehabilitated, not in the least, hence his 4th trip to prison. And he's only 32! The system is broken, and yes he bears much of the blame, and no, I don't know what the answer is, but it's certainly failed him, and I'm convinced will continue to do so.

Friday Mar 28th

No sooner was Ollie out the door, than another inmate come marching in, bags, mattress, and attitude. As my boss Chief R said one day, "Ah, job security, it's a beautiful thing; fresh product comes through those gates every day." While it may sound mean- spirited and a little heartless, the fact remains, it's true.

America ranks as the number 1 incarcerator in the world; one out of every 99 adults found themselves in prison at the start of 2008. Those are stop -you- in- your- tracks numbers, the chief is 100% right, he might not have the best job, but it's damn secure!

It's Friday so you know what that means, another week down. I've said it before and I'll say it again; the weekdays are over before you know it, while the weekends are akin to watching grass grow. This Saturday will be a welcome one however, my parents, along with brother's Joe and Jack are arriving for a visit. God willing it will be their final trip to Mohawk. As you can imagine, I can't wait to walk in the Visitor's Room and see their loving and familiar faces.

Saturday-Sunday Mar 29-30th

Earlier this Saturday morning (10:00) I had what I hope will be my final visit at Mohawk. Perhaps Eileen will make the journey once more, but other than her, God willing it's a wrap. My parents along with brothers Joe and Jack arrived in Rome, NY last evening, spent the night at the local hotel, and thankfully the mob scene which is the visitors room, never fully materialized. Don't get me wrong, it was still loud, but I've seen the place a whole lot worse.

Anyway, back to the visit; it was all the usual cadre of emotions. Even after close to ten months these visits are fraught with anxiety, sadness, and at least one bout with tears. My elegant Mother and Father sitting amongst this collection of inmates; talk about your, 'What's wrong with this picture moment.' Now I don't know how much longer I will remain here, but I do know I don't want to subject them to this experience any longer. And not for a minute is this about me, but for them I feel such a wave of remorse and emptiness when those chairs are pushed back and the final hugs and kisses begin. From there we head towards our respective exits; theirs leading to the outside world, freedom and reality. While my door leads me back into this awful nightmare.

Sunday brought sunny skies, however the temperatures remain cold. But we're getting there; forecast for the week brings a day or two of fifty degree weather. I know this change will do wonders for my outlook and psyche. To get back to where I can run again; to borrow a lyric from an old Beatles song, "....little darling, it's been a long cold, lonely winter."

Monday Mar 31st

I almost always complete my writing following my afternoon program. Upon returning to the dorm, (at 2:45 p.m.) I have three solid hours to record the day's events and my impressions towards them. This morning (currently 6:00 a.m.) however, with the dorm mostly silent (a few early risers sitting in their cubes, having coffee) I decided to share before going off to breakfast (6:30) and then work at 8:00 a.m.

I awake around 5:30, morning prayers are soon to follow. I head over to the community hot- pot and make instant coffee. Back to the cube where I put the head phones on and listen to the local news, one of the only 3 stations that come in clearly enough; the others being a Country- Western station, along with the BBN, which stands for Bible Broadcasting Network.

I think about my two sons who will soon be waking up back home, it's now going on ten months since last I saw them. As I sip coffee in the dark, I reflect on our separation; I can't help but think of the countless memories I could have partaken in these past months, now lost to me forever. Unlike the majority of my fellow inmates, statistically speaking 83% of them, I know that I will never return here. I think the pain of another period of time away from Brooks and Philip would be too much for me to bear; I don't believe I could overcome another round in prison. This applies to the entire family of course, especially mom and dad whom I will refuse to ever let down again. They've all witnessed my sinking to the very bottom, I so want them to absorb and witness every day of my rising back to the surface. I hate this place!

April

Tuesday Apr 1st

The first day of the new month. Ahh, to an inmate "another month down" are three of the most magical words you could utter. Yes, yes I know, live each day to its fullest and don't wish your life away. Right, I am totally on board with that, and after ten months so far in here, truer words have never been spoken. But while here, I do indeed wish my current life away....that is, until I am released.

As I have said, the jokers you see laughing and having the time of their lives (and there are many) they are the habitual returnees, who view being locked up as simply a way of life, or just the cost of doing business. They don't come back here to better themselves or rehabilitate, but rather to hook up with 'ol familiar faces, play a little basketball, scam a few dudes here and there, then go home and lock up a corner.

So when I hear that sweet, welcome sound of a page being torn from my calendar, well to me it means I am that much closer to getting out of this depressing, menacing, and negative hell hole.

Wednesday Apr 2nd

With the arrival of April it means the two outside yards will be open full time, right up until October 1st. I can't describe to you how anxious I am to get out for some air and exercise. I plan on hitting the yard this evening, at 6:00.

It's been a little over two months since last I spoke with Dino. I've gotten used to it, although considering our cubes are directly across from each other; it can at times be uncomfortable. He continues to operate on a different plane than I, always the hidden agenda. With Dino it's all about making moves, pulling fast ones and preying on the weak. I never saw it at first; I was too preoccupied on simply trying to survive. Dino was only too happy to take me under his wing. But he miscalculated, he mistook my kindness for weakness (I was more than generous towards him with the food packages Eileen would send). And yes, while I am angry, I pity him more than anything. Being locked up for over 13 years (and counting) absolutely must do things to your mind. I mean just imagine all the moments that have taken place in your life the past few years; now try to imagine taking every one of them away, experiencing nothing other than a cell and the harshness of prison for thirteen years. I'm well rid of someone like Dino, whom I have not witnessed pursue a single ounce of rehabilitation in the past eight months.

Still no word on work release from Albany, has to be any day now. In the meantime my stomach (mail is about to be handed out) is experiencing the pangs and knots that arrive everyday at this time. Hmm, no way that can be good for my system.

Thursday Apr 3rd

The warm spring weather seems to be bringing out the Mohawk psychopath's. A few nights ago in the dorm next to mine, an inmate got up from his chair to change the TV channel which was set to the black sit- com, Bernie Mac. Unknown to him it happened to be another guy's favorite show. Cooly and calmly the psycho then heads over to his locker where he has hidden a weapon, a shank. He walks back in the TV room where he proceeds to stab the poor slob who changed the channel.

efore you know it, the C.O.'s are all over the place; two inmates lying on the floor in a pool of blood, one from a homemade knife, the other a result of the officer's nightsticks.

So what do you think the inmates in the dorm were upset about; that someone was badly hurt, that violence and ugliness stared them right in the face? No, not quite, but rather that they had to all return to their cubes, the dorm and TV shut down for the rest of the night.

Friday Apr 4th

Time for those magic words again…… "Another week down." The lack of any word from Albany regarding work release has begun to weigh heavy. It hit me especially hard yesterday, I couldn't tell you why all of a sudden (well it was right after another mail handout with no letter from Albany) I felt an urgent need to call my parents, hear the safety in their voices. Nor could I explain why for the first time in weeks I broke down in tears.

Wait a minute, what am I talking about, of course I KNOW why: I hate this place, I hate everything it represents, and I ache for the day I walk out these gates to reclaim my life. THAT'S why I cried and why I felt the anxiety and tension were going to smother me yesterday. I'm down on myself for doing so, but breakdowns happen and I thank God for the strength He's given me, otherwise it would happen every day.

Saturday-Sunday Apr 5-6th

Every waking minute I'm reminded of the difference between my former life and the one I am currently experiencing. On occasion however, there will be particular moments that especially drive this point home; today at lunch for example.

Back when I was working on Wall Street I would share lunch with bankers from Ivy League schools, mathematic PHDs disguised as traders who would quant this or macro that, everyone with their slicked back hair, Brooks Brothers shirts and Hermes ties.

In the mess hall today however, I sat with Jon, the only other normal man I've met here who is in the middle of his six year sentence for robbery. We were joined by 'Goodwilly' a white 27 year old, baby faced, slightly pudgy teddy-bearish type, who already has five children with three different women. Unfortunately the last woman was only 13, hence he is serving a 4 year rape sentence. Also at our table was 'Mikey-Kids,' the dude who used to live in my dorm who molested his 12 year old nieces. Rounding out the table was James, (aka, Jimmy Waldorf) whose company I enjoy very much. James is also about half- way finished his sentence of seven years for burglary at the Waldorf- Astoria Hotel in NYC. As I took a second to look around the table, observing and listening to my 'new prison friends,' for some reason this moment just struck me with a "wow, I'm not in Kansas anymore" realization.

Of course I accept that I'm here, geez you would hope so after close to ten months. I get through the day keeping my head lowered, staying as far under the radar as possible, and yes understanding that I am surrounded by people I never would have come across during my life otherwise.

But every now and then I am jolted, I have to pause, everything going on around me stops and I don't hear a word being spoken. It only lasts a few seconds (seems like hours though) this blackout, before I snap back to attention and digest the reality of where I am. The days of Wall Street lunches are nothing but a distant memory now, eating with a degenerate like 'Goodwilly' is my current world.

Monday April 7th

Yesterday's warm weather brought a case of 'Spring Fever' to one particular inmate in my dorm. I'm embarrassed to say I don't even know his name, but really that's not so unusual. Obviously I've seen him around but with never an occasion or reason to speak. Remember, no one is here to make new friends, but simply to complete our time and get the fuck out.

So with the sun shining and temperatures in the 60's, this guy decided it would be a nicer plan to skip his mandatory afternoon job, and instead sit out in the yard with a blanket and a good book. Playing hooky so to speak, what the hell, people do it out in the real world. Well sure enough, about an hour into "his plan" the C.O.'s came looking for him. I happened to be nearby, the exchange went like this:

C.O.: What the fuck do you think you're doing, you're supposed to be at work.
Inmate: I don't feel like it man, it's too nice out.
C.O.: Fine, you don't want to work?
Inmate: That's right man.
C.O.: No problem, stand up and turn around.
C.O. I said stand up!

Inmate: Quit hassling me son.
C.O.: You got five seconds to stand up.

Well, sure enough, the inmate gets up off the blanket, puts his hands behind his back as ordered, & is cuffed. His case of spring fever earned him two weeks in the box. In prison, there is no such thing as playing hooky.

Tuesday Apr 8th

It can only be a matter of days until I receive word from Albany regarding work release. I mean it has to be. Or does it? It's just about all I think of, and trust me, as hard I try to block the 800 pound elephant, it's simply not possible. As I've said before, this isn't just any 'ol letter, this is my freedom, my (literally) get- out- of- jail- card.

Earlier this afternoon (3:15 p.m.) when our dorm officer screamed out "mail call," I put down my pen (was writing a letter), said a quick prayer, and gingerly walked over to find out if this would be the day I learn of my fate. Quickly I discovered it would not be the day. For a few minutes the anxiety level subsided; it will be a short hiatus though, because all I have to do is look around at my surroundings which instantly reaffirms how much I despise this place. Not long after I will begin to hope and pray that tomorrow's mall will bring news of the first day of the rest of my life.

Wednesday Apr 9th

The dorm has had more turnover than usual the past couple of weeks; why I don't know, it just seems to be happening. A couple of guys were sent to the box (a.k.a. Special Housing Unit) and once that happens your cube and locker are immediately cleared out, you're gone. We've had a few go off to begin their ASAT program, which means you pack up and move to the 22 Building, otherwise known as the "projects." It's a six month program and the chances are slim that you'll return to this

(74- D) dorm upon completion. And the best scenario of all: two guys have finished their sentences and headed for home.

Wanna know the one constant in each and every of these moves? No sooner has a bed become vacant, than there is "new product" (as my boss, Chief R refers to new prisoners) ready to walk through the doors. I have literally yet to see a lone, empty bed, in this dorm for more than a few hours. It's like they're waiting in the woodwork, or right outside the door, mattress and pillow in hand just ready to come on down. Fresh product indeed.

Thursday Apr 10th

While I still await word regarding work release, I did learn from my counselor that I have been approved for outside clearance. Hmmm, perhaps it portends more good news on the horizon. Gaining outside clearance is definitely a positive; I'm told it's rare to receive it on the initial go- around as I did, and the number of inmates granted this are beyond miniscule.

Okay, what does it all mean? Well basically that I can go outside the gates (escorted of course) if my job requires, which it does from time to time. Before all that however, I have to get a new I.D. and fill out reams of paperwork. Hey, not a problem, whatever it takes.

When I finally do step out into the real world after nearly ten months, it's no doubt going to be an odd, but exhilarating sensation. Can you imagine what it will feel like when I really have my freedom again? No, unless you've been locked up, or are a former POW, you simply can't fathom the experience. Consider yourself lucky.

Friday Apr 11th

As the cold and flu season draws to a close, I think the Lord that I have not once been sick the past ten months. Considering where I have ventured it is nothing short of a miracle. I look back at my first few days at Rikers, especially the initial 24 hours: being moved from holding cell to holding cell, one dirtier than the next. I slept on the floor that first night, the cells filled to capacity, no room on the wooden benches. I drifted in and out of consciousness, I remember being jolted awake by the crawling of, what turned out to be, a cockroach on my arm. Each room was a place of degradation, despair, germs, and abasement. A cacophony of hacking coughs, guys spitting and flicking their snot on the brick walls. I thought for sure it was only a matter of time until their sickly germs infected me, how could I possibly elude all the filth I was surrounded by? I remember washing my clothes in a bucket or the sink, then rinsing them out in the shower room. Never got sick though.

When I was eventually moved into a dorm at Rikers it only got worse- now I was living with 50 germ carriers instead of the 20 in the cells. Getting outdoors to take in in fresh air was limited to one hour a day, so that wasn't going to help much. There was no escape so I had resigned myself to being infected, I could only hope to limit the number of eventual visits to sick call. Try to imagine the collection of disease covering and surrounding the four toilet stalls and four showers, God only knows when they were cleaned last.

But as I said, here I am ten months removed from those dreadful days, with not even a case of the sniffles. A miracle? Well, maybe not quite, but close to it.

Saturday-Sunday Apr 12-13th

Another dreaded weekend. Monday through Friday I'm kept occupied with my job at fire & safety. You stretch your imagination hard enough and it almost feels like heading off to work back in the real world. The reality of being in prison isn't quite as impacted on the weekdays, because I'm busy, it's only on the weekends where even the most vivid of imaginations can't take you away from here.

Saturdays used to mean going to my son's Little League games, a trip to Starbucks, mowing the lawn, raking leaves, spending money at Home Depot, or perhaps taking in a movie. Now it means cleaning my seven by seven cube, receiving a new cheap razor, toothpaste, toilet paper, and envelopes to last me the week. The weekends hit you hard; while I'm always aware of the beautiful moments lost to me back home, saturdays, more than any other, are the most heartbreaking. No matter how hard I try to allow the tendrils of my mind to 'take me someplace else,' I can't seem to gather enough trickery to pull it off. There is no escaping on a weekend.

Monday Apr 14th

Everyone has their own way of dealing with the amount of time left on their sentence. I've come across a few guys who try to lose track and block out the number of days left; to other inmates who know the exact amount of hours until the day they walk out these gates. I'll never forget the lunatic I met at Down State who was already counting the days until Friday September 13th, 2013, when he'd be released, and was planning to head directly to the bar; where he would proceed "to get fucked up all weekend long" because he didn't have to see his parole officer until Monday. Six years down the road and he could already taste his first drink.

My friend Jon counts down the months he has remaining, but the day he has planned for his release is far different. He said to me this morning at breakfast, "Jerry, 34 months from today I'll be leaving here; I'm planning on surprising my children by picking them up at school." That's what keeps him going, the thought of that day, seeing the look on those faces when he shows up to greet them. He started counting down at 65 months and as of today, only has 34 left.

Tuesday Apr 15th

As I inch closer towards the one year anniversary of my sentencing (6-22-07) I can't help but look back on what was my wretched mental state at the time. Each day was bringing me closer to the fate that awaited me; literally my days were numbered. At this point a year ago I hadn't yet mustered the courage to inform the boys that their Dad was soon headed off to prison; obviously a moment I was dreading.

Zombie- like I would muddle through the day, constantly berating myself for the irresponsible actions and the procession of poor choices which led me to this point. I did my best to tie up the loose ends- paying down bills, cancel subscriptions, disconnect cable and phone services- and hold on long enough during the day, until an appropriate time to throw back my first cocktail. Funny, each day that cocktail hour seemed to arrive earlier and earlier.

Beyond all this finality however, I simply wanted to spend every available second with Brooks and Philip. Clinically I could probably have been diagnosed with a mild case of shock or a severe case of depression. I would catch myself staring off somewhere, dazed, in a trance. The tears would begin to fall, I was helpless to stop them. They were such wasted months, what I was doing certainly wasn't living, the best part of the day was turning out the light, putting my head on the pillow; only then I could escape, for a few hours at least, the sadness of my life. Looking back, I wish sometimes I had just pled guilty at my arraignment and gotten this damm thing over with. Would have saved my family a lot of money in legal fees, thats for sure.

And all I can say now is, what a difference a year makes........even here, in spite of all this, I love my life, I am truly blessed. I can't wait to start over.

Wednesday Apr 16th

In fear of sounding (too much) like a broken record, yet another day without word from Albany. It will be six weeks tomorrow my appeal was sent to the NY State Temporary Release Committee. You begin to get the feeling they've forgotten about me, that I've officially fallen through the cracks. Perhaps it was a clerical error, never to be rectified. My fate has been sealed. It's just so damn easy to let your mind get away from you. I repeat: staying mentally strong is the most important key to survival!

So I will head my own advice, put aside today's lack of news and continue to hope and pray that perhaps tomorrow these nerves will finally be calmed. Remember; I can handle them telling me no (after a few tears that is), the agony comes from the not knowing, this state of limbo I find myself in. Please Lord, let all this waiting be worth it.

Thursday Apr 17th

A friend asked me in a letter recently what (if any) my favorite point of the day was. It's an easy answer: 10:00 p.m., each and every day, when the lights go dark. The first true silence of the day takes over the dorm, I flip on my reading lamp in order to read for about 30 more minutes, then prepare clothes along with my coffee, for early the next morning. In addition I'll say prayers, then comes the best part: the realization I have completed another day of my sentence, one they can't get back. I am now a step closer towards coming home. The bed and pillow welcome me and aid me in escaping from this place for the next seven hours.

Friday Apr 18th

Early next week (Tuesday 22nd) will mark month number ten. As the months continue to pile up (along with the moments back home lost) I look at the milestone of time, and must admit, in spite of many, many hardships, it's moved along rapidly. How far removed from those early days at Rikers I now am. The top job in the facility is mine, I live in the best cube in the best dorm, and I possess an ever so thin degree of seniority, with hopefully a smidge of respect from the very few people here who "get" what it's all about.

However, there is one threshold, no matter how much time elapses, that can't be assuaged. This would be the......I surrender to my surroundings, emotionally the heart can't take any more pain every three week breakdown........threshold. Yup, seems every 3 weeks I melt down. Like clockwork. It happened last evening, as I was at first talking with Brooks and Philip, followed by a call with my parents. Whatever the "it" is, it hit me: all of a sudden I began to cry, no matter how hard I fought, the realization of where I am (and have been for ten months), the mystery of when I might ever be leaving, plus the constant shame and sorrow associated with my being here in the first place, took hold.

But I must shrug all that aside, I must, it's vital. And I will; for twenty- one days, at least, until that trigger returns again, and I'll have to "let it all out" once more.

Saturday-Sunday Apr 19-20th

It seems like just weeks ago I was lamenting about "the long cold lonely winter." Now all of a sudden we're in our 5th straight day of 80 degree weather. Not complaining mind you, the sunshine feels terrific, along with getting out to the yard for fresh air and exercise

I notice however there are about ten inmates from the dorm who never set foot out to the yard, no matter how beautiful the day. Silently (and sadly) I refer to them as "the surrender's." Exercise and fresh air is of no import to them; lying on their beds staring at the ceiling is their more desirable option.

Willie P., behind the walls for 30 years now is one of them. With that amount of time served I would not begin to try and comprehend what kind of mental state he is in. It's been an especially difficult week for Willie; he went before the parole board with the chance of gaining his release, but was denied. He got "hit" for another two years, at which time he'll be eligible to apply again. His original sentence was 25-to life, but after the 25 is served, he's eligible for parole, but once again was struck down, I think for the 6th time he's been denied now.

I can somewhat understand and certainly sympathize with his surrender, but the other dudes who seem to have thrown in the towel, I cannot. I want to shake them, screaming "don't give up hope, you can do this." But of course that will never happen, not my place to do so nor my business. Each man really is an island here, no matter how much love and support you have 'out there.' The life boat off this island is maintaining a strong frame of mind, the most important tool we possess.

Monday Apr 21st

Jon and I took full advantage of yesterday's beautiful weather and walked five miles on the track. We had a chance to cover a variety of subjects; one of them being his constant reminder: "Jerry, right now you are living in a place literally like no other." What prompted this was my telling Jon how I had participated in a Racquetball game the previous day and one of the guys I played against questioned a call I made on an out ball, twice. He is competitive and so am I, but I knew I was right, so the situation got a bit heated. When the game was over I went for a walk to clear my head and thought, "What the heck did I put myself in that position for?" Playing with 3 other career criminals, all hot- headed, with no regard for the slightest code of conduct. Shit, guys get stabbed over things like that. Yes, I'm doing my time, but in an entirely different fashion, I'm not here to engage in prison games, laugh and have fun. Geez, what the hell was I thinking.

During my ten months I've taken pride in avoiding being snared into the prison culture, the prison way of thinking. And here I was mixing it up in the yard, concerning myself with a psycho on the paddle court.

Jon with three years under his belt was quick to see the situation clearly. I'm still learning he told me, "These aren't normal people here, you're not at the Country Club playing with Skippy, there is no honor among thieves. Avoid situations, keep to yourself, remember; you're just passing through, most of these dudes are here for a long time!"

Tuesday Apr 22nd

I've been taking full advantage of both this continued perfect weather and the reopening of the Rec. yards. This past Sunday, making the most of my 3 yard visits, I speed-walked and ran, a total of 11 miles. Needless to say I had no trouble falling asleep come lights out time (10:00 p.m.).

On the weekdays I work a morning and afternoon shift, so the only available exercise time is from 6:00- 9:00 p.m., with an early go- back option at 8:00 p.m, which I usually take advantage of so I can prepare for the remainder of the night (shower/shave) along with getting ready for the morning. You see the key is to get the jump start in the early morning, to avoid the mad rush for the five sinks used by 39 inmates. Dudes spitting, gargling, picking their noses, well it's a sight I don't need to see (or hear) first thing. Call it the "early bird gets the clean sink."

Oh, and I can't forget the hot- pot for instant coffee; dilly- dally too long and you'll find this thing as dry as the Sahara. The rule is: the last person to use it before it goes empty is expected to refill the darn thing. Well, as you can imagine, in a place like this, rules are made to be broken. The pot takes about 20 minutes to heat up, an awfully long time in the morning; therefore another incentive to be an early riser.

P.S.....Ten months ago today I was sentenced.

Wednesday-Thursday Apr 23rd-24th

The gritty, hard-edged reality that is prison reared its ugly head earlier this evening. A young black man (from my dorm) was beaten silly out in the yard. Let me try to explain why. He sleeps two cubes away from me, but I'm embarrassed to say I didn't even know his name; he was relatively new to the house. That's the way it is, new guys don't count for much the first few weeks when they enter the dorm.

About 15 minutes before the 6:00 p.m. movement out to the yard, I noticed an anguished look on his face as he spoke with his bunkmate. I then overheard this exchange, "Hey man, I have no choice. I have to go out, either these dudes are going to get me, or the guys in the gang will." He then began to return cassette tapes and books he had borrowed from some other guys. I realized what was happening. He knew he was walking into a fight, and no matter what the outcome, he would never be coming back to this dorm. Apparently he had "disrespected" some loser from another gang, and was now being called out. If he had chosen to turn the other cheek (the sensible move) his fellow gang members would have thought him a coward and settled this matter with their own twisted prison logic, by slashing him across the face!

So off to the yard he went. There is a tiny restroom off to the side, a brick building with two sinks and one stall. To avoid the guard in the watch- tower, plus the other C.O.'s walking around, this is where fights takes place. Sure enough about an hour into the Rec. period, this all went down. While I was indeed out there (running on the track) I witnessed none of it. However one inmate who was present described the outcome in his own eloquent style, "Yeah son, this nigger got his shit busted wide open, mad crazy blood all over the place."

So that's how it ended, a stupid mindless act of brutal violence, concluded the "prison way." On top of getting badly hurt, this guy is now in the box for at least sixty days. His locker had been emptied, his name crossed off the board an hour after this all occurred. Just like that, he's gone.

The sad thing is; I believe he didn't want to fight. Observing what little I did of him, I noticed he was quiet, kept to himself, and seemed happy in 74- D. I overheard him talk proudly of his hard- working mother and preacher father. If I had known him better I would have tried to talk him out of this end game. In his mind though there was no way out, get slashed at the hands of your own gang members, or go into battle merely to save face. That's prison. That sucks.

Friday Apr 25th

A trip to the mess hall is always an adventure, and occasionally the source of a few laughs; sometimes you just have to find the humor out of a prison moment. The inmates who work in the kitchen are 99% black. Okay fine, no problem with that. The amusing part (although some guys don't find the amusement) is when the white boys like Jon and I present our trays for filling; the portions we receive are at least half as much as the black guys. We always get the crusty end slices of pizza, the last dregs of a bowl of rice, and the over- ripe, bad looking fruit will come our way too. But don't even think about arguing, these are the meanest collection of dudes in the facility. Give them a hard time and God only knows what you'll find in your food next time around.

Personally, I find it funny- hey it's prison, what are you going to do. Jon's a big eater so he gets pissed off, half our meal is spent with me trying to calm him down. What I have always found so disconcerting are the C.O.'s patrolling the mess hall, watching you eat, pressuring you to finish up quickly (I'd say on average we get between 5- 7 minutes) and head back to the dorm. On your way out, in too for that matter, be prepared to be put up against the wall and frisked.

Someday, soon, I'll get my dignity back. Scenes like this will be a distant memory, a memory (or nightmare) I will never forget.

Saturday-Sunday Apr 26-27th

Cross off another week. Another Saturday morning endured; as I've mentioned numerous times, my least enjoyable hours of the week. Just a short time ago I had to fight off the tears.

I received some very discouraging news in speaking with my lawyer last night. Given that it has now been seven weeks with still no word from Albany regarding my work release appeal, Celia decided to call and see if she could find anything out. Unfortunately what she discovered is that my appeal hasn't even been reviewed yet. Probably just sitting up there in Albany on a desk somewhere, they don't give a shit. And to think, here I was anticipating mail call these past weeks, like a fool running up to the front of the line saying to myself "okay, today has to be the day." Little did I know.

In allowing the window of hope to open a little I have only myself to blame for the sadness I'm experiencing now. I let "hope" take the lead; I was only too happy to jump on its bandwagon. This little thing called reality then got in the way and sent me tumbling back to earth.

There will be no more sprinting for the mail, not for the time being at least. I made the grave error of projecting and hoping, this morning I have paid the price with my tears.

As a result of Celia's call, one thing is now certain: I must see Brooks and Philip. I can't hold out any longer, I am desperate for them. I will call my ex wife tonight, she'll look at their schedules and hopefully they can be here within a weekend or two. While I've never wanted them to possess a memory of visiting their father in prison, tonight as I write these words, my longing to hug them once again trumps all.

Monday Apr 28th

The perfect stretch of weather we had going came to an abrupt halt today; one of which brought rain and sleet. More of the same predicted for the next few days, looks like I won't be making any trips to the yard.

While my work release appeal seems to be on the back burner for the next few weeks at least, today did bring a consolation prize; I was called in to complete my outside clearance paperwork. By the end of the week I'll have a spanking new picture ID, signaling me as one of the privileged few to venture beyond these walls. I believe only 10 or so inmates out of 1000 have this status. So I feel pretty good about that.

Will it aid in the pursuit of work release? Hmm, who knows, but I figure it can't hurt.

Tuesday Apr 29th

I had to laugh following up on what I wrote about the other day regarding the discrepancy in portions for the white inmates versus the black ones. Well this morning for breakfast, coffee cake was on the menu and I must say it's actually (for state food) not bad. So while I was looking forward to a piece, I had prepared myself for a "white- boy slice." "Just watch," I said to Jon as the line snaked closer. Now there happened to be a black inmate in front of me, the server (also black) gave him a nod, grabbed his spatula and proceeded to hack off a piece of cake that could feed the entire offensive line of the NY Giants. Now it was my turn. He took one look at me and presented a slice that could have fit in a thimble! I stood there in shock as he screamed out- NEXT. And that's it, there is nothing you can do. Most of these guys working mess hall have life sentences, it would phase them not in the least if given back talk, to reach over and beat you silly until a guard could pull him off.

So I took my few crumbs and washed them down with a glass of milk. There will be no recourse or sympathy from anyone. Who cares, you're a prisoner, deal with it. As one particular heartless C.O. likes to say, "Hey asshole, you shouldn't have to come to prison."

Wednesday Apr 30th

Almost always the dorms are evenly divided amongst whites, blacks, and Hispanics. Within an inmate or two, there is rarely a majority; until just recently that is. In 74- D (my dorm) there are a total of 38 inmates, and as of last night, 17 of whom are white. I asked Willie P.(in prison since 1978, in this dorm the past six... double murder) if he's ever seen this discrepancy before. "Are you kidding, I feel like I'm at a KKK meeting, I better not see any white robes come out," he said kind of jokingly.

The reason behind the influx of white inmates is that Mohawk now offers a Sexual Offenders Program (SOP) which is predominantly white, 80% as a matter of fact. The "Rape-o's" as they are affectionately called, are now being sent here in greater numbers (isn't that special), hence you begin to see the shift. I mean what do I know, I've only been here a short period, but I will say I've never seen a gap like this either. Right now in this dorm there are eight or nine rapists- all white. Some you could spot right off, others you'd be shocked upon discovering, they look and act so normal. We have one old man, has to be at least 70, to look at him you'd think he was this sweet old grandfather, who wouldn't hurt a flee. Think again. His name is Jack, and Jack is here for committing sodomy against a 12 yr. old boy next door. I kid you not.

May

Thursday May 1st

Another month down! These have become three of my favorite words. Each day in itself is an accomplishment; so in that case you have to view the months as a milestone.

The day brought two new developments. On my way out of the dorm this morning I heard my name being called, "Hey Jerry, wait up." I turned and saw Peter (the diamond thief, serving a 3-9 year sentence) coming out of 75- A, the reception dorm, his mattress slung over his shoulder and carrying 2 draft bags containing all his prison possessions. Peter has only served about a year so far, he can't be going home I thought. "They're sending me to a camp, minimum security," he said. Just like that, a man whom I had come to know, share sentiment and tears with for the past eight months, was moving on, and I had about one minute with which to say goodbye. We hugged and promised to stay in touch, although we probably knew that wasn't ever going to happen.

Primarily because ex- cons, while on parole, aren't allowed to have any contact with each other, but also there are just too many painful memories of why we met, & the sadness associated with it all. Our friendship, solid by prison standards, probably couldn't sustain the real world.

Friday May 2nd

The other development which occurred yesterday was Jon being hired for the fire and safety office, the best job in the facility, and he starts Monday. He had been working at Walsh Hospital (on the grounds here at Mohawk) as a porter, and probably one of the worst jobs. Walsh is maximum security; this means you get frisked entering and leaving. You are not allowed to carry anything in (for fear of distributing to the inmates living at Walsh) or out. If you do, and are caught, it's a one- way ticket to the box.

When an opening became available (currently only Dee and I work at F/S) I mentioned Jon's name to Chief R who wants someone comfortable with computers, smart, and reliable. Oh yeah, Mohawk is just overflowing with guys like that. Luckily for the chief, Jon is the proverbial needle in the haystack.

As I was leaving the office this afternoon I happened to see to DOCS bus unloading. Eight pieces of fresh meat disguised as inmates, hand- cuffed at the wrist, shackled at the ankles. Shaved heads and blank stares, a look I know all too well. Exactly nine months ago today, that was me. God, I will never forget that day, and ya know what: I don't want to.

Saturday-Sunday May 3rd-4th

The weekend brought a return to cold and dreary weather, as if weekends weren't depressing enough around here. Rain or shine however I was determined to get out to the yard at 1:00 p.m. for exercise and fresh air. I head over to the track area and proceed to run- walk- run- walk, etc... I keep moving; physically I am behind the walls, but I place my mind far away. I allow it to wander anywhere that contains happy memories. I latch onto them, relive and savior them, and convince myself they will all return to me someday. For two hours I practice this bit of survival. My eyes are focused straight ahead but I do my best to take in any of the few signs of nature's beauty around- blue sky, birds, green grass. I avoid glancing over at the weight- lifters, their prison macho and stature about the only things they deem important. They could never fathom how I spend my time in the yard, nor I them. Their vision is cloudy and distorted; they have yet to look inside their hearts. I recall a quote from the philosopher Carl Jung, "Who looks outside, dream; who looks inside, awakens." I feel a tinge of sadness for them, nothing more. They are grown men who could certainly improve themselves, make better use of their time here. But they have chosen another path.

This being the first Saturday in May, brings the Kentucky Derby. I managed to pull a few strings (ok, I bought him some candy) with

Willie P. and got this iconic event on the TV for about an hour. The pageantry and the beauty of the race transported me out of Mohawk; just as my time outdoors earlier today did.

Monday May 5th

Monday morning, the beat goes on. I can't stress enough how welcoming the start of each week is. For one, obviously, it's a step closer to getting the hell out of here, and two, the end of a long tedious weekend.

Speaking of weeks, will this (finally) be the one in which I learn of my fate and work release? Of course I hope and pray that's the case, but I have a feeling next week will be the one bearing the long awaited news. Just a hunch I have, based on nothing really.

It was a beautiful sunny spring day, made even better by the Chief having to go to the Dentist this afternoon. That translates to no afternoon work, which then means I head to the yard at 1:00 p.m. to run and walk, and lose my thoughts. I wish you could see that sight, about 400 men in the yard, most lying in the sun, soaking up the rays, basketball being played, weights lifted. Brought to you and paid by the taxpayers of New York. There has to be a better way.

Tuesday May 6th

Here's one tiny example of how blessed I am when it comes to love, faith, and support. As I mentioned a few days ago I've been here at Mohawk for nine months now. Well for the first time in that span, on back to back days, I was shutout in the mail department! Pretty good track record I'd say. After all these many days, nearly close to a year, and only now am I not ripping open an envelope.

That everlasting support has meant so much, carried me along during the numerous and inevitable dark days that creep up on you. Some inmates (many actually) are lucky if they get one letter a month. Once the mail arrives (around 3:30 p.m.) I'll pick it up from the Officer on duty, then head to my cube where I can read in 'privacy.' I make it a point to savior each one, reading them slowly. Certain letters bring a tear or two, it can't be helped. Once I'm finished they don't go far, as I always plan on reading them over again, right before bed.

So tonight I'll pull out an old letter or two, just to fill that void which came my way today. Now if I don't receive any mail tomorrow, then I'll start to worry.

Wednesday May 7th

No matter how strong you aim to be, there's no getting around that some days are harder than others and you have to just take what comes washing over you. Today has been one of those days.

I was feeling so- so and blah throughout the day, only to become more so with the 3:00 p.m. mail call. And while yes, I did receive mail (3 letters) and as much as I loved the ripping into the envelopes, for some reason, I had allowed myself to think, "Okay this is the day I'll hear about work release." Well, I didn't. And today that lack of news hit me right between the eyes. I needed someone to talk to, someone away from here. I usually almost always will dial my parents around 6:00 p.m., but since today was "one of those days," I picked up the phone at 3:15 p.m. When they heard my voice immediately mom and dad thought something was wrong or perhaps even that I had good news to share.

Since being sentenced I've never given my parents reason to fear for me, no matter what might have gone down I keep it positive, I keep it upbeat. So I wasn't going to lose it now, I simply needed to hear the comfort of their voices. We spoke for about 20 minutes, towards the end though I could feel myself about to break when my mom (never have I seen such faith, in anyone) said "Jerry, your strength is our strength." I was on the verge, I had to hang up quickly before I lost it.

So I'll head back to my seven by seven cube, dive into a book and count the hours until the lights go out. Bouncing back is the only option I know. I accept that & will be determined to wake up tomorrow and make it a better day.

Thursday May 8th

I had an active day at fire and safety (fire drills and paper work) which kept my mind "in the now" and away from depression and negative thoughts. Until around 3:00 p.m. that is, the continued saga of still no word on work release. All day I keep waiting for that one moment, that piece of paper which will lead me thorough these gates. Your emotions take over and you begin to conjure all the beauty that awaits you, anywhere but here. And then you discover, as the mail is passed out, the magic letter did not arrive today; all those images dashed, gone, just like that.

Seven more hours to go until lights out at 10:00 p.m.! Thankfully I have Rosary Class from 6- 8, that will help tremendously. I have to pick myself up when I begin to dip, lately those "dips" are becoming all too frequent.

As I've mentioned we have about 8 guys in the dorm serving a sentence for either rape, sodomy, or some other deviant sexual behavior. From age 68 (Jack who sodomized a 12 year old next door neighbor- a boy) to Joey who was sleeping with a 13 year old girl, while he was 21. Well it seems almost every night, starting around 8:00, serious harassment of these dudes starts up. No holes barred, some of the hard core inmates bring it. Now I don't condone what these 8 did, but I also don't sign off on the abuse that comes their way. To witness grown men being humiliated and tormented on an almost nightly basis, well, I hate to see it. The look of sorrow, loneliness, and shame on their faces. Yes they've committed a terrible crime, and now they are here paying for it, leave them be. Considering, the C.O.'s look the other way, almost giving the abuse a green light, means that the ridicule won't go away anytime soon.

Friday May 9th

A very special "moment" is occurring today, another one of those I am obviously missing out on and one I will never get back. My mother turns 82 today! As I sit in this depressing prison all I can think of are birthdays past, my loving family gathered for the occasion; hugs, laughs, tears of joy to celebrate Mom. I dwell on the guilt I'm feeling, the sadness I've caused my parents. As if my mom deserves the pain she no doubt is experiencing, her youngest son now almost having been locked up for eleven months. She would lay down her life for me and trade every earthly possession to have me at her side this day. There is 100% truth in those words.

I can't bear to think of my family this evening, it's just too painful, and doing so only makes matters worse. Blocking the thought of them may seem harsh, but no, what it, is survival.

Saturday-Sunday May 10-11th

As I write (Saturday, 5:30 p.m.) there is upheaval in the dorm. A razor is missing, the sergeant is investigating, and before this is over, at least one person is going to the box. The inmate whose razor has disappeared is 'Sloppy Joe,' all 6'3, 310 lbs. of him. A giant couch potato never without a bowl of food in his hands, constantly with a disheveled look and an unruly full head of salt and pepper hair parted down the middle, serving a sentence for rape. He's been the target of abuse since the day he entered the dorm. Yes, Sloppy Joe did a horrible crime, but compared to most of the cats in here, he's just a harmless, giant teddy-bear. Joe is a Christian, consumed with remorse, bothers no one, and is simply doing his time until released this coming December, after serving 5 years.

But there are vicious, mean- spirited men here, men who plain and simple won't tolerate rapists. And if the opportunity presents itself to steal a razor, get the guy sent to the box, and at the same time out of the dorm, well then you can bet your ass that razor is going to vanish.

Two days ago was Joe's birthday, and earlier today I was with him at the Christian festival held at Mohawk. He had four family members come visit, he couldn't have been happier, and now this.

I know who stole Joe's razor, he told (bragged to) a few people and has no remorse. I'm so outraged it's tempting to drop a slip to the C.O. and reveal his name. How dare he do such a thing! Where is the outrage amongst my fellow inmates, why would they allow such an act to be committed? Just when I begin to think there is a touch of camaraderie in the dorm, this heinous act occurs.

As Joe was being led away, right before he was to be frisked, cuffed, then taken to the box, he began to scream out in anger, "You bastards, how could you, I didn't do anything wrong." And other than being a shade careless with his razor (he must've left it out, or perhaps forgot to lock his locker) he absolutely did nothing wrong. Right now I hate this place more than I ever have. I hate the culture, what is deemed acceptable, to 99% of the people, and most of all I hate how it's beginning to affect me. I'm getting so negative, no matter how hard I work at finding 'the good.' The event which took place this weekend sets me right off track.

Monday May 12th

The injustice of yesterday continues to eat away at my conscience. Why do I not accept the company line given by other inmates, "Hey, Jerry, it's prison, shit happens." Or this other popular one, "I've seen worse." Oh, you have? Great, good for you; but what does that have to do with anything? Does that make it okay for Joe's razor to be stolen and his being shipped to the box? No of course it doesn't, don't feed me that bullshit about signing off on this vicious act.

It has outraged me to the point that I crossed a prison line so to speak; I "dropped a slip" on the inmate who stole Joe's razor. Yeah, I did. I've thought long and hard about what the right thing to do is. I went to see the Deacon earlier, an emotional wreck I was. I told him what I knew, how I felt. "Please don't look upon me as a rat," I said. I had to follow through on what I believe is right. Deacon C. understood, this is not exactly new territory for him, he's seen it all before. "I'll make a call to the Lt, your name will never be mentioned," the Deacon assured me. And so he did.

Where this goes from here I am not sure, Sloppy Joe will remain in the box regardless. All I can hope for is this piece of shit joins him soon enough.

When I left the Deacon's office I felt good about my decision, no matter what happens. If any inmate gets word on what I did though, I could be in for some serious repercussions.

Tuesday May 13th

It seems my actions from early yesterday brought immediate results. A little after 6:00 p.m. last night two of the biggest badass C.O.'s in the facility came into the form to conduct a cube search. Yes, 7- bottom (the razor stealer lives in that cube with bunk beds) was about to be tossed. You have to give these guys credit, it was only hours earlier that I had "dropped a dime" on the dude who caused Joe to be thrown in the box.

One of the cops, Officer S. is never without his trusty night stick, I think he might even sleep with it. He'll wear a shirt at least two sizes small, and in the dead of winter you still won't catch him wearing a jacket, just so he can show off his muscles. Go on make his day, give ol' Smitty a reason to bring that club right down on your head.

So anyway, they march over to 7- bottom where Brian (the guy who stole the razor) now knows the jig is possibly up. But listen, if you steal a razor you're not going to still be holding it 48 hours later. I mean no one is that stupid. In fact one of the very first things you do is get rid of it.....anywhere. It was probably gone by Saturday night. And these cops know that too, but by tossing a locker they might just find something else, and at the very least send a message of, "Hey dirt bag we know you did it, count on your life being miserable for awhile," As expected, no razor was found. His cube though looked like a bomb had hit, shit was thrown around everywhere. For the time being this cat is on some very thin ice. But they'll get him, yes one of these days they will.

Wednesday May 14th

A combination of the events the past few days, plus there still being no word coming out of Albany, have left me in a deep funk. Throw into the mix next week will mark eleven months, my youngest son's 15th birthday, and in one month Brooks will be graduating from High School. The boys moving on in life and their dad continues to wish each day away, confined to Mohawk.

Am I feeling sorry for myself? Yes, I am , so sue me, I can't help it. My momentum seems to have come to a screeching halt; the prospect (probably false hope) of work release has caused me to retreat. I carry around a sense of helplessness. I hate myself for this weakness, I've come so far, but I'm in the thick of some serious hurt.

Hopefully a trip out to the yard later on (6- 8 p.m.) where I can leave my troubles behind will center me a bit.

Thursday May 15th

Two days ago one hundred fourteen inmates appeared before the Parole Board. They get the opportunity to convince the 3 members how they're rehabilitated and deserve this shot to re-enter society. Get approved and you'll be packing your bags in about two weeks, freedom awaits you. If the board feels you're not ready, you'll get "hit," which means two more years at Mohawk, end of story.

Well, the mail will be distributed any minute now and with that these 100 men will learn of their fate. Talk about anxiety. There are a couple from this dorm waiting, they've had no sleep, and are walking around with dazed, catatonic looks in their eyes. I say can you blame them? One guy is Gene whom I see at church often, he's serving a 10 to life and has been hit the last 3 appearances, 16 years in so far. He can barely speak right now he's so nervous. A few months ago I helped Gene compose a resume, he really feels this time around the Parole Board's gonna let him go. When he opens the letter I won't even dare to ask him the result, I'll instantly know by his face. For his sake, I hope he makes the grade.

Friday May 16th

At breakfast (Rice krispies- apple juice) this morning I spotted Gene a few tables away. Since you're not allowed to get up from the table once you sit down, I tried to catch Gene's eye and get a sense of what the parole board outcome was. He seemed to be staring into the bowl of cereal, lost in thought, not a good sign I began to think. Finally Gene did look up and glanced in my direction, he knew what I was wondering. A far- off look and a shake of the head no said it all: Gene was denied and got hit for another two years. Gone, just like that, all the plans he had envisioned; reunion with family, the prospect of a job, and most importantly, reclaiming your freedom.

Carrying my tray I got up and began to head out the mess hall, my path would take me right by Gene's table however. What can you possibly say? I looked at him an simply said, "I'm really sorry," and kept on moving (no stopping and talking permitted).

A total of 114 went before the Board, the two men I know of were denied, and eventually I will learn what percentage of the rest got hit. I can only imagine the level of sadness that was reached in many a cube last night. No doubt tears were shed, not only here but in all the houses of loved ones, and bedrooms of sons and daughters. No need to leave a light on, daddy won't be home for a while.

Saturday-Sunday May 17-18th

I focus hard on adhering to Willie's credo: "You do you and I do me." Obviously being down 30 years it has served him well. But in my mind you can't completely be an island, hence I got close with a few men here. Gordon was one of them, then Dino who turned out to be nothing more than a can man. I did strike up a bond with Fritz, the laundry porter, and then six months ago, Jon came into 74- D. I knew right away he was someone I could talk to, share feelings with, and commiserate about our poor choices which led to eventual incarceration.

The percentage of people here who I would ever remotely consider a "friend" is beyond tiny. How easily I could serve my sentence never uttering a single word towards 99.9% of the population of Mohawk! I can't stress that enough. I talk frequently of how blessed I am, that while here I've been able to discover so much of what was missing in my life. I will one day (soon?) walk out of these gates a much different and profoundly better person. There is no doubt.

My friend Jon learned yesterday that he will be heading to Marcy C.F. (one of the 4 prisons in this hub) to undertake the six month ASAT programs. Ironically he had just recently said to me how everything was coming into place here: He loved being added on to the F/S team, was settled into a strategy for coping, and was in the best dorm in the facility. "Jerry, I could easily do the remainder of my bid (33 months) right here." And then the phone call telling him, "Jon I., get ready to pack your bags, you're outta here in a few days."

Whatever day he ends up leaving I'll thank him for the connection we made; one that can't be duplicated in the real world, it's such a unique bonding in prison. Amidst all this turmoil, depression, and negativity we came together, carried water for each other, and someday will come out on the other side.

It will be a while (while on parole there is no interaction allowed between ex- cons) but I hope our paths cross again. What an amazing world awaits us, one we will appreciate so much, and oh the memories of Mohawk that will never fade away.

Monday May 19th

For today at least, Winter has returned to the Central New York Area: Rainy, cold, even a glimpse of sleet. Ugh, and it's a Monday. But remember, I love Monday's, it's a start to the work week (F/S) which keeps the day moving, and the anticipation of mail call. Could this (finally) be the week word filters in from Albany, the long awaited decision on work release? This cold, shitty weather makes such a difference, mostly it means I won't head to the yard where I can lose my thoughts & drift far away from here.

I'll need to stay strong this week, Philip turns 15 on Friday, and I have a feeling towards week's end I'll get word. If denied it means at least another 4- 6 months at Mohawk. Oh God, I don't know if I can handle that. Not only for my sake, but I know how devastated Mom and Dad will be, heartbroken.

Tuesday May 20th

In calling my parent's last night, Dad informed that Celia (my lawyer) had learned from her contact in Albany that my case was "to be reviewed towards the end of this week." Yes, that's right, finally, after all these months my family and I will receive an answer.

Of course all this hope and glee could be for naught, a huge letdown may await; my spirit crushed for the long holiday weekend ahead. To put into words how ready I am to depart Mohawk is way beyond any talent level I possess. So let me keep it simple; I literally ache for the next chapter of my life to begin.

Today was one of those rare 'no mail' days, thank God they're few and far between. Boy have letters gotten me through many a rough day and night. I know at least five dudes who haven't once been called for mail since I've been here. Someone told me early on to be sure and tear the return address's to shreds. If not, some of these guys will actually write your people, say something like, "Hey, Jerry's my man and said it would be okay if I wrote you, etc..." Don't laugh, while pathetic, it's definitely happened, a lot more often than you'd believe.

Wednesday May 21st

The phone rang at 7:15 a.m., officer B screamed out, "Johnny I. come see me." "Pack your bags, you're on the draft," he further added. Finally, the call Jon knew was coming had arrived, it was time to go; he now had twenty minutes to get all his belongings (3 years worth so far) and stuff them into draft bags (reinforced large Glad bags), bring them to processing (where they are searched and repacked) where they'll sit until tomorrow morning at which time, 8:00 a.m., they are loaded on the bus taking Jon to Marcy C.F.

Tonight Jon will move out of our dorm, mattress, pillow, state sheets in hand and head over to the Reception Dorm (75- A) where he will spend his last night. We'll be able to have breakfast together tomorrow (6:30 a.m.) and then upon leaving hug good- bye. Once he completes the ASAT program he'll be returned to Mohawk, six or seven months from now. By the grace of God I won't be here, knowing this, my "good-byes" to Jon will most likely be forever. I'm sorry, call me sentimental, soft, whatever, but it is a moment I won't ever forget.

Thursday May 22nd

The day started with Jon and I having breakfast and saying so long. I gave him a big hug, he looked at me and said, "Stay strong Jerry." Shortly afterword he was gone.

After lights went out last night (10:00 p.m.) I turned on my lamp to read for about 30 minutes. But before I picked up my book I wanted to reflect for a little. I glanced over at Jon's cube, now occupied by someone else, thinking how the days will be altered with him gone. Besides sharing meals, we sometimes cooked together, attempted to complete a crossword puzzle each night, exchanged books, and most importantly, expressed our hopes for the future, the better life that eventually awaits us.

I also noticed two empty beds, that's an unusual site; for a day now they've been empty, surely they'll be filled soon. After that I continued my routine, put the book down, said evening prayers, and then listened to relaxing music until 11:00 p.m. That's it I said, another day down, another day I've given the state of New York.

As I expected, those two empty beds I wrote about earlier, well, they are now occupied. On the 6:00 p.m. movement two "New jacks," fresh off the bus, with their shaved heads, terrified stares, and dressed in State Greens from head to toe, stepped through the door to begin serving their bids. Eleven months ago this very day, that was me!

Friday May 23rd

For much of the day my stomach has felt like a bowl of spaghetti, the nerves jangled and frayed. When I feel this way I often wonder what the long term effect is physically; whatever it is, it can't be good. Prison grates on you, day after day the angst and sorrow you endure, the shitty processed state food, cameras everywhere, barbed wire, no privacy, and the tinkering sound as the C.O.'s walk by of nightsticks and handcuffs.

For the most part I've gotten used to it, but then today throw into the mix that my youngest son Philip is 15, plus there is a good chance I will learn of the decision by Albany. Other than coffee and a doughnut at 6:30 a.m., I've eaten nothing all day (currently 5:30 p.m.) and still feel like I'm going to be sick to my stomach.

I kept a stiff upper lip when I spoke with Phil; he had a few friends over and his Mom was planning a small celebration tonight. Phil sounded like a happy teenage boy, that's all I could ask for. His strength is my strength.

The long holiday weekend looms; hopefully the sun will be out which means I head to the yard where I can escape for a few hours. In saying my prayers at 10:30 p.m. (creature of habit, always the time when my knees hit the ground). I'll ask God to watch over my family and grant me the courage to get through another weekend.

Memorial Weekend
Saturday-Sunday May 24-25th

Getting right to the heart of the matter, yesterday (Friday) brought no word regarding Work Release. Racing to the phone around 6:00 p.m., dialing madly to reach my parents who were supposed to have received the news; well they hadn't, and this being a holiday weekend I'll have to sit tight until Tuesday, same time.

So my stomach feels a shade better, hopefully I won't have to go through that again. And remember, there's no such thing as a private bathroom, you're talking stall, out in the open, front and center.

Sunday brought gorgeous sunny weather, inspiring enough to get me out to the yard for the 9:00 a.m. and 1:00 p.m. movement. In between running 4-5 miles I rested and overheard a brilliant, typical exchange. The setting: two inmates playing basketball in the midst of a heated argument.

Inmate #1: Listen man, quit your free- styling, I tell you what is. The score be tied 6- 6, then you scored twice, that makes it 9- 6!

Inmate#2: That's official tissue! You be right, you be right.

I had to get away, quickly. I couldn't let these two math experts witness my look of disbelief, mouth agape. Six plus 2 equals 9? Huh? But really, if I wanted, I could literally fill pages and pages of dialogue that would make you on one hand laugh out loud, and the other shed tears for the lack of basic smarts, the ability to complete a sentence without using: shit, fuck, nigger or bitch. Simply put; these guys can't do it. Eleven months down, you'd think I'd be used to it by now, well I'm not.

Monday May 26th

Memorial Day......another holiday spent behind bars. Am I used to them, do I handle the day better, am I any less sad? An emphatic NO across the board! My memories of this day are so vivid; from early childhood attending the local parade with my father, to the opening of the Country Club pool, the final days of school and eventually going to the very same parade with my own sons.

Thankfully the sun was out, and so was I; keeping as busy as one can possibly be in prison. Taking full advantage of the yard I walked and found a secluded spot to be alone with my thoughts.

Tomorrow could very well be the day word from Albany comes down. The thought of this has triggered the ol stomach to kick into full flip- flop mode; there will be no, dinner consumed tonight, lunch was a PB&J made and eaten in my cube.

Whenever the day I leave is upon me and I return home, after all the phone calls to family and friends are complete, the very next call will be to a Doctor, for I shudder to think what the daily grind of this place does to your insides.

Lights out at 10:00 p.m., my legs exhausted after 10 miles in the yard, I read until 10:30, the eyes refusing to obey any longer, got on my knees and prayed this would be the last holiday spent in prison.

Tuesday May 27th

Having been told by my lawyer that Albany was reviewing my case "towards the end of last week" (to me that means Thursday or Friday) and here we are Tuesday night with a big zero in the word dept. It was another episode of not eating all day then rushing to the phone around 6:00 p.m. to call home only to discover- once again- that indeed no message has been handed down. I wish I had the ability to describe the sense of letdown, the emptiness I now feel. I'm almost numb, dazed you could call it; like a fighter sitting on his stool between round, a blank look, weary and worn out. You wanna shout "I don't fucking care anymore, " but of course I won't shout and I so do care. Why else would I be feeling like this?

So for almost the first time since I began recording my story, I don't care to write anymore this evening, the power to conjure up words, the energy required, escapes me. For tonight anyway, I surrender. A soft cry, dare anybody overhear, awaits me, my pillow is calling.

Wednesday May 28th

The influx of sexual offenders continues; on average I see 2- 3 new white guys enter the reception dorm each day. From there (usually you'll spend only one night in that dorm) they are filtered throughout the facility. As I've mentioned, their crimes come with an automatic bulls-eye on their backs; they are the target of constraint ridicule, scorn, hate and theft, as in the case of Sloppy Joe's razor, which not only got him ousted from our dorm, but also sent to the box for thirty days. They huddle amongst themselves both in the yard and the mess hall, groups of four to six.

Well something happened the other night which proves that people can be pushed around just so far. An inmate, sentenced for molesting a young boy, reached his own personal breaking point; turning the table on his tormentors, he fought back, stabbing one of them (a white guy, bully, name is Kevin Mc.) badly enough to send him to the hospital.

I had a feeling an incident such as this would occur, and it's a safe bet it won't be the last. The sexual predators are easy targets (coming back to Sloppy Joe) not normally known to strike back. The shit inmates who abuse them know this and in the process gain a bit of stature and respect (such as it is) from their peers. But the "SPs" are gaining in numbers, everyday. With that, comes some new found courage, the notion to take a stand; hence the severe stabbing of Mr. Mc'S.

To a degree I feel sorry for the "SPs," let them be man, they're here doing time, no better no worse, than any of us. I mean would you blame Joe, when he comes out of the box, where he's been for 30 days for something he absolutely did not do, would you blame him for attacking the two dudes who <u>did</u> steal his razor? I wouldn't.

So like I said, I foresee this "drawing a line in the sand" approach taking place again. More guys will be hurt.

Thursday May 29th

As I often do when I leave the F&S office in the afternoon (2:00) I spotted a group of new inmates, fresh off the bus, all their possessions stuffed into draft bags, with mattresses slung over their shoulders, headed for the Reception Dorm – 75 A. What struck me about this collection of 'New- Jack's' was the number of them- 21! By far the most I've seen; usually "fresh product" (as Chief R likes to refer to them as) comes in four or five at a time.

The shaved heads with the deer in the headlight faces, spanking new state green polyester from top to bottom, and the black work boots (picture Herman Munster's boots), with nary a scuff on them. Oh how I don't envy these guys, just starting their bids, an ocean of the unknown awaits. On average I would guess their sentences are between 4- 8 years; a few of them no doubt returning for a second or third time, and probably a parole violator or two.

As I (hopefully) wind down my stay here, I know exactly the anxiety coursing thought their system right now. That first day and night, the first week, and all you can think of is: 'Oh God, how will I get through this, how will I last a month, much less four years, or longer?'

Friday May 30th

It seems with the arrival of warmer weather, tempers, fights, and general nastiness has escalated. Two dorms over, a case of snoring too loudly has gotten one guy (Don G.) a broken nose and eye socket. I would see Don at church and playing handball in the yard, yes a bit of a wise guy, but no one deserves to get beaten up because you snore!

Even with three fans blowing 24 hours a day, the sleeping area in the dorms are awfully warm, and smelly. Luckily I have two windows alongside my cube, ones that open. This definitely helps, but still........

A dude I had never said one word to was sent to the box earlier today. He had a shitty demeanor, never took a shower, and sang homemade rap lyrics. His mistake was mouthing off to Officer B. He was told to zip it, but instead choose to mutter a few words of disrespect under his breath. Next thing you know the Sergeant is called for & this idiot is up against the wall, handcuffed, then led away to the box for at least 30 days.

June

Saturday-Sunday May 31st-June 1st

I've talked often about the weekends in prison and the toll they take: sadness, depression, and an extreme sense of helplessness prevails. This weekend particularly so.

In speaking with my parents earlier today (Saturday) I learned my brother Jack was in a plane crash when the pilot attempted to land at the Honduras Airport. Ten people were killed as the plane split in two and flames took hold. Thank God he escapes with a broken shoulder and facial cuts. How I wish I could speak with him, but I can't. Or be with my parents, to aid them in dealing with this near tragedy.

I also received news that my work release appeal is "still being processed." This after a nerve wracking week of awaiting the final decision which I was told was coming 8 days ago. Now it's another week or two before they decide. I am reminded of that lyric from a famous song, ".....waiting is the hardest part." Truly it is.

The last happening of the weekend is my son Brooks heading to Burlington, VT for a two day pre- orientation for incoming freshman. Abby is accompanying him. Without a doubt, if I had not landed here, that would have been me taking Brooks. Of course I couldn't be any more excited for this wonderful young man; the college experience lying in wait. How I wish I was with him now.

Throw all the above into the mix and you have a recipe for emptiness and longing. At least I know what I'm facing, the key is to be ready and just like the 4 weekends prior, I'll do my best to get through. It can't be much longer now, it can't, I need to get away from the negativity here. The world is turning, please God let me part of it again.

Monday June 2nd

Oh I forgot to mention I heard a beautiful sound yesterday- the sound of the month of May being torn from the calendar.

I often think back, early in my prison days, to David whom I met briefly at Down State. I remember someone asking him the length of his sentence, his reply, "Twelve years, I'll end up doing nine." What I still find so shocking was how casual and nonplussed David's tone and demeanor was: as if he was discussing the weather! And this was a guy no more than 25, with a wife and two kids. I was like where is the anguish, where is the heartache, we're talking 9 years man.

We have a substitute C.O. for the 2:30- 10:30 p.m. shift, a female, young and relatively attractive. What's that all about? Why in the hell would a woman want to work here, amongst all this negativity, filth, not to mention murderers and rapists? It'll be interesting to see how she handles the evening.

Tuesday June 3rd

As it turns out there ended up being no difference between the woman C.O. and all the others: she cursed like a truck driver, did as little as possible for her eight hour shift, made sure to be rude and obnoxious, completed a series of Soduko puzzles, then went home. Hey, not the best job in the world, but $50k a year to sit on your ass isn't too bad.......especially in this economy. She's back for a repeat performance tonight.

The only excitement of the evening was caused by one of the dorms brain surgeon's; he turned the microwave on full blast, but then forgot to put any food in! Twenty minutes later- boom- explosion time. He'll be getting a ticket for that stupidity, probably loss of Rec. privileges for two weeks.

Saw a forecast for the weekend, temps heating up, 90 degrees both days. Ugh, even with four fans you can imagine how the dorm is going to heat up, and smell!! Thirty- eight guys and about ten of them refuse to take showers. Lovely, I can hardly wait.

Wednesday June 4th

An inmate who I was at best, mildly friendly with, left here 21 days ago after serving a two year sentence. Guess what. Today he's back! That's right, I saw him marching into the reception dorm, head down, looking ashamed; as he should be. Back in on a parole violation. Simply amazing.

Here's another crazy story; a dude was sent to the box earlier today for stealing a piece of chicken- and he was scheduled to go back home in five days. I mean could you be any more stupid? Now he'll probably still be released, but who wants to spend their remaining days in the box? Apparently this guy.

Broken record time: still no word regarding my possible work release- 3 months now the appeal had been in. I can say these past few weeks, the waiting, has taken a toll. Not just on me, the entire family, we're all hurting.

Thursday June 5th

Earlier today, at 12:30 p.m., for the first time in 348 days, on a magnificent sunny Spring day, I stepped outside the gates. I wasn't wearing hand cuffs, nor shackled to another inmate. I was as close to being free since the day I walked into the court house at 100 Centre Street to be sentenced.

The reason for being outside was to flush a few hose boxes in the Admin Building. From there, Dee and I ran the hose out onto the courtyard. My outside clearance made this all possible. I saw civilians driving their cars and jogging along the street, I saw planted flowers, picnic benches and a barbecue grill.

Unfortunately, I was a "free man" only a short time, the job took about 45 minutes, and then it was back to my current reality. I had to be frisked (making sure I didn't steal anything while walking through the Admin Building) then heard the dreaded sound, electric gates being opened, and it was time, like a dog, to be herded back inside the gates.

When I was approved for outside clearance (two months ago) I couldn't wait for this day to arrive. Now, after briefly experiencing freedom, I almost wish I hadn't gone outside. It was a tease. A bittersweet moment to be sure, getting a small taste of something I took for granted my entire life.....freedom. How I ache to have it returned.....forever!!

Friday June 6th

It seems temperatures have fast forwarded straight to the height of summer- 90 degrees today and throughout the weekend. After the long cold winter I'm not complaining mind you. A full day at work, actually the entire week we were busy- mostly flushing hose boxes within the facility; a total of 88.

While at work this morning (8:30) the chief yelled out, "Byrne head over to sick call." What the heck could that be about I thought. Well, since my work release papers are very much in the pipeline, I was summoned to see the Mental Health Doctor in conjunction with my mental stability. You see, when I arrived at Rikers (50 weeks ago) I was placed on anti- depressants (Prozac) along with suicide watch- which I firmly believe they label all white men entering that shithole for the first time.

So I told this Doctor how I now feel better than I have for many years, my new found appreciation for every aspect of life, and the yearning to start again. We met for ten minutes, I thought it went well, and left thinking, "Okay, this has to be a positive, why else would Albany arrange a meeting, perhaps the final cog in the selection process, if they weren't pretty certain about granting me work release." No, I don't want to get ahead of myself, but I've examined the meeting every way possible- I can't find any negatives. For the very first time in this agonizing and brutal process, I believe I will hear- for sure- from Albany in the weeks ahead. And dare I even say it; I think I'll be approved. Oh God don't let me be wrong.

Saturday-Sunday June 7-8th

I have no doubt that the longer you remain in prison, you become immune towards the feelings and tales of woe of other inmates; you simply don't give a shit. In spite of nearly a year under my belt (no, not a lifetime but a life changing length of time) I am far from what you would label a veteran, so I guess that's why I find myself still affected upon hearing sad stories- especially when they frequently involve son and daughters whose dad is imprisoned.

I was running (slowly considering it was 90 degrees) in the yard yesterday (Saturday) and came across Rod, a guy I knew only slightly when he lived in our dorm. He was there for only 4 weeks and then got moved to the mess hall dorm. After making small talk about the heat we got around to discussing the hardship of prison. Rod, who is white and no more than 30, is serving a ten year flat sentence, with 5 ½ remaining. I'm not sure what his crime is (the rumor is rape) and not knowing him all that well I was hesitant to ask. "Somedays I don't think I'll make it through," Rod said. He's quiet, mild- mannered and would be considered "soft" within these walls. When he says something like that, he means it. Rod is also a father of 3 children, 2 young girls and a boy. His wife left him, has re- married, and her new husband, (so Rod no longer has to pay child support,) has adopted his children. He hasn't heard "boo" from them in all this time. Not long ago he had a good paying job, the house, a family dog and cat, the Volvo wagon and now this…....

"I fucked up," he kept repeating to himself, as he smoked cigarette after cigarette, the sun beating down on us. I'm not condoning whatever it is that Rod did, he's being severely punished, but I still can't help but feel sorry for the innocent victims- his children. What I've always referred to as the "ripple effect" of a man's prison term, the lives that become forever altered, the suffering they endure.

Monday June 9th

After the seemingly endless snow and cold of winter, I never imagined I'd be bad mouthing the heat and humidity Central New

York is currently experiencing. But soaring (record) temperatures take on a whole new meaning in prison. And if that wasn't bad enough, one of our three toilet stalls is broken!

For a reason I can't fathom, about 8- 10 dudes in the dorm refuse to shower, so the past few day they've given off an odor which takes your breath away. It's gotten so bad officer B made an announcement, "Listen, there's no charge for the water, it's free… use it." If they continue to refuse, it's a ticket with a potential trip to the box awaiting.

In addition, the ice machines are on the blink- no cold water the past few days. The four fans, on full blast throughout the day and night, do little more than blow the hot air around. Falling asleep has been a challenge.

With the heat, along comes short fuses- nearly three fights this past weekend, and one this afternoon, over the TV of course. If this weather keeps up much longer (2 more days predicted) someone's going to snap.

Tuesday June 10th

Couldn't fall asleep last night. With the third straight day of sweltering 90 degree heat, the dorms ice machine not working, and a handful of guys who refuse (for religious reasons) to take showers, the place felt more like Guam on a hot night. I was literally sticking to the sheets. Take away the first couple of weeks at Rikers and it was my worst night yet.

Perhaps a final test of the resolve before I venture on? Hmm, could be, if so bring it on as many of those sleepless evenings as possible. Because if I haven't cracked by now, well it's not going to happen. Amazing what you learn to endure if you have faith; upon sentencing I didn't think I would last a week within prison walls. But "one day at a time" really did work. Of course accepting early on that I had control over nothing helped, otherwise you'll be miserable. Can't get writing paper, stamps, or a pen- tough shit, deal with it. No toilet paper, the phone doesn't work, can't get all the items in your package? Well screw you, should've thought of that before you came to prison.

That's why my life will never be the same- for the better. Those little things thrown at you, "the small stuff," the shit which used to drive me crazy; man, after this past year- it's all nothing.

So I will deal with the heat again tonight, yeah it's uncomfortable but I'll fall asleep eventually.

Wednesday June 11th

My oldest son Brooks will be graduating from high school a week from today. It could be the most difficult day of my incarceration; I am devastated to miss the sight of him clutching his diploma. The following is a copy of the letter I just wrote to Brooks..........

Dear Brooks,

Since you already know how emotional your Dad can get, I'll try and keep this light and breezy, otherwise it will be too difficult for me to finish. I want to wish you a Happy Graduation! I could not be any more proud of you, and of course so sorry that I won't be there to see you receiving that diploma.

During my time away I've had the opportunity to discover so much of what was missing in my life: I had forgotten to live each day to its fullest, seize every moment, and most of all; count my many blessings. Chances are you will probably hear those words at your graduation. The commencement speaker might even sprinkle some of them into his/her speech. Having lost my freedom for the past year, I can tell you, without question, how true those words are. Brooks, I beg you to follow them, an incredible world awaits you; you have the ability to become anything.

Okay, I knew it, starting to get emotional, so let me close with a favorite quote by Henry James:

"Live ALL you can; it's a mistake not to.It doesn't so much matter what youdo in particular, so long as you haveyour LIFE. If you haven't had that,what have you had?"

I love you,
Dad

Thursday June 12th

Continuing the waiting game, silence from Albany has put me in a foul mood. Mail call came and went, not a peep regarding work release.

If my brain had a bullhorn which could shout out what I'm thinking at the moment, first and foremost would be – fuck this place! Fuck these guys who wear their pants below their ass, what's that all about, pull your pants up you piece of shit. Fuck these morons who can't put a sentence together without saying at least one of the following: you heard... nigger... whas up son... my baby mamma... pussy... shit. Fuck most of these assholes back in prison for a second, third or fourth time! Stop selling drugs you fucking idiots, get a job. Fuck these guys who can't walk 10 yards without spitting, and fuck all of them who walk slower than a 90 year old man. Fuck these dudes who refuse to take showers. Fuck all the beggars who come to my cube time and again asking for a shot of coffee and creamer. Fuck these guys who sleep all day and haven't spent a minute of their bid trying to rehabilitate themselves. Fuck the child molesters & rapists. Fuck the crappy food they serve here and fuck the lazy, good ol' boy, overweight C.O.'s who don't do shit for their $50k per year. Fuck the Hispanics who can't seem to speak to each other without screaming at the top of their lungs. Fuck all the muscle heads, lifting weights day and night as if that will help them, in any way, in the real world, read a book, get a clue. And fuck you too Jerry, for fucking up your life, forgetting to count your blessings and ending up here. How could you!

Friday June 13th

Cross off another week; that makes 51 of them so far. A year ago this Friday was supposed to be my sentencing date. I, along with my 2 brothers and my lawyer were at the Manhattan Supreme Court, 100 Centre Street. The day's weather was exactly the same as today: clear blue sky, abundant sunshine. We were there to ask Judge Obus to extend the sentencing by a week so I could celebrate Father's Day with not only Brooks and Philip, but my father. In addition Philip was graduating from middle school and I desperately wanted to attend. The prosecution let it be known they were planning to object.

We walked from the subway to the courthouse; my mouth was dry, legs rubbery, and mind in a million other places. Walking up the steps there was no guarantee I'd be coming back out. I had hugged my parents earlier in the morning, none of us sure when the next time we'd be together, perhaps that evening, or years from then. My mother, ever faithful always positive, even made dinner plans for that night, confident her boys would all be returning from NYC.

Judge Opus, fair from day one, much to the cold hearted ADA's dismay, granted me an extra week, I had seven more days of freedom. Yes, I would be returning to that courtroom in a week. Bnd the next time I wouldn't be leaving through the front door, but rather the back, shackled for the bus ride to Rikers.

I got off the train in Short Hills, hugged my brothers, told them I would see them later for dinner (Mom was right, as always) and went directly to see the boys, only a matter of days with them remained.

Saturday-Sunday June 14-15th

Eileen came to visit Saturday, a quick day trip, hopefully her last at Mohawk. It was great seeing her and catching up. Purposely she planned on Saturday, as Father's Day (tomorrow) is the busiest- craziest- day in the Visitor's Room. A very high percentage of inmates have children with different women, then throw into the mix all the "baby mamma's" and you have yourself quite a scene. The room is chaotic, ear splitting, and cramped on a normal visiting day. Today there was probably a 2- 3 hour processing wait just to get in. One guy in our dorm has 7 children with four separate women; two of the ex- wife's were going to visit. He's been a nervous wreck all morning, afraid they might show at the same time, considering they hate each other, it won't be pretty.

I spoke with my boys Sunday afternoon, did the best I could and tried not to dwell too much on our separation; the first Father's Day we have ever been apart. I gather my strength, remain stoic, and let them know once again how much I love and miss them. Right now I am helpless to do anything more.

Monday June 16th

I witnessed the zero tolerance policy in action last night. To run the loop around the yard you have to pass the basketball courts. On the first few trips I overheard the usual trash- talking, moronic comments screamed back and forth, I didn't pay them much attention. A few more laps later I began to sense the joking had a harsher tone, less cordial (as cordial as prisoner's get) and the pushing ramped up. A quick, but what I thought harmless slap was thrown by one guy, next thing you know, 3 C.O.'s, alerted by the cop in the watch tower, are on the scene. In an instant these dudes are on the ground, hands behind their backs about to be cuffed, and looking at a trip to the box.

Tuesday June 17th

The heat wave of last week has given way to much cooler temperatures- barely 60 degrees. Thankfully I find myself no longer sticking to the sheets as I had been.

I seem to be operating on auto- pilot these days, fumbling my way through; the mind constantly seems to be elsewhere. The long awaited work release news still has not arrived, the constant worry of the outcome has worn me down, the sadness of missing Father's Day, combined with tomorrow being Brooks' high school graduation has all weighed heavily.

Spending more time than usual in my cube reading, or at least trying to, as I am easily saddened and distracted. My mind takes over and begins to play tricks.....will I ever leave here, has system forgotten about me and I've fallen through the cracks? Allowing this to happen is so damn easy. Jerry, don't you let it, you've come too far this past year- stay strong!

Need to get some air, escape the negativity of the dorm, exercise will help, it usually does. I don't care that it's cloudy, cool with rain predicted, I'm headed to the yard from 6- 8 tonight. I need to fix this state I'm in.

Wednesday June 18th

I remember early on when a veteran inmate offered advice in dealing with the separation from family and loved ones: "This might sound harsh, but you have to almost forget all about them, otherwise you'll go crazy," he said. Immediately I dismissed him as 'institutionalized and shot.' Gradually though, to a degree, I found what he offered made some sense......you have to immerse yourself in this world, so as you don't go insane thinking of your children/family back home, how much you miss them. You do indeed have on occasion have to block them from your thoughts.

For weeks now, all I could think about is my son's graduation at 5 p.m. today, and my absence from it. I couldn't summon the will power to refrain from dwelling, but I should have as it's caused me nothing but heartache.

I should have because in speaking with Brooks this afternoon- around 3 hours before the big event- he was so reassuring, so strong, and all that mattered to him was telling his dad not to worry, high school graduation "isn't a big deal," and that he loves me! Within minutes of our chat, my 18 year old son lifted me from the depths, our roles reversed; his maturity, strength and courage has made me feel alive again.

As hurdles go, I always felt this one today would be the last serious obstacle, that I can handle what lies ahead from this point on. I'm proud of the race I've run so far, I can see the finish line, stay focused and I will cross it someday soon.

Thursday June 19th

Being surrounded twenty- four hours a day, by inmates only, is wearing me down. How I long to have an intelligent conversation, to talk about the economy, politics, religion, the weather, oh please anything. Or how about to see a pretty girl walking down the street, a simple "hello" or even a passing glance would make my day. Take me away from here so I can be running late for a train, reading a fresh newspaper, ordering an iced latte at Starbucks. Let me know what it feels like to start up my car in the morning, to turn on a TV without worry, to sleep with both eyes closed. Any of these events, always taken for granted, would be heaven.

What heaven is definitely not, is listening to the word "fuck" used in each and every sentence, no matter what the topic. If overhearing "fuck" represented a $1 in my pocket, an average day would make me at least $1000 richer. Easily. And it's not a market cornered solely by the inmates, the C.O.'s are just as bad, in some cases worse!

Just a few days short of a year, oh God I want to go home so very much. A new life awaits, please allow it to happen soon.

Fri-Sat-Sun June 20, 21, 22

The memory of my sentencing and the immediate aftermath, exactly a year ago, I will carry forever. Looking back upon the events of that day; at times they seem so fresh in my mind, at others almost like they never happened, a bad dream perhaps. While I didn't think so at the time, truly I know now it was the first day of the rest of my life.

There I was, on a beautiful sunny Friday, as I boarded the train from Short Hills to Penn Station, most of my fellow commuters dressed casually, some carrying canvas bags, no doubt headed for the Hamptons, their cell phones and Blackberry's already in full swing. I looked at them thinking, "that used to be me." But not anymore, now I was headed to 100 Centre Street, the Manhattan Supreme Court, to be sentenced for securities fraud and grand larceny. I stared out the window, numb and in shock, still contemplating the idea of not showing up. Screw it, I'll get in my car and drive out West, begin a new life. I even toyed with suicide. Alcohol and pills; no mess, nice and easy. What the hell, my life was finished anyway- how the fuck was I going to survive Rikers Island, (being possibly raped) followed by God knows how long in state prison? Ugh, how could I ever do that? Easy answer, I couldn't. Never!

I didn't have the courage to tell a few friends what was my soon to be fate, so as I got closer to Centre Street I began to call them, praying I would get only their answering machine. What a pathetic sight, "Hi it's Jerry, look I wanted to tell you, if you try to e-mail or call me, I won't be able to get back, yeah, you see I'm going to prison for a couple of years. Okay, I guess that's all, gotta run now......" Good grief.

Before walking through the courthouse doors, I looked up at the clear blue sky thinking I could still make a run for it. Fuck it, c'mon Jerry run. The thought of losing my freedom, locked behind bars haunted me. But deep down I knew I couldn't, I had to face this I had to be a man, not only for myself, but for my family and most of all my sons. Not to mention my cousin- George Maguire- would have lost the $250,000 bail he put up. I just couldn't do that, I couldn't. It was face the music time.

The twenty or so minutes before actually being sentenced and led away, remain a blur. My lawyer spoke, followed by the prosecution, and then my turn to beg for leniency, these minutes I can't fully recall. Looking back, I think I was in shock. I know I was sobbing, telling the Judge how sorry I was, hurting everyone so, letting my family down, and how devastating the separation from my boys would be. Not to mention financially for my ex- wife whom I had been paying child support to for the past ten years. How in the world was that going to be paid now?

The only clear moment in court was when the Judge hit me with a 2 1/3 – 7 year sentence! My lawyers had been hoping (as I and my family had) a 1 to 3 year sentence. No sooner had the sentence been handed down that I was surrounded by 3 court officers, one who asked, "Sir, please put your hands behind your back." And that was it, it was over, and there was nothing anyone could do for me now. The 3 court officers led me through the side door of the mahogany court room; I glanced towards my family members, tears running down my cheeks, so helpless all of us. No words spoken, but the show of pain emanated through our faces. I now only had a few seconds to look at them before being led through the door. The door opened and I was gone. Awaiting me there was a cold, hard wooden bench with a bar to the side where they attached one of my handcuffs to. And that's how it all began, and it truly was just beginning.

The next few hours consisted of being moved from holding cell to holding cell, one more crowded than the next, the smell of urine and stale vomit in every corner. Perhaps I spotted another white guy, I don't recall. I do know there weren't more than a few of us. Lunch consisted of two pieces of hard moldy bread, in the middle a slice of cheese which had a greenish tint. I couldn't look at it much less eat it. Sensing my disdain for "lunch" I was soon swarmed upon; my cellmates, who all appeared to be veterans at this type of thing, were more than happy to take my unwanted sandwich. I'm going to starve I thought.

Next thing I knew it was 3:00 p.m., time to get me on the bus to Rikers- looking back, I can honestly say the worst trip of my life. Stepping out into the 95 degree heat, shackled as if I was Hannibel Lector, I was herded onto the 1950 looking school bus, bars on windows which would not open, making the temperature inside at least ten degrees warmer. The person they cuffed me to for the ride, Carlos, was a recovering meth addict coming off a 4 day binge; well, he hadn't (which he shared with me, talk about TMI) gone to the bathroom or washed himself in all that time.

As the bus inched its way through Friday afternoon traffic in Chinatown, some young school kids passing by thought it would be funny to mock and taunt us, "Have a good time in prison, die there you scum bags." I had never felt lower.

Just my luck Carlos decided that now- on the bus, handcuffed to me- was the right moment to relieve himself. "C.O. I have to take a shit" he began to yell. This went on continuously, other guys on the bus screaming at Carlos to "shut the fuck up," had no effect. The C.O.'s ignored him like he was a piece of dirt. Carlos began to look at me for help; what the heck am I going to do Carlos?

Finally, after about two hours we pulled into Rikers, never thought I'd be glad to see the place, but I had to get off that bus, away from the filthy smell, away from my traveling companion. It was about 5:00 p.m., the rest of the night consisted of being moved to various holding pens, all overcrowded, hot and disgusting. Oh my God I thought, how will I survive this, I'm not coming out of here alive, am I going to be raped tonight? Trying to find a seat on the bench, to no avail; which meant lying down on the sticky, urine- coated floor. It's where I slept my first night, on more than one occasion water-bugs scurried past me (one crawled up my arm) while I tried to sleep, but of course I did not.

It wasn't until 4:00 p.m. the next day I was finally assigned a dorm. Where upon someone trying to "help" me, immediately stole my pin # with which I needed to make my first phone call. I wanted to let my parents know I had survived so far. The C.O. on duty seeing how desperate I was took pity and put five minutes on toward my account, so I could make the call. And that's how it all started.

Monday June 23rd

Over the weekend in one of the dorms a fight broke out (just like the Elton John song says, "Saturday night is alright for fighting") involving four inmates. Apparently it was another case of the weak saying, "I'm not going to be pushed around any longer damn it," as two dudes who had been on the receiving end of constant abuse, jumped their tormentors while they watched TV; kind of a sneak attack. And you know what, as far as I'm concerned, more power to them.

This place is overrun and dominated by bullies and tough guys who feel the need to be forever fronting their machismo. Fuck them! In case you hadn't noticed asshole, you're in prison now, not back on the streets dealing. They've never come to terms what led to prison in the first place, again for many, the time spent here is merely the cost of doing business, and while here they choose to act just as if they were back home- wherever the hell that is.

So all four went to the box, serving at least 30 days, probably longer. I say hat's off to the two inmates, pushed to their limit, at last drawing a line in the sand.

Tuesday June 24th

I get a kick observing guys entering the dorm for the first time; that doesn't mean they are rookies necessarily, just new to 74- D. In a heartbeat you can spot a veteran, the old- timer, the repeat offender. They've got this prison thing down, they move with ease while carrying all their essentials collected over the many years of doing time.

They've got the fan, the lamp, hangers for their shirts, plenty of food, coffee, an extra blanket, cooking bowls, their radio, and even some have a typewriter. Every square inch of the locker will be accounted for, they unpack with little effort, obviously the result of having done so numerous times. To them it's simply a move to another "home."

I count my blessings all the time- for many reasons- as I've only moved once. My first night at Mohawk in the reception dorm, then 74-D ever since. I write about this because the other day a guy named Matt M. sauntered in. As I watched him unpack I knew right off, "Oh he's done this before." Besides the lack of even a hint of trepidation, he had all the tools; everything I mentioned above. A dead giveaway are the headphones (deluxe ones) on while he sorts through his belongings, rocking away to the music as if he was literally n his room back home.

Turns out my call was pretty damn accurate: Matt has been arrested 40 times, (no joke, he told me) is doing a fourth state bid (one in Ohio as well) spanning most of the past twenty years, and he's all of 37 years old.

Out of 38 guys in the dorm, I'm one of just five serving their first sentence. It astounds me how many return, how many don't learn.

Wednesday June 25th

Just to follow up on my last point from yesterday, the Parole Board was here early last week interviewing a large contingent of inmates (140) to see if they might be released early. Three guys from my dorm appeared and after waiting four (must have seemed like a lifetime) days, they learned all were denied, as were five dudes from the dorm next door. Not a good sign, but the problem is they are all serving at least a second or third bid. Their inability to conform once back on the street speaks volumes to the Board.

A bad case of nerves today, my stomach has been acting up nonstop. It's a constant sharp pain affecting every bit of me. While the shitty almost uneatable food is partly responsible, mostly it's brought on by anxiety; awaiting word from Albany. This delay, this being jerked around is nothing but cruel. I've written about what prison does to your insides, the never ending nerve wracking moments and the damage it causes. God only knows the toll my stomach has taken, hopefully I can get to a Doctor soon to assess what's been done.

Thursday June 26th

Two guys from my dorm have been sent to the box this week; with perhaps more to follow. 'E' was the first sent packing- a dirty urine did him in. I didn't know E well except for the occasional hello when out paths crossed; but I liked him. He was always polite, a smile (those are rare) and possessed good manners, the result of an upper middle- class upbringing. In addition E was white, married with two children. So what's E's problem? Drugs; he couldn't stay away!!

On Tuesday he was called to the Tier Office for a piss test- he failed, heroin in his system. Where he got the stuff from I have no idea, and don't want to know. Apparently it's not hard to come by though. So E gets sent to the box and is looking at 90 days minimum. The disciplinary Lieutenant approaches him (this is standard practice) and says, "Look, make it easy on yourself, give us a few names, other dudes who are also using, where you got the shit and we'll go easy on you." E takes the bait and caves, starts signing like a canary. Next thing you know 4 guys from our dorm get called up to the Tier Office- piss test! Gulp.

Friday June 27th

You get 3 hours (max) to produce urine, if you can't produce they assume you're guilty and it's off to the box with you. The problem is that the cop's are watching you while you try to piss, the pressure is on, the clock is ticking. What if you have a bashful kidney? And you don't get much help, only a shot glass full of water to drink and hour, that's all. You sit in the waiting room, handcuffed, praying you'll be able to piss soon.

While all this is going on, you can bet that your locker is being searched back in the dorm. When they have you in their cross- hairs, chances are you're going down. That's what happened to one of the dudes, he didn't fail the piss test, but they found 200 stamps in his locker (you're only allowed to have 50) so off to the box he went.

The other 3 weren't found dirty either, possibly the drug was already out of their system. So for now the heat is off. No doubt they'll be forced to produce urine again in the near future. Worse, these three are in play, on the radar screen, just where you don't want to be.

As far as 'E' is concerned, he's finished at this facility. After giving up all those names he'll either be assigned to protective custody (after his time in the box) or sent to another facility).

228

Saturday- Sunday June 28-29th

Allow me a stream of consciousness following my 53rd weekend in prison:........They don't get any easier, each & everyone is difficult.......during my twenty- seven years out in the working world, I never came across a lazier collection of workers than the C.O.'s here, making $50k a year and they do practically nothing.......I long for the day when Albany sends someone undercover to expose this scam........I'm sorry, I don't mean to sound harsh, some of them are decent, really decent, I've been fortunate to come across those guys, they've treated me well, sadly though I think the bad far outweighs the bad........it's probably the environment here, I mean who could enjoy working in this element??........two new inmates arrived at the dorm, one a serial rapist, the other beginning his third state bid, he's all of 27 years old, lovely....... it amazes me to see dudes laughing and joking throughout the day; hey asshole, you're in prison, what's so funny about that... how do so many drugs get smuggled in......I guarantee 7 out of 10 (maybe more) guys would not know who the Presidential Nominees are, but they sure as shit would know the title of Beyonce's latest single......83 percent recidivism rate, I understand that now... there's that pant thing again, why do guys wear them below their ass, I don't get it....it's the dead of summer, take a fucking shower man.......I hate prison, I hate being an inmate, and hate being looked upon as if I'm less than human... my sons are coming to visit on July 19th, I can't hold out any longer, I can't wait to hug them... ....I am blessed with so much love and support......I wonder how Jon is doing....... privacy, I really miss that......a miracle I haven't gotten sick at least once these past 13 months.......thank God for books, the Bible too... they give us toilet paper that is more akin to sand paper, my ass hurts every time I use it.......I miss my bed and pillow back home... I'm tired of living with men, I want to touch a woman's face again, feel her lips... don't give up Jerry, you've come too far...... will I get a letter from Albany this week?

Monday June 30th

For over a year now a constant theme (worry and sadness would be more like it) on these pages has been the heartache of my separation from Brooks and Philip. Never could I have imagined not seeing them for this length of time; prior to prison not more than a few days ever elapsed in between the three of us doing at least something together-even homework.

I just couldn't bare them to witness their Dad dressed in his state greens, surrounded by fences, barbed wire, and then worst of all, them getting up to leave the Visitors Room without me. God knows how I'd react, the tears might never stop, I could possibly crush them right now with my hugs. No I thought, I'll wait, I can hold out a little longer. Well as you know that wait continues, and geez, that could still take months. Besides, thankfully the boys are holding up, keeping busy with teenage boy stuff: school, sports, video games, girls, and computers. They've received love and support from all avenues during this nightmare. Yes physically I have been absent from their lives, but between the weekly (at the very least) phone calls, and one letter (to each son) per week for the past 54 weeks, I pray I've been able to touch their minds and hearts; touch in a way that they know how much I love them.

In spite of all the above, I can hold out no longer- I must see B & P and in fact have already set a date for that to happen. My brother Jack will drive them up on Saturday, July 19th. The 'unknown' release date I face caused this to occur. Literally it could be a week, and at the same time possibly over a year. Otherwise we could have dealt with a firm date, something to latch on to, to strive for. I can't deal or bargain with a black hole. Of course the grace of God could make July 19th a moot point; there remains the chance that I will be granted work release between now and then. My encounter with the boys would then be free of barbed wire, our first get together in thirteen months surrounded by ordinary citizens instead of murderers, rapists and drug dealers. I think I'll get on my knees now and pray to God......again.

July

Tuesday July 1st

A new month is here, cross off June, days gone by that you can't get through fast enough. Wishing your current life away, really, that's about all you do in prison. No phrase seems to be uttered more, by C.O.'s and inmates alike, it transpires like this, you see someone and say, "Hey, what's new?" The universal reply, "Same old shit, different day." Spend a week inside these fences and you understand how that exchange can't go any other way.

So will this be the month work release comes knocking on my door? Truly, yes I believe it will be; it just has to. How much strength do I have left, how much fortitude and will power? An endless supply I like to imagine, but there have been days, especially as of late, when I feel myself slipping.

Wednesday July 2nd

Even going back to the earliest, darkest days of Rikers and Down State C.F., I always anxiously awaited when I could snag paper and pen to record my thoughts onto this blog. The hour or so I would spend on each day's happenings and how I managed to deal with them, was sanctuary; my hour of normalcy. And now, about 13 months later, even thought I have all the paper I need, I struggle to sit down and continue my daily diary, I seem to be losing my edge, my focus.......questioning if I will ever get out of here. Was this whole work release thing just a pipe dream, should I have been more realistic? No, I don't regret for one second my pursuit of it, the thought of going home one day must continue to be my mission.

Thursday July 3rd

Lately it seems like almost every night out in the yard, when I'm either running or walking with my friend and dorm-mate Bob, along comes a quick little rain burst......followed by an incredible, bright and clear rainbow. I look up at it and begin to think it's 'a sign;' there is some light at the end of this rainbow, I'm almost convinced of it. Yes it's true, I've been saying this to myself for the past few weeks, but nonetheless the feeling seems so strong, so real. I can't explain it. I circle & circle around the track, looking up at the fading light of day, another one almost down. I only pause to do my push-ups, 50 at a clip. For the past 8-9 months I do them everyday, either within my cube, or out in the yard. Whenever the time comes for me to leave here, I'll be doing so in probably the best shape of my life, at least since college/swimming days.

The usual yard activities are taking place; Fritz standing tall at the handball courts, getting such joy out of his games, almost like he'd rather not be anyplace else. The soccer & volleyball games in full swing. Basketball of course, always a basketball game to be found, and the touch football teams are practicing up as the season is about to begin. Take away the barbed wire and you have a summer camp for wayward adults.

It's hot and humid, I get back to the dorm and the evenings ration of ice is all gone, I'll have to settle for room temperature powdered gatorade, followed by a shower, followed by reading my book.......lights out at 10:00. Another day down.

Friday July 4th

My second Fourth of July in prison! I recall so vividly last year on this day; I was at Rikers, still in a bit of shock, living in that horrible, stifling dorm with 50 other men. In the evening I could see a glimpse of fireworks, off in the distance. I tried to peer out of this tiny window, hoping the bars wouldn't cover up most of the view. Funny, tonight I did practically the same thing, except my window (and I now have two of them) is a lot bigger, but still covered with steel bars. I did indeed see fireworks off in the distance.

Lunch was hot-dogs, chips, and pie. Now even in prison, can you get any more All-American than that!! They give you 3 hot-dogs, I can barely stomach two, usually I'll give the last one away. There is never a shortage of takers. The heat and humidity continue. Catholic services tomorrow, 1:00pm.....I'll be there.

Saturday July 5th

The moment I've been dreaming of arrived earlier this afternoon. I HAVE BEEN APPROVED FOR WORK RELEASE AND WILL LEAVING MOHAWK ANYDAY NOW!!!! Yes, yes, it's true, I can barely contain myself, I am so incredibly overjoyed. And the way I found out was so very special. Oh my God I can barely contain myself!!!! I'M COMING HOME.

Allow me to circle back for a minute: I'll never forget the first time I attended Catholic Services here. I had just arrived the day before, clueless and scared out of my mind. I hurriedly inquired about when and where the mass was, and made my way to the makeshift chapel. Towards the end of the mass, the Deacon preforms a tradition by honoring those inmates who will be leaving the prison in the upcoming week. (Apparently he receives a sheet with the names of those specific inmates going home) It's never more than 1 or at the most two guys, but they stand up in front of the room, we all say a prayer of hope acknowledging their return to society, followed by a round of applause. The first time I witnessed this I was so moved, it's such an emotional scene observing these grown men, who have come to the end of their time, weeping with joy upon hearing the news they'll be leaving in a matter of days. I thought to myself, "My God, some day, and I'm not sure how long, but that will be me." So for every service I've been to since, for the past 11 months, I've been waiting for that day.......AND TODAY WAS THE DAY!!

This afternoon I left the dorm for services at 12:50 p.m., which was the first movement. Nothing seemed out of the ordinary as I made my way down to the classrooms, where the chapel is set up. Arriving before most of the other guys, I was sitting down previewing the days Gospel, when all of a sudden the Deacon walks by me and says, "Come up at the end for your blessing, you're leaving this week." Not quite sure if I heard him correctly I looked up (hoping beyond hope that I did hear him correctly) and asked, "Excuse me Deacon, what did you say?" He stopped, looked back down and said, "Yeah, I saw the sheet, you're leaving this week, congratulations." And there it was, just like that, I received the news I had been living for. I was stunned.

I sat through the rest of mass basically in shock, with an inner sense of utter joy and happiness practically bursting out of me. Hours later, as I record todays events I couldn't tell you what happened during the mass, it was a total blur as I held back the tears, and thought about how this was the last time I'll be in that room, attending a catholic service. This was it, my days at Mohawk were down to a precious few. I couldn't wait to get back to the dorm and phone my parents, followed immediately afterword with a call to the boys.

At the end of Mass I stood up in front of the room for the Deacon's blessing, and my fellow inmates round of applause and well wishes. I cried of course.

Sunday July 6th

My parents shrieked with joy when I gave them the news yesterday. I was crying, they were crying. The same emotions repeated themselves right after, when I dialed my sons. This would be the last time they would have to accept a collect call with the recording from the NY State Dept. of Corrections, stating they were accepting a call from an inmate. Each time I have called these past 13 months that's been the drill. Humiliating.

I spent this sunny and hot day out in the yard, doing my exercise, but mostly sitting on one of the cement benches reminiscing about my time here. On one hand how hard it was, on the other how quickly these 11 months have come and gone. I will be leaving a changed man, one who sees and lives life differently from now on. I will never take a single day for granted, I will never complain or sweat the small stuff again. Each time I look up at the sky I will appreciate it so much more, along with everything in front of me now, the grass, trees, open roads, fresh air, and on and on. I can't soak it up fast enough.

I want to keep my news a secret as much as possible, the only ones I've told are Fritz, Willie P, and Bob. I have heard that if word gets around it can easily trigger jealousy in another inmate, one who might not be going home for a long time, and takes an instant dislike to you, perhaps trying to trap you off or lure you into a fight, thereby negating your leave. I will sit on this news. The only other person I'd like to tell is Joe, whom I arrived with 11 months ago. I hope I get to see him before I leave. I already know I'll be emotional when I walk out of here, can't help it, thats who am I. This place has impacted me so. My gosh, I'm probably going to be the first prisoner in the history of New York who cries walking out of prison!

As an aside, Dino and I have made up, we are now speaking. I saw him out in the yard earlier and we just looked at each other....it was time to mend the fence. I explained my reasoning for backing away months ago. I think he respected it. I also respected his side, the fact he has been incarcerated for 13 years now, how he sometimes forgets his bearings, looses focus, along with the difficulty of breaking away from the prison mentality he has needed to survive all these years. He has a good heart & Dino helped me immensely during my first few weeks, I'll never forget him for that.

Monday July 7th

As my co-workers and I were going through our usual chores at the Fire & Safety office, the chief yelled out, "Byrne, get back to your dorm and pack up, you're on the draft." That was it, I was officially leaving, this was my last day @ F&S. My last day of working for 24 cents per hour. For all his bluster and at times obnoxiousness, I am actually going to miss Chief R. He treated me well, no two ways about it. One thing for certain, I'll never forget him, just as I won't forget all the CO's whom I came across on a daily basis. Most of all Officer B, who took me under his wing, never failed to treat me with respect, and could not have been more fair in our dealings. Tough when he had to be, but behind the veneer of his prison guard aura which he must give off, he was an extremely decent man. Thanks as well to Officer R, whom I enjoyed talking about world events with each evening after watching the NBC nightly news. And thanks to Officer W., a regular all around good guy, who filled in for the chief from time to time. He was very cool.

My writing will be sporadic, as I have to pack all my belongings, this includes pen and paper. I'm not even sure when I will able to chronicle what's happening, but trust me, I won't forget a single detail.

As I get back to the dorm to pack, the word is now spreading around, 'I'm leaving Mohawk.' The guys I know are happy for me. Thanks to the countless visits and never ending generosity of Eileen, I have accumulated quite a collections of shirts, sweaters, socks, magazines, books, etc......and I don't want to bring any of it home. The exception being the one or two essentials I'll need for the bus ride back, although for that I'll be dressed in my state greens. As I start to throw a few things into the draft bags the vultures form around my cube, hoping for handouts, mostly clothes or food. I give the majority of my candy/coffee to Willie P, and clothes I'll have no use for, to Fritz. He knows that whatever he doesn't want to keep, he can always barter down the road.

I have to hurry, the CO's don't give you much time to gather your shit together.

Tuesday July 8th

I have learned that I'm headed to Lincoln CF in New York City, on 105th street, overlooking Central Park. OMG, someone pinch me, is this really happening!! At 6:00 this evening I will be moved over to the reception dorm, where I will spend my final night at Mohawk. Like it was yesterday I can recall my first night in that same dorm, 11 plus months ago. After I sign in, I will quickly head over to the yard, also for the last time. Wonder if I'll see that rainbow?

Friday July 11th

Where do I begin? Well for starters I am currently a long, long way from Mohawk. I am in NYC. Yes that's right, so long depressing Central

New York, hello Big Apple. Two days ago I had one last breakfast @ Mohawk, with Bob. These past few months he has been such a source of strength for me. This hulking, intimidating looking man, who has at least 8 years remaining on his sentencing for drugs, had nothing but encouragement for me. Ever since Jon left Bob was the guy I had shared my frustrations and sadness with. He would never allow me to remain down for long. Not a single time.

After we ate I walked back to 74-D one last time, to say so long to a few of the guys I had become close with. I knew this was going to be emotional as I hugged Willie P. He had befriended me, no questions asked on that 2nd day here. I'll never forget how he handed over his extra baseball cap, so my shaved head wouldn't get anymore sunburn. You just don't show kindness like that in prison, but he did. I also hugged Fritz, the laundry porter. He was a good man, we worked out and ran together, we opened up about our faults and wishes, and became friends. These men, who had been front & center in my day to day world these past 11 months, well I knew after this moment I would never lay eyes on them again.

The usual routine for the bus ride, I am shackled at the ankles & wrists, DOC procedure, coming or going. I just don't have the mastery of the english language to describe the feeling as the bus pulled away from the gates of Mohawk, but I'll never forget that moment. I looked back over my shoulder as the bus made its way, one last look at the prison gates. Quickly they began to fade away as we turned onto the main road.

Our route takes us to 3 other Correctional Facilities picking up other dudes who are also being released. Eventually we reach Ulster Correctional Facility where we will spend the night, and then head to Lincoln CF, NYC in the early morning. At Ulster there is a baseball game on, I watch it just like I did my very first night at Rikers, 13 months ago. But this time, I'm going home, I made it. I did my time, & did it well. No one can ever take that away from me.

Sunday July 27th

At 10:00 this morning I walked out the door, for the first time in thirteen months, a free man.....for three hours anyway. Yes, I have a three hour pass. This is the day I have dreamt about from the beginning, since the day I was standing before Judge Obus. I am going to be reunited with Brooks & Philip.

I hail a cab as quickly as I can, after all the clock is ticking. I don't have a lot of time. As the cab heads down 5th Avenue I can only stare out the window in amazement; the people strolling around, wearing normal clothes, no "state greens" to be seen. There are vendors hawking tacky souvenirs, children running around the park, laughing and smiling. These sights I had taken for granted a million times before, but no more. It all looks so different now.

My destination is the NY Athletic Club, courtesy once again of Eileen, who has arraigned for me to have lunch with the boys, my brother Jack, and sister Virginia. This will be the first time I have seen the boys since the night before I was sentenced. The typical NYC traffic moves slowly, we are just inching along. I can't stand it anymore, I can get there quicker on foot, I ask the cabby to pull over and let me out. I run the rest of the way. In the distance I can spot Jack standing in front of the building, waiting for me, the boys are inside. I hug Jack, then he guides me inside to where they are sitting. I see them, I am so nervous, but also becoming overwhelmed.

I grab hold of Brooks, squeeze him tight, and marvel at how big he's gotten. I begin to cry. I don't want to let go. Philip comes over, I bring him into the fold, my arms reach around both of them. This exact moment is the one that has carried me through my darkest of days. Finally this moment has arrived. They've grown, matured, and are looking like young men. I have missed out on 13 months of their growth. I pull back a bit so I can look into their faces. The tears continue to run down my cheeks.

Virginia suggests the boys and I take a walk around the block, before lunch, so we can catch up. It's a perfect idea. On this hot & sunny summer late morning, we begin our walk. I want to hear about everything they've done. Phil begins to talk, then Brooks wants to speak about stuff, all of a sudden they are both talking, and I can't get enough, I soak it all up. I want time to stand still, please Lord freeze this exact moment, don't let it end. I tell them how great they both look and how much I have missed them. And that their Dad is going to be just fine.

I spot a Starbucks on the corner, this being NYC you don't have to go far to find one. Aaaahh another first, I'm going to have fresh coffee, with real cream. I quickly think back to the last time I drank real coffee, it was the Friday of my sentencing, 13 months ago. I kind of feel like I'm closing a circle.

I want to savor every minute of this. I can't stop stealing glances at the boys. Brooks blurts out, "Dad I've never been happier." During the slow walk around the block we cover a whole slew of topics; girls, schoolwork, sports, new music they're listening to, and how great it is to see me again. I have dreamed of this exact moment, everyday, for the past thirteen months. It's finally here!!

Given that I only have a three hour pass we have to move things along quickly. We head back to the NYAC for lunch, where Virginia & Jack are waiting. Virginia wants to take a picture of the boys and I. Around my neck is a St. Christopher medal my Mother bought for me. On the back contains the date I left Mohawk, along with an inscription stating my parents never ending love.

We all sit down at the table overlooking Central Park. I just can't believe this. Only a short time ago I was sitting across from a murderer, rapist, kidnapper and child molester. I take a quick look at the menu, there isn't anything I wouldn't love to have. Well maybe not anything, because for the past 13 months I've consumed more rice than I care to remember. So I order fresh asparagus salad, with bacon and blue cheese. Followed by a thick juicy cheeseburger. I wanted to hold onto this moment forever, but the clock was ticking, I had to be back at the work release facility in an hour.

But there were no tears this time, for there was no need. Just hugs and kisses. I had survived my 13 months of hell and had gotten to the place where I had dreamt about the entire time. I knew I was a different person now, one who would no longer be caught up by all the small stuff, and who would never take for granted what was in front of me, like I had done for way too long. I had been stripped of my freedom at Mohawk, what a horrible thing to lose. But I have it back now, and I know for certain, I will never lose it again. My journey was over. I am truly blessed.

The End

CPSIA information can be obtained at www.ICGtesting.com
Printed in the USA
239423LV00002B/92/P